U0882078

翻译本科及研究生推荐教材
山东省社科科学规划研究项目“《西方翻译传统》翻译本科教材建设”(12CWJJ21)最终成果
教育部规划基金项目“中国译论的社会文化批判”(14YJA740060)部分成果

社会文化视角下的西方翻译传统

A Socio-Cultural Perspective of Translation Traditions in the West

赵 巍 编著

山东大学出版社

图书在版编目(CIP)数据

社会文化视角下的西方翻译传统/赵巍编著.—济南:山东大学出版社,2014.11

ISBN 978-7-5607-5175-7

Ⅰ.①社… Ⅱ.①赵… Ⅲ.①翻译理论-研究-西方国家 Ⅳ.①H059

中国版本图书馆 CIP 数据核字(2014)第 278588 号

责任策划:张晓林

责任编辑:王 潇

封面设计:张 荔

出版发行:山东大学出版社

社 址 山东省济南市山大南路 20 号

邮 编 250100

电 话 市场部(0531)88364466

经 销:山东省新华书店

印 刷:山东和平商务有限公司

规 格:787 毫米×1092 毫米 1/16

12 印张 271 千字

版 次:2014 年 11 月第 1 版

印 次:2014 年 11 月第 1 次印刷

定 价:36.00 元

版权所有,盗印必究

凡购本书,如有缺页、倒页、脱页,由本社营销部负责调换

序

面对赵巍的书稿《社会文化视角下的西方翻译传统》(*A Socio-Cultural Perspective of Translation Traditions in the West*),感慨良多,虽觉孤陋寡闻,不堪为序之重任,然盛情难却,也有些话要说,遂欣然命笔。

任何一位翻译学者的研究,都有一个基本立足点的问题,不立足于本民族的语言文化传统与现实,即立足于他民族的语言文化传统与现实。著名翻译理论家刘宓庆将翻译学方法论的基本原则高度概括为"本位观照,外位参照"①。也就是说,做研究首先要立足于本国、本民族、本语种的社会历史和文化,外在翻译理论则应成为参照、借鉴,即令它十分完善、极其先进、特别时髦,也不例外。

不过,参照、借鉴绝非可有可无;相反,它极为重要,不可或缺。不论在翻译的行为方面还是理论探讨方面,都是如此。历史上,如果英国没有翻译大量的拉丁语文献,就不可能诞生伟大的莎士比亚;如果德国没有把《圣经》译成平民可观的德文本,现代德语便无由产生,影响深远的宗教革命也不可能爆发。在现代中国,如果没有翻译就没有共产党及与之相联系的一切。在译界,不借鉴西方就没有翻译事业的大发展,也不会有科学、系统、深入的理论探讨。

《社会文化视角下的西方翻译传统》以英语编写,系我国第一部西方翻译史专门教材,又是翻译本科及研究生推荐教材。翻译史在翻译本科和翻译硕士层面,都被列为专业必修课或专业必选课,西方翻译史如以英语讲授,学生透过英语直窥西方翻译史实,自然有其优越性,所以这部英语行文的西方翻译史教材应能发挥其特有的作用。

作者认为:"当代翻译理论正日益突破文本研究,表现出更加宏阔的社会—文化研究取向,因此有必要全面搜集英文翻译史资料,按照'翻译是一种社会文化活动'的基本思路,形成一部面向翻译本科专业的西方翻译史教材,同时补充原教材中的部分遗漏,并改进原教材中详略不当之处。这样的教材编写不仅对翻译史研究和当代的社会-文化研究取向的翻译研究有借鉴意义,在翻译方向本科生及研究生培养中也可以发挥作用,对国内翻译本科教学有直接的实用价值。"②

我在阅读了该教材后确信,作者的初衷一定能够实现。

本书的主要特点,我想可以概括为如下几点:

---

① 刘宓庆:《翻译与语言哲学》,中国对外翻译出版公司 2001 年版,第 41 页。

② 本书"前言"。

一、立意较高。按照“翻译是一种社会文化活动”的基本思路,教材突出翻译活动的社会文化属性,指出翻译在西方不同国家之间传播知识、推进文明、促进交流的过程中发挥着巨大作用。立意高使教材具备了较大的学术价值。

二、尊重史实,避免以先入之见剪裁和切割历史。按历史分期进行阐述,从社会文化背景、翻译的目的、翻译策略、译本的短期效应及其对译入语语言文化乃至人类文明的深远影响等各方面着笔。遵循理论和实践并重原则,必要时援引重要评论,或结合当前翻译界的理论兴趣进行述评,

三、各章末提供参考书目信息,并含讨论题3~5个,有利于读者进一步思考和查阅相关信息,从而有助于学术论文的撰写。

我相信,各位本科生、研究生通过本教材的学习,不仅能够获得大量有关西方翻译史的知识,且可开拓思路,提高理论思考能力。

此外,还有几句话想说,供各位读者参考。中西译学各有其迥然相异的源流,我们在引进西方译论,学其长处的时候,决不应当无视甚或丢弃自己的传统。可惜的是,不少人,特别是青年学者,一味跟风,而对中国自己的文化传统却不甚了了。2012年8月,我曾拜读张传彪教授的《“道”与“逻各斯”的对话》一书的书稿并为之作序,从书中可以看到,张教授以很大的学术魄力,在中西译论之间进行了一种别具特色的散点式对比,堪为青年学者的楷模。书中内容涉及从汉字语境质疑后现代解构主义、中西诗歌迥异根植于汉字本源、译诗贵传神而非机械转述、凡语言均有其局限性、冷思考异化翻译策略、翻译基本属性为变通等重大议题,实在难能可贵。写作如此论著,一靠学养深厚,二靠目光深邃,三靠熟悉中西翻译史。

打开中国译论史料库,我们看到,先贤留给我们的是一大笔精神财富。古代从支谦《法句经序》、道安《道行经序》开始,经科学翻译时期西来传教士利玛窦“译《几何原本》引”、我国先贤徐光启“《几何原本》杂议”,再经近代马建忠《拟设翻译书院议》、严复《天演论·译例言》,到现当代鲁迅《域外小说集·序言》、郭沫若《谈文学翻译工作》、茅盾《为发展文学翻译事业和提高翻译质量而奋斗》等,琳琅满目,精彩纷呈,作为后人我们没有理由不去继承。对于西方的传统译论,我们的态度亦复如是。而我们作为中国学者,自然要以中国为本,借鉴他国,这样才能为世界译学宝库增添新物。

从历史源头方知,哲学基础不同,翻译观、理论形态自然也会呈现根本性差异。比如翻译策略中的归化异化问题,按许多西方人的见解,二者必居其一,非此即彼;而以中国哲学为基础,归异虽对立却必然互补才是正确的,合乎实际的。

希望本书给各位读者带来多方面的裨益。

是为序。

孙迎春
2013年12月于山东大学(威海)

前言

翻译史是翻译领域的基础知识，是翻译本科知识结构必不可少的一部分。在全国率先开设翻译本科和翻译硕士的院校中，翻译史都被列为专业必修课或专业必选课，但翻译方向教材建设相对滞后，目前仍然没有较为详尽的面对国内翻译专业的西方翻译史专门教材。

西方翻译史撰写及研究在国外已经有丰硕成果，Mona Baker 1998，Douglas Robinson 2006 和 George Steiner 2001 主要撰写翻译实践或理论通史，而更多学者从某一角度阐述翻译史。Lawrence Venuti 2004 从意识形态角度阐述翻译史，Willis Barnstone 1993 从翻译诗学角度描述翻译史，Louis. G. Kelly 1979，Jean Delisle 和 Judith Woodsworth 1995 等从译者角度梳理翻译史，Flora Ross Amos 1920 和 Peter France 2000 专门记录英语翻译史，Benson Bobrick 2001 则专门研究圣经的英语翻译及其影响。这些研究成果均体现了独到的研究角度和学术视野以及现代译学的研究兴趣和研究理念。但总体而言，国外翻译通史的内容过于宽泛，编排体例也过于单一，而翻译专史过于专深，作为翻译专业翻译史教材都不尽适用。

国内的西方翻译史研究以译介综述西方研究成果为主，主要成果包括谭载喜主编的汉语教材《西方翻译简史》(2004)，谢天振主编的《中西翻译简史》(2009)等。《西方翻译简史》用汉语行文，粗略描述了自古希腊罗马至今的西方主要译本，至今仍然是西方翻译史方面的主要参考资料。该书按照时间先后和国别，以翻译历史事件和翻译人物为线索来编排、叙述历史，较为连贯地勾勒出西方历史上的主要译事译论。但该书只是按照时间顺序罗列堆砌史实，没有一个一以贯之的中心思想来串联史实，因此无法就翻译现象得出任何整体性、规律性认识。在编排思路和体例方面，语言学和文艺学派的分立、国别和地区线索在翻译史实的编排中并没有一贯地体现出来，在一定程度上忽略了教材编写的整体性和系统性原则。更主要的是，按照语言学和文艺学派的分立来阐述西方翻译史，已经无法反映当代翻译研究的最新发展。当代翻译理论正日益突破文本研究，表现出更加宏阔的社会—文化研究取向。最后，该书对翻译史实的剪裁、取舍不尽合理，对某些翻译事实的译述也不尽完整和准确。尽管如此，作为国内第一本西方翻译史，该书仍然是西方翻译史研究的基本参考书目，在很多高校作为翻译史指定教材使用。后出的翻译史仍然不同程度地、乃至不加区别地借鉴《西方翻译简史》。(《中外

翻译简史》高华丽,2009,《中西翻译简史》谢天振,2009,《翻译简史》孙迎春,2011)

“翻译史撰写是现代翻译理论的首要任务。”(Berman, 1992: 1) 翻译史是构建现代翻译理论的基础性工作,而翻译史撰写不仅在于阐述过去,更主要的是结合当下的翻译学学科发展状况,更好地为翻译学学科建设服务。按照克罗奇的说法:“一切历史都是当代史。”因此,翻译史也需要与时俱进,在如实呈现基本翻译史实的基础上,按照当下翻译界全新的理论兴趣和宏阔的学术视野对历史上的翻译活动做出新的阐释,以便及时反映并跟进翻译学的最新进展。当代翻译理论正日益突破文本研究,表现出更加宏阔的社会—文化研究取向,因此有必要全面搜集英文翻译史资料,按照“翻译是一种社会文化活动”的基本思路,形成一部面向翻译本科专业的西方翻译史教材,同时补充原教材中的部分遗漏,并改进原教材中详略不当之处。这样的教材编写不仅对翻译史研究和当代的社会—文化研究取向的翻译研究有借鉴意义,在翻译方向本科生及研究生培养中也可以发挥作用,对国内翻译本科教学有直接的实用价值。

从远古时代人类最早进行交流开始就有了翻译,翻译史几乎和世界文明史一样悠久。世界翻译史实证明,翻译不是一种孤立的活动,而是特定社会历史背景下整体文化学术思潮的一部分,翻译只有在整体的社会历史文化语境中才能得到充分理解。本教材按照“翻译是一种社会文化活动”的基本思路,试图说明翻译在西方不同国家之间传播知识、推进文明、促进交流的过程中发挥的巨大作用,翻译活动的发生、译本的流传和接受取决于特定的特定社会文化条件,大规模翻译活动的整体翻译策略受制于特定社会文化条件,而翻译理论更是反映了特定历史时期的社会文化背景。整体而言,本教材的基本思路是突出翻译活动的社会文化属性。

其次,本教材按照西方、特别是欧洲的一般历史分期阐述西方历史上的重要译本、翻译人物、翻译事件、翻译文献等,涉及古代翻译、中世纪的翻译、文艺复兴时期的翻译和近代翻译。各个历史时期按照统一体例进行叙述,尽可能包括翻译发生的社会文化背景、在该背景影响之下翻译的目的、翻译策略、译本的短期效应及其对译入语语言文化乃至人类文明的深远影响等等。本教材理论和实践并重,有必要时援引相关重要评论,或者参照当前翻译界的理论兴趣进行述评,但历史叙述中会尽量尊重史实,避免以先入之见剪裁和切割历史。为配合教学需要,本教材列出翻译名词术语,提供规范解释,帮助读者加深理解,把握重点。并总结各章、设置思考题,以加深读者对翻译的社会文化属性的认识。各小节末提供参考书目,以方便读者进一步研究。

本教材中的“西方”以欧洲国家为主,但不限于欧洲,也包括中国以外的其他国家和地区。由于涉及国家和地区广,时间跨度大,本教材不得不按照翻译活动的规模和影响有所取舍。而教材中提及的某一翻译活动中的翻译策略,一般是指整体策略。由于翻译是一种主体性很强的个人活动,任何时期的整体翻译策略都不排除有例外情况,但这和某一翻译活动中的整体翻译策略并不矛盾。

需要注意的一点是历史史实本身是连贯的,历史叙述中的分期则是人为的。因此本教材中的历史分期只是为了便于讨论的权宜作法，不能僵化理解。实际讨论中，常常需要照顾历史翻译实践或理论发展的连贯性而打破历史分期。

本教材编写过程中，得到了山东大学(威海)翻译学院教师的积极支持，在此向他们由衷地致谢。其中薄振杰负责全书的审订，崔莹辉提供了早期英国翻译理论的电子资料(Flora Ross Amos1920)，崔英和曹春玲负责文字润色，陈怀凯和谷秀春负责体例的统一，王苏华、孙萃英和李楠负责第二章的资料收集工作。

赵 巍

2013年12月于威海

FOREWORD

History of translation is an indispensible part of translation studies and an essential aspect of knowledge to the students of translation and interpretation. While translation has gathered momentum as a young and promising undergraduate and graduate program in China, there is no generally accepted textbook on Western translation history, which has caused much irregularity and uncertainty in the teaching and evaluation of the course.

Research on history of translation has been fruitful in the West. Mona Baker 1998, Douglas Robinson 2006 and George Steiner 2001 recount the general history of translation, and more researchers address particular problems or periods in translation history. Lawrence Venuti 2004 gave an account of history of translation from ideological angle and Willis Barnstone 1993 from poetics. Louis. G Kelly 1979, Jean Delisle & Judith Woodsworth 1995 examined the translator's role. Flora Ross Amos 1920 and Peter France 2000 focused on translations made into the English language. Benson Bobrick 2001 specialized in English translations of the Bible. A general history of translation is too broad and usually presented in a strictly chronological manner too monotonous for Chinese undergraduates and graduates. A more specific history of translation, on the other hand, is too specialized and therefore unsuitable for undergraduates and graduates program as well. Also these books are more theoretical and academic than interesting as textbooks for Chinese students.

In China, research on Western history of translation is informed by the researching findings in the west, primarily in the form of *A Brief History of Translation in the West* by Tan Zaixi 2004. Written in Chinese, the book is a chronological presentation of the important translation events and people from the ancient Rome and Greece up to the 20th century, the first one of its kind in China. It is not without problems, though. Apart from some factual errors, it does not follow a clear central idea, so that after reading the book we would only have many sporadic and separate facts, without any idea what these facts together reveal to us about the nature of translation. In the arrangement of the historical material, the book is inconsistent in the division of linguistic versus literary schools of translation studies. More importantly, this division of linguistic versus literary is out of step with translation research today, which is expanding into socio-cultural domains. For all these defects, up to now the book is still widely used as the most important sourcebook for research on translation history or as the appointed textbook of translation history. Later publications on translation history (Gao Huali, 2009; Xie Tianzhen, 2009; Sun Yingchun, 2011) draw heavily on Tan Zaixi.

"The construction of a history of translation is the first task of a modern theory of translation." (Berman, 1992: 1). History is written not only in the context but also in the best service of the author's own time, namely, with due regard to the current dominant ideas of the present so as to interpret the past for the benefit of contemporary translation studies. In the words of Benedetto Croce, "All history is contemporary history". This book is an attempt to present translation history in the west "as an activity addressing questions of concern to the present" (Pym, 1998: 123). In response to the growing social-cultural approach in modern theory of translation, this book is to present translational facts in the history of the West as socio-culturally conditioned undertaking. It is hoped that such a textbook will provide the information on translation in a more comprehensive manner for translation undergraduates and graduates alike, playing an important role in the development of undergraduate and graduate translation program in China. Hopefully, it will also be an inspiration to translation history research and an improved sourcebook for translation research in general.

Translation happened when there was first contact between different peoples in ancient times. The history of translation is as old as the history of world civilization. Studies of translation traditions show that translation is not an isolated phenomenon, but a by-product of the general intellectual movement of a certain historical era. As a fundamental element in the history of language, literature, or philosophy, translation must be understood within the general historical and cultural context. This history of translation illustrates translation as a social-cultural event in a particular historical period as much as possible. It aims at establishing the point that translation played an active part in disseminating knowledge, advancing civilization, and promoting communication between different cultures, that translation happened, circulated and took root in a particular social-cultural context, that translation strategies were determined by various social-cultural factors, and that translation theories reflect the general social-cultural tendencies of the time. In one word, the underlying scenario for this book is mainly social-cultural.

As a secondary line of development, all the translations, translation people, translation events, translation articles, etc, will be presented in a chronological order following classical history division, i. e., Antiquity, Middle Ages, Renaissance, Modern times, etc. Each historical period will be divided into sections with consistent format of presentation, which will cover the following aspects wherever possible: under what socio-cultural context, for what purpose these translations were made, what translation strategies were employed, what actual effect was achieved through the strategy, what socio-cultural significance they produced on the advancement of human civilization in general and on translation theories in particular. Important remarks on these translations will also be presented for the reader's reference. Before each section the relevant translation terms will be listed in separate with explanation. At the end of each discussion section, a number of questions will be asked about the translations, translation people, translation theories or translation events, etc, in order to deepen the students' understanding of the contents. For those interested in related topics, some important sourcebooks will be included for further reading.

"West" in this book mainly refers to Europe, but in the actual discussion all regions outside China are included. As the materials to be covered are too vast to be amply dealt with in a book of this length and depth, we have to focus on the countries that are better known for translation activity and whose translations have greater influence upon world civilization. Translation strategy in a translation movement is used in the most general sense. As translating is essentially an individual activity, exceptions to the general translation strategy of a historical period are not uncommon. But it does not follow that the general translation strategy does not hold true.

Here we need to caution ourselves that history itself is a continuous whole and cannot be understood as being rigidly divisible. The periods above, therefore, are more for the convenience of discussion than real and enough emphasis will be paid to the continuity of translation events and translation theory per se.

I would like to extend my gratitude to all those people from the School of Translation Studies, Shandong University (Weihai) who have contributed to the formation of this book. One is Bo Zhenjie, who reviewed the outline of this book. Cui Yinghui photocopied *Early Theories of Translation* by Amos, a book that I quoted extensively in the accounts of translations into the English language. Cui Ying and Cao Chunling worked as the English editor of part of the book. Chen Huaikai and Gu Xiuchun were in charge of the consistency in documentation format. And Wang Suhua, Sun Cuiying and Li Nan collected some valuable material for the drafting of the second chapter.

Dec. 2013

Contents

Chapter One
Cultural Transmissions in Ancient Times

1.1 Earliest Translations in Ancient Times

Translation Terms

Inverse translation 逆向翻译

Also reverse translation. Translation can be divided into two kinds in terms of the direction of translation. The translation that is made from one's native language into his acquired language is inverse translation and the translation from one's acquired language into his native language is direct translation 顺向翻译. Although direct translation is the more commonly used method of translation, inverse translation is still used. The direction of translation is determined by various factors: the translator's language competence, the text type, the translation purpose and the relative status of the two languages.

Collaborative translation 集体翻译或协作翻译

Also collective translation, team translation. It is the translation that is made by multiple translators simultaneously in a highly organized manner. In this kind of translation, multiple participants can collaborate on the same book, each of whom has been assigned a part of the job and participates simultaneously with shared resources.

1.1.1 Socio-cultural Background

General socio-cultural conditions were unfavorable for translation enterprise in ancient times as illiteracy was widespread in almost any culture until long after the end of ancient history. Prior to the recorded history of written translation in the West, there must have been a long tradition of oral transmission, which started with the first contact between peoples who spoke different languages. But as these earliest oral translations were largely unrecorded, they could not be counted on as the reliable starting point of translation history. Our discussion about translation, therefore, has to begin with historical periods that are more verifiable.

As early as the third millennium BC, there appeared in Assyria[①] the earliest trace of written translation. The Assyrian emperor ordered the scribe, normally a polyglot, to sing his imperial exploits with elaborate embellishments in many languages of his empire. During the reign of Hammurabi[②] (about 18th century BC), Bagdad, capital city of ancient Babylon, was a cosmopolitan city that spoke many different languages and conducted state affairs with the assistance of corps of translators. These translators were in the position to put state documents, codes and laws into different languages so that they would be understood by the common people. They were also in charge of making wordbooks with equivalents in many different languages of the empire, and these wordbooks are very much like multilingual dictionaries today. Some of these "dictionaries", as it were, were preserved intact on tablets engraved with cuneiform scripts[③]. *Esther*[④] 8: 9 makes a mention of the activities of translators in ancient times, saying that the king's scribe was summoned to send royal edicts "to all the satraps[⑤] and governors and princes of the provinces from India to Ethiopia, a hundred and twenty-seven provinces, to every province in its own script and to every people in its own language, and also to the Jews in their script and language" (quoted in Nida, 2004: 11). During the Nehemiah's[⑥] reign (about the end of the 4th century BC) a special form of translation appeared in Jewish community. It was believed that all city people assembled in the square before the Water Gate of Jerusalem, listening to the laws and rules to be read and interpreted to them in public.

1.1.2 The *Septuagint* and the *Letter of Aristeas*

Bible is the most translated book in the world and currently is being translated into many different languages. *Bible* consists of *the Old Testament* and *the New Testament*. *The Old Testament*, the holy book of Judaism[⑦], is mostly written in Hebrew, the language of the

---

① 亚述:亚洲西部底格里河流域北部文明古国,公元前9世纪至前7世纪为强盛时期,疆域从地中海跨越阿拉伯和亚美尼亚地区。

② 汉谟拉比:巴比伦王国国王,使巴比伦王国称霸美索不达米亚地区,并把美索不达米亚和苏美尔人的法律编辑成法典。

③ 楔形文字:古时的苏美尔人、阿卡得人、亚述人、巴比伦人和波斯人的书写符号。

④ 《圣经·以斯帖书》:以斯帖是《旧约》中波斯犹太人的皇后,曾经将人民从大屠杀中拯救出来。

⑤ 总督:波斯帝国一省之统治者。

⑥ 尼希米:《圣经》中公元前5世纪犹太领导人和朱迪亚地区的统治者。

⑦ 犹太教:世界三大一神信仰中最古老的宗教,也是犹太民族的生活方式及信仰。犹太教的主要诫命与教义,来自托拉(Torah),即《圣经》的前五卷书,又称《律法书》或《摩西五经》。犹太教虽然只是一个民族性宗教,但在宗教史上有很大的影响。

Jews[1], substantial parts of two books (*Daniel*[2] and *Ezra*[3]) in Aramaic[4]. The earliest recorded complete translation in the West is the *Old Testament*, a collection of religious writings of ancient Israel that form the major and first section of the Christian *Bible*.

Conventionally the classical antiquity is taken to start with the earliest-recorded Greek poetry of Homer (roughly the 8th century BC), continue through the emergence of Christianity and end with the decline of the Roman Empire and the dissolution of classical culture (the 5th century AD). The culture of the ancient Greeks, together with some influences from the ancient Orient, prevailed throughout classical antiquity as the basis of art, philosophy, society, and educational ideals. In about the 3rd century BC, Alexandria was the main Greek city of ancient Egypt, with an extraordinary mix of Greeks from many cities and backgrounds. Alexandria was not only a center of Hellenism[5] but was also home to the largest Jewish community in the world who were so thoroughly Hellenized that their knowledge of Greek was better than their native Hebrew language. Hence there was the increasing demand for the Hebrew *Bible* to be translated in the Greek language for the benefit of those Jewish communities. Besides, the early Ptolemies[6] developed its museum into the leading Hellenistic centre of learning (Library of Alexandria) but were careful to place an emphasis on Greek culture in part to exclude and subjugate non-Greeks. In literature, non-Greek texts could only be kept in the library once they had been translated into Greek. As an essential collection for the library, the Hebrew *Bible* had to be translated into Greek. At first there were many sporadic Greek translations of the Hebrew *Bible*, but by the end of the 2nd century BC, a standard collection, called the ***Septuagint***, appeared. It was translated into Greek in Alexandria between about 280-130 BC, which over time had expanded into many books in a variety of genres and on a wide range of Hebrew life.

There was mystery about the making of the translation and the details of the translation are recorded in the ***Letter of Aristeas***. This mysterious *Letter* was written in about 130 BC by an anonymous Jew. It carries an eyewitness account of the translation of the *Septuagint* known as *The Legend of the Septuagint*. As the *Letter of Aristeas* was written about one and a half century after the making of *Septuagint*, it is difficult to determine whether the statement about the

---

① 希伯来人、以色列人和犹太人大体上指的是同一个民族,是该民族的不同历史时期有不同的叫法。现今使用时也有一些约定俗成的惯例:希伯来主要用于称其语言、文学;以色列多用于与政治、历史有关方面;犹太则指其民族和宗教。

② 《圣经·但以理书》。

③ 《圣经·以斯拉书》。

④ 阿拉姆语:又译为亚兰语、亚拉姆语、阿拉米语、阿拉美语,是闪米特语族的一种语言,有3000年的历史,是《圣经·旧约》中《以斯拉书》及《但以理书》所用的语言。

⑤ 希腊化时期:指公元前4世纪末至公元1世纪初希腊文化向东方传播以及与东方文化交流的时期,又称“泛希腊时期”。这一时期的希腊化促进了东西方宗教的融合及世界宗教和中东文明圈的形成。

⑥ 托勒密王朝:是在马其顿君主亚历山大大帝死后,其将军托勒密一世所开创的一个王朝,统治埃及和周围地区,历时275年。亚历山大港是托勒密王朝首都,也是当时希腊化世界的重要文明中心以及贸易枢纽。

translation is factual. Undoubtedly, however, the essay is historically important because it documents the making of the *Septuagint* translation, the earliest extant Greek translation of Hebrew *Bible* in ancient times. Besides, it gives the author's view about the methods as well as the procedures of translating the *Old Testament*. Hence the epistle is called "the oldest extant book on the history and theory of translation" (Barnstone, 1993: 166).

The letter relates that the translation was initiated by Demetrius of Phalerum①, who was devoted to the establishment of the great Alexandria Library of King Ptolemy II②. For the formation of such a library, he intended to collect all the important books in the world then, and Jewish laws were an essential collection. As the Jewish laws were written in a foreign language and in a careless manner, they need to be translated into a standard copy in the popular language of Alexandria.

The king was convinced that an immaculate Greek copy of Jewish laws was necessary for his library, so he sent a letter to Eleazar the High Priest of Jerusalem③, asking him to translate the *Old Testament* into Greek. At the request of Egyptian King, Eleazar the High Priest sent 72 Jewish translators from 12 important Israelite④ tribes, 6 from each, to Alexandria. Under the direction of Demetrius of Phalerum, these 72 noble Jewish scholars translated the *Old Testament* from Hebrew into Greek. The final version of the work was called the *Septuagint*⑤.

By the *Letter of Aristeas*, there was a general anxiety about translating a sacred text; upon their arrival at Alexandria, the 72 translators were immediately admitted into the King's presence, a rare occurrence that showed how much importance the Egyptian King had attached to the event; Eleazar the High Priest and the multitudes under him offered sacrifices before the sacred undertaking began; the translators, as a rule, washed their hands in the sea and prayed to God before their work each day; they worked in a mansion especially built for that purpose in isolation from other human settlements, all the appliances well provided for; they divided themselves into 36 groups, working simultaneously in separation from each other; they all translated the whole text, and all translations turned out to be identical; then they met again, put their translations together, compared and checked until they came to an agreement about the final version; the transcription of the work was completed, as if by design, in 72 days; upon the completion of the work it was read out at the place of the translation to the general public who warmly received it as the law of God; a special gathering of senior translators and priests was held which decided that as the translation was piously made with accuracy it should stay in its present form and not a word should ever be changed; whoever added, deleted or

---

① 法勒鲁姆人德米特里(约公元前350~前280年):雅典杰出的演说家、政治家、哲学家、作家。

② 托勒密二世:托勒密王朝是由马其顿国王统治的埃及王朝,托勒密二世(公元前285年至前246年在位)利用巧妙的外交手腕扩大权力,发展农业和商业,使亚历山大城成为艺术和科学的中心,是托勒密王朝较有作为的君主。

③ 以利亚撒:《旧约》中亚伦之子和继承人,以色列的大祭司。

④ 古以色列(人)的,犹太(人)的。

⑤ 《七十子希腊文本》:拉丁文前缀septu-意为"七十",指参与翻译《旧约》72位犹太学者。

transposed what had been written down in the translation would be cursed.

The *Letter* defends the strict literalism in the translation, hinting that the literal version is achieved with the help of divine inspiration. Philo Judaeus① was the first Christian scholar who, after a close reading of the document, proclaimed that the 72 translators who produced identical versions in isolation from each other were divinely inspired. This claim, although under constant attack, continued well into the Renaissance until it was overthrown by Juan Lius Vives②(1492-1540), etc. in the 16th century. Although most Christians sincerely believe every word in the *Letter of Aristeas*, much of the contents were attacked as pure fabrications. One piece of evidence against is that by the 3rd century BC, the legendary 12 Israelite tribes as a unit had long disappeared from Palestine. It is generally believed that the actual process of translating took almost 75 years.

Be that as it may, the *Septuagint* is important as the first complete Greek translation of the Hebrew *Old Testament*. In the history of translation, it is noteworthy for a number of reasons. First it marked the verifiable beginning of translation in the west. Second, it started the tradition of **collaborative translation** in world translation history. Collaborative translation ensures accuracy as too many translators put their hearts in it; on the other hand the translation is uneven and varied in style, as it is done by too many people that have different language habits. As a matter of fact, the styles of the various books of the *Septuagint* vary considerably, some departing frequently and freely from the Hebrew texts. Third, the translators of the *Septuagint* translated out of Hebrew, their native language, into Greek, which they acquired. This kind of inverse translation had undesirable impact on the quality of the translated text because the translators took pains to make the version faithful in meaning, with little regard for stylistic elegance. The translation they produced was obsolete in diction and awkward in style, impressing one as non-Greek or bad Greek. For all these defects, *Septuagint* enjoyed a high position in world translation history as the most faithful and complete translation of the Hebrew *Bible* and for many years it was kept unchanged and remained the only reading for earlier Christians. Despite many textual variations from earlier scriptural texts, the *Septuagint* remains the basis of the *Old Testament* in the Eastern Orthodox Church③. Fourth, as the *Septuagint* was substantially quoted and referred to in the *New Testament*, the Hebrew culture was absorbed into Christian culture. Today, the *Septuagint* is still used by the Greek Church, and serves as the basis for translation into many other languages of the Mediterranean world.

---

① 斐洛:希腊哲学家,早期基督教教父。参见第 17 页。

② 斐维斯:西班牙人文主义者,持有基督教人文主义观念的教育家。

③ 东正教:又称正教会或正统教会,是基督教的主要宗派之一,是由东罗马帝国所流传下来的基督教传统的教会。它是与天主教、新教并立的基督教三大派别之一,信徒主要分布在东欧国家。与天主教不同,正教由一些被称为“自主教会”或“自治教会”的地方教会组成,这些教会彼此独立,但却有着共同的信仰。

1.1.3 The *Rosetta Stone*

Another famous translation from the ancient world is the ***Rosetta Stone***. It is 1.14 meters long and 0.72 meters wide. The stone was believed to be carved in 196 BC, but was discovered by French soldiers who were rebuilding a fort in the town of Rosetta, Alexandria, Egypt in 1799; hence its name the *Rosetta Stone*. It fell into the hands of British Army in 1801 and is now on display at the British Museum. On the stone was engraved the text in honor of Egyptian pharaoh Ptolemy V. The stone lists all the good things that the pharaoh had done for the welfare of the priests and the people of Egypt. It carries two languages (hieroglyph① and Greek) in three scripts (hieroglyph, Greek and demotic②), which were used in Egypt then. The hieroglyphic was the high script used for important or religious documents and the demotic was the low script of common usage. Greek was the language of the rulers of Egypt at that time. The *Rosetta Stone* was written in all three scripts so that the priests, government officials and rulers of Egypt could read what it said. There is still debate as to which text is the original and which the translation, the Egyptian hieroglyphic or Greek. This stone is historically significant because the scholars, by making a comparative study of the scripts, deciphered the ancient hieroglyphic and opened up the door to the mystery of ancient Egyptian civilization.

Further Readings

Barnstone, Willis. *The Poetics of Translation: History, Theory, Practice*. New Haven and London: Yale University Press, 1993.

Nida, Eugene A. *Towards a Science of Translating*. Shanghai: Shanghai Foreign Language Education Press, 2004.

Shuttleworth, Mark & Moira Cowie. *Dictionary of Translation Studies*. Shanghai: Shanghai Foreign Language Education Press, 2004.

谭载喜:《西方翻译简史》,商务印书馆2004年版。

Topics for Discussion

1. Did the earliest translations in the West happen orally or in writing?

2. What is the *Septuagint*? Is the *Septuagint* religious or secular translation? What method was used in the making of the *Septuagint*? What is its historical significance?

3. Why is the *Letter of Aristeas* an important document in the history of translation? Is everything in the letter verifiable?

---

① 象形文字。

② 古埃及象形文字的简体和通俗用法。

1.2 Secular Translators in Ancient Rome

Translation Terms

Romanization or Latinization 罗马化

It is the translation strategy in which Greek culture was incorporated into Latin framework through cultural assimilation and linguistic adaptation. It is a target-oriented translation strategy that strives for the acceptability of the translation, often at the cost of stylistic faithfulness and cultural transmission.

Adaptation 改编

It is a loose term for any translation that has been made with great latitude to accommodate the target readers. In the adaptation process, the target text has been recast into a different form from the original text to achieve a particular purpose in the target culture. The changes may be so considerable in the adaptation process that the target text is no longer considered a translation.

1.2.1 Socio-cultural Background

Located along the Mediterranean Sea and centered on the city of Rome, Rome was a close neighbor of Greece, with a large Greek population very early in ancient history. The Romans were the most cultured population in the ancient world when literacy was widespread in almost any other culture. For a long time in history, there had been contact between the two peoples on day-to-day basis. After the founding of the Roman Republic (early 6th century BC), Roman rulers began to attack other regions in pursuit of economic and military profits. In 146 BC Greece was annexed into the Roman Republic and lost its political independence, but Greek society and culture continued and remained essentially unchanged until the appearance of Christianity. As a matter of fact, Greece was one of the ancient civilizations in the world, rising far superior to Rome long before the Roman conquest. The Roman emperors and nobles maintained an admiration for Greek culture. The seminal ideals of the Greek were preserved and imitated by the Romans through massive translation movement.

1.2.2 Roman Translation of Greek Secular Culture

The Romans started with translating Greek theater, which the Roman soldiers grew to love during their garrison in East Greek. When these soldiers returned to Rome with a taste for Greek play, some scholars, to address the popular need, began to translate and adapt Greek plays into the Latin language. Translations made then and afterwards constituted the first tidal wave of translation movement in Western translation history, which began in the 3rd century BC and continued well into the 5th century AD. In this period the Roman translators translated Greek culture, particularly its literature and philosophy and later the *New Testament*. Through the translation movement, Greek cultural tradition was preserved in the Latin language and the Roman culture was greatly enriched by Greek culture. Ancient Greek and Roman civilizations were interlocked, collectively known as the Greco-Roman world. This Greco-Roman cultural foundation has been immensely influential on the language, politics, educational systems, philosophy, science, art, and architecture of the modern world.

The earliest translations made during the monarchy period were largely literal and slavish. After the conquest of Greece, the Roman translators began to regard Greek works as *literary prize* that they could take liberty with. Translation was not made to be faithful to the original, but to outshine the original wherever possible. Most of the earlier translations were anonymous. Translation was considered a literary apprenticeship to the entertainment of Roman audience with a more mediocre taste. This attitude was wrought about partly by the consensus that, with their rise in battlefield, the Romans should act as victors in cultural aspects, too. The general translation strategy was free **adaptation**. The Roman translators of Greek theater borrowed most of their plots and all of their dramatic techniques from Greece. Even when writing about themes that are distinctively Roman, they presented them in Greek forms, setting, and dress, without any qualms. In the days when copyright or plagiarism was unheard of, this kind of practice was customary and even commendable. The translations made under this policy were fragmentary, full of flagrant mistakes, omissions and additions. Greek literature was compromised as a result, but Roman culture and language were greatly enriched by Greek philosophy and literature. Theoretical discussion on translation appeared in this period.

1.2.3 Andronicus, Naevius, Ennius and Plautus

The pioneer translator of this period is Livius Andronicus①(285-204 BC).

Livius Andronicus, father of Roman epic poetry and drama, was born in Tarentum in south Italy. His ancestral home was Greece, though. He was captured and made a slave at the fall of Tarentum into Roman hands. Later he was freed from slavery and received the name of Livius Andronicus from his master, a Livian noble. As a freeman, he gained his living by teaching Latin and Greek to his pupils, mostly children of his former master's and other nobles'. As in the course of his tutorship there was no standard Latin textbook, Andronicus translated Homer's *Odyssey* into crude Latin Saturnian metre②, which was stylistically awkward and not without mistakes. Yet it was significant in Western translation history as the first important translated Latin poem. His translation of *Odyssey* offered the young generation of Rome the first access to Greek culture. Up to the 1st century AD, this translation was still used as the most important

① 译为安德罗尼柯。

② 萨图尼乌斯诗体:以轻音重音为标志,后来在希腊诗歌的影响下,又增加了长音、短音的因素。

textbook in schools.

In 240 BC, he was commissioned to translate a Greek play for the annual games honoring Jupiter①. This was the beginning of Roman Drama. Since then, Andronicus continued to write, stage, and sometimes perform in both tragedies and comedies, often in rivalry with his contemporaries. Most of his translations got lost, except the fragments and titles that are preserved in quotes. Fewer than 40 lines of the 10 tragedies have survived, among them the tragedies by Aeschylus②, Sophocles③, and Euripides④. Only one fragment is known from each of his three remaining comedies by Menander⑤. Cicero⑥ and Horace⑦ quoted lines from his translation. As he played an active role in the production of the first Latin comedy and the first Latin tragedy, he was honored as "founder of Roman epic poetry and drama".

Andronicus' translation method was rather flexible. When translating the gods of *Odyssey*, Andronicus used not the original Greek names, nor did he produce a Latin transcription of the Greek pronunciation. Rather he replaced all the Greek gods with Roman mythology. He translated Zeus⑧, for example, with Jupiter, Hermes with Mercury⑨, and so on. This **Latinization** of Greek gods is highly controversial today, but it accelerated the marriage of Greek and Roman mythology and enriched the character of Roman gods and of Roman culture in general. Largely through his efforts as well as similar efforts by later translators, ancient Greek plays were carried onwards as the most felt influence on European theater and culture.

Concurrently, translations were being made elsewhere by some other translators, among them the noteworthy were **Gnaeus Naevius**⑩ and **Quintus Ennius**⑪.

Gnaeus Naevius (270-199 BC) was born in Capua, Campania (Italy) and died in Utica (now in Tunisia). Naevius chronicled the events of the First Punic War (264-261 BC)⑫, basing the facts upon his own experience in the war. He is the first poet who based historical plays on Roman historical or legendary figures and events. Together with Andronicus and

① 朱庇特:罗马神话中统治诸神、主宰一切的主神,古罗马的保护神,朱诺的弟弟和丈夫。也作 Jove。

② 埃斯库罗斯:与欧里庇得斯和索福克勒斯齐名,一起被称为"希腊最伟大的悲剧作家",代表作有《被缚的普罗米修斯》《阿伽门农》等。

③ 索福克勒斯:古希腊剧作家,著有《俄狄浦斯王》等。

④ 欧里庇得斯:古希腊戏剧家,著名作品包括《美狄亚》《希波吕托斯》和《特洛伊妇女》等。

⑤ 米南德:古希腊戏剧家。

⑥ 西塞罗:古罗马政治家、雄辩家、著作家。参见第 12 页。

⑦ 贺拉斯:公元前 1 世纪罗马诗人、批评家。

⑧ 宙斯:希腊神话中的主神,天堂的统治者,诸神和世间英雄的父亲。

⑨ 赫尔墨斯:希腊神话中掌管商业、发明之神,也是众神的信使、书吏及报信者。墨丘利是罗马神话中诸神的信使,掌管商业。

⑩ 涅维乌斯:古罗马历史剧作家。

⑪ 恩尼乌斯:古罗马最有影响的拉丁诗人,被誉为"罗马文学之父"。

⑫ 布匿战争:公元前 264 年至前 146 年古代罗马与迦太基之间的三次战争。罗马人称迦太基人为"布匿",故名。第一、二次布匿战争是作战双方为争夺西部地中海霸权而进行的扩张战争,第三次布匿战争则是罗马以强凌弱的侵略战争。

Ennius, they are styled "the three fathers of Roman poetry". He is an important poet after Livius Andronicus who imitated the Greek models. Unlike Andronicus, who worked on commission, Naevius translated under the patronage of the influential people of the Roman society. For as long as 30 years, Naevius produced half a dozen tragedies and more than 30 comedies. In the course of doing so he created a genre of comedies later called *fabula palliata*① ("play in Greek dress"). He was the first one to introduce song and recitative, transfer elements from one play into another, and add variety to the meter. In his adaptation of Greek plays, he introduced his own critical remarks on Roman daily life and politics. His character and plot and the apt and colorful language were recognizable in Plautus②.

Quintus Ennius (239-169 BC) is a most brilliant poet from ancient Roman Republic and is proclaimed as the father of Latin poetry and the founder of Roman literature. Born in the meeting point of three civilizations—Oscan, Greek, and Latin, Ennius was at home in three languages, i. e., Oscan of his native place, Greek he learned in school and Latin he grasped in his military service in the Roman forces during the second Punic war. He wrote comedies, satires, and epigrams. Ennius was best known for his great history book *Annales*③, but his achievements in translation were also remarkable. Like Naevius, Ennius translated under the patronage of the influential people of the Roman society. His ambition was to be a Homer in the Latin language. As a matter of fact he introduced himself as a reincarnated Homer and translated the meter of Homer in dactylic hexameter④. He adapted 20 tragedies from the Greek, mostly Euripides whose pathetic appeal and rhetorical effect he greatly admired. But most of them are known only by their titles and only about 420 lines remain. Yet these fragments show notable deviations from the originals and display the translator's great skill in adapting the native Latin meters to the Greek poetry form. They also heightened the rhetorical effect and the pathetic appeal through skillful use of alliteration and assonance. He created the elegiac couplet⑤, softened the roughness of Latin diction, and gave Latin poetry a definitive artistic quality. His innovations proved important in the development of Latin poetry. Virgil⑥, Lucretius⑦ and Ovid⑧ borrowed freely from Ennius. Lucan⑨ studied him, Cicero and others admired his work throughout the republican period. He was still widely read up to the 2nd century AD. By the 5th century, copies of Ennius were rare.

---

① 长袍剧:长袍即希腊人日常穿的长袍,该剧种根据希腊剧典型服装命名。

② 普劳图斯:罗马喜剧作家,其作品影响了莎士比亚和莫里哀。

③ 叙事诗《编年史》:记叙了从特洛伊战争中的英雄埃涅阿斯的漫游一直到到作者生活时代的故事,在《伊尼特》面世以前一直被奉为罗马民族史诗。

④ 六音步长短格。

⑤ 挽歌对句:希腊罗马诗体,六音步长短格加五音步长短格组成。

⑥ 维吉尔:罗马诗人。他最伟大的史诗《伊尼特》讲述了伊尼阿斯在特洛伊陷落后的流浪经历。

⑦ 卢克莱修:古罗马哲学家和诗人。

⑧ 奥维德:罗马诗人,以其《爱的艺术》和《变形记》而闻名。

⑨ 卢坎:罗马诗人,他写的《法撒利战记》是关于凯撒和庞培之间内战的史诗记录。

Some other writer-translators of this period include, among others, Plautus, Terence[①], Cicero, Catulus[②] and Horace.

Titus Maccius Plautus (254-184 BC) was the greatest Roman comic playwright. Plautus succeeded in writing comedies by using puns and slapstick gags to make plays entertaining to audience. Like his predecessors and contemporaries, he borrowed most of his plots from plays written by Greek authors of the late 4th and early 3rd centuries BC, notably by Menander and Philemon[③]. Plautus was rather innovative when treating Greek originals. In his representation of Greek life he incorporated Roman concepts, terms, and usages, "referred to towns in Italy; to the gates, streets, and markets of Rome; to Roman laws and the business of the Roman law courts; to Roman magistrates and their duties; and to such Roman institutions as the Senate."[④] But Plautus was a careless translator; he was once criticized by Terence, a more disciplined translator of his day, for being inconsistent in **Romanization**. Plautus did not stop at this, though. He allowed himself greater freedom by combining scenes from two Greek originals into one Latin play. Even more noteworthy was Plautus' mastery of Latin language. In his hands, Latin became racy and colloquial, verse varied and choral, almost to the point of vulgar and crude, but they proved to be the best possible vehicle for his action, which is lively and slapstick.[⑤] In general, Plautus's translations, or rather, free adaptations, impress one as superficially Greek with Roman flavor, or Roman originals based on Greek theme. His command of the Latin tongue was even admired by Cicero. By loosely adapting his works from Greek plays, he established a truly Roman drama in the Latin language. Some of the plots of his plays can be recognized in the comedies of Shakespeare. The popular modern stage and screen comedy "A Funny Thing Happened on the Way to the Forum" is also based on Plautus.

During the reign of Augustus[⑥], a translation office was set up as part of the imperial house to help with administration of the empire. And up to the late 4th century and the early 5th century it was still in operation. Similar organizations were being established in Papal administration.

In sharp contrast with the flowering of translation practice, theoretical discussion on translation was scanty. The only kind of translation theory was a word or two in refutation of other translator's method or in defense of one's own. In the 1st century BC, Cicero began to argue that translation should overtake the original and the translator should have more freedom than the writer.

---

① 泰伦斯:生于希腊的古罗马剧作家。其喜剧如《福尔弥昂》和《阿德尔菲》以其巧妙的幽默和精彩的对话为特征。

② 卡图鲁斯:罗马将军,演说家,散文家。

③ 斐利蒙:雅典新喜剧诗人,享有比米南德更高的声誉。

④ Plautus. Encyclop dia Britannica. Encyclop dia Britannica Inc. 2012-03-16. http://www. britannica. com/EBchecked/topic/464334/Plautus.

⑤ Plautus. Encyclop dia Britannica. Encyclop dia Britannica Inc. 2012-03-16. http://www. britannica. com/EBchecked/topic/464334/Plautus.

⑥ 奥古斯都:罗马帝国第一任皇帝(公元前27 年~公元14 年),尤利斯·凯撒的侄孙。他于公元前31 年打败马克·安东尼及克莉奥帕特拉,于公元前29 年称皇帝,并于公元前27 年被授予奥古斯都荣誉称号。

1.2.4 Cicero

Marcus Tullius Cicero, also called Tully in English, was born in 106 BC and was murdered in 43 BC at the hand of Octavian. Born into a wealthy family, Cicero was able to receive systematic education in rhetoric, law, literature and philosophy. He was, among other things, an orator, rhetorician, lawyer, politician and philosopher. He wrote great works on a wide range of topics like invention, rhetoric, republic, laws, friendship, old age, fate, and so on. His life coincided with the fall of the Roman Republic, and he was an important actor in many of the significant political events of his time. His political writings not only record his personal views on political events of his time but also provide reliable source of information for history study.

Cicero was a prolific translator who translated, among other things, Homer's *Odyssey*, Plato's *Timaeus*① and Protagoras's② works, Xenophon's③ *Economics*, and made a verse translation of Aratus's④ *Phenomena*, etc. He was a Roman encyclopedist who summarized in Latin the important works of Stoic⑤, Academic⑥, peripatetic⑦ and Epicurean⑧ traditions. In the course of his translation, Cicero created a Latin philosophical vocabulary, many of the words still in use today. Among these terms are *quality*, *individual*, *vacuum*, *moral*, *property*, *difference*, *element*, *definition*, *notion*, *infinity*, *comprehension*, *induction*, etc.

Cicero's contribution to translation theory was equally noteworthy. In *The Best Kind of Orator* (46 BC) he was much quoted as saying

> *And I did not translate them (the most famous orations of the most eloquent Attic orators) as an interpreter, but as an orator, keeping the same ideas and the forms, or, as one might say, the 'figures' of thought, but in language which conforms to our usage. I did not hold it necessary to render word for word but I preserved the general style and force of the language. For I did not think I ought to count them out to the reader like coins, but to pay them by weight, as it were.* (quoted in Robinson, 2006: 9)

In his another book *On Definition of Good and Evil*, he further elucidated his idea, putting more emphasis on a flexible translation. Cicero nicely expressed the translator's dilemma:

---

① 《蒂迈欧篇》:古希腊哲学家柏拉图的晚期著作,是关于宇宙论和自然科学的一篇对话。

② 普罗塔哥拉:公元前5世纪希腊哲学家,智者派的主要代表人物。

③ 色诺芬:古希腊将军,历史学家,著有《远征记》《希腊史》《回忆苏格拉底》等。

④ 阿拉托斯:古希腊诗人和天文学作家,他将天文学著作《物象》改写成韵文。

⑤ 斯多葛派:希腊哲学流派,为芝诺约于公元前380年创立,他们认为人不应为情感所动,应把各事情当作神意或自然法则的不可避免的结果来坦然地接受。

⑥ 学园派:柏拉图创立学园(Academy)作为讲学之所,后来引申为柏拉图学派或学园派哲学,宣称理念是绝对实在和永恒实在,而现象世界只是绝对实在和永恒实在的不完美的、暂时的反映。

⑦ 原意为"漫步",由于亚里士多德常在古雅典学园中一边漫步一边讨论问题,后来引申为亚里士多德的哲学思想或教育方法的逍遥派。在其哲学体系里,理论服从实地观察和逻辑,以三段论为基础,基本上是理性研究方法。

⑧ 伊壁鸠鲁:古希腊哲学家、无神论者,伊壁鸠鲁学派的创始人。主张要达到不受干扰的宁静状态,提倡感官享受和享乐主义。

> *If I render word for word, the result will sound uncouth, and if, by necessity, I alter anything in the order or wording, I shall seem to have departed from the function of a translator.* (quoted in Bassnnet, 2004: 49)

It can be inferred that Cicero opposed word for word translation and approved a strategy that could reproduce the force of the original in conformity to the target language usage. His version of *Odyssey* was a good illustration of his translation concept. Cicero held that literal translation is the work of the unskilled and should best be avoided; translation is a form of literary recreation; translator of Demosthenes① should be a Demosthenes himself.

Ever since the publication of his views on translation, translation was considered as a form of literary creation, and incessant debate arose over three dichotomies: original versus translation, form versus content and the translator's rights versus his responsibility. His division of translator *as an orator or as interpreter* basically defined the *literal versus free* opposition, which is still under debate in translation community today. To quote Wilss, Cicero formulated two basic methods "which decided the course of discussion in the field for those who followed... Since the time of Cicero, a continuous thread has been woven through the history of translation theory by the argument over normative points of reference for the activity of translating" (Wilss, 2001: 30, my ellipsis).

1.2.5 Horace, Pliny the Younger and Quintilian

Horace is a famous poet and art critic in early Roman Empire. His father was a freed slave. In his early life, Horace received his education in Athens, took office and served in the army. In his *Arts of Poetry*, an important work in world art theory, Horace expounded creation of poetry and play as well as the qualifications of poets and playwrights. Horace's *Arts of Poetry* not only influenced literary creation of later generations but also gave impetus to the development of translation theory. He mainly followed Cicero's translation tradition and advised the translators not to "trouble to render word for word with the faithfulness of a translator" (quoted in Robinson, 2006: 15). He said in his *Arts of Poetry*

> *A theme that is familiar can be made your own property so long as you do not waste your time on a hackneyed treatment; nor should you try to render your original word for word like a slavish translator, or in imitating another writer plunge yourself into difficulties from which shame, or the rules you have laid down for yourself, prevent you from extricating yourself.* (quoted in Bassnnet, 2004: 49)

Horace maintained that the playwright should better translate and adapt great Greek plays than write about the strange subjects of their own. He also emphasized that translation may help enrich the translator's native language and culture. Translators of Horace's time had a habit of

① 狄摩西尼:希腊演说家,因号召雅典市民反抗马其顿国王腓力二世的一系列演讲《强烈抨击》而知名。

creating or borrowing Greek new words without constraint, while Horace cautioned them about the use of new words. The addition of new words and removal of old ones were compared to the change of leaves in spring and autumn that would be natural provided the translator used them with moderation. If, on the other hand, the original was learned and deep and had to be expressed with a new word in the target language, the word must be coined with great circumspection. Like Cicero, Horace held that the art of translation consisted in judicious interpretation and representation of the original text sense for sense, instead of word for word, and in the translator's concern with the target readers.

Pliny the Younger①(62? -113 AD) is a Roman consul and writer, the nephew of Pliny the Elder. His letters provide valuable information about Roman life of his time. In his letter to Fuscus Salinator he suggested that translating from Latin into Greek or Greek into Latin is a good literary exercise that requires careful reading, cultivates perception, and develops critical sense. He believed that it does no harm to rival the original, improve on it, revise it, retaining, or deleting as the translator thinks proper. This exercise is difficult but profitable to rekindle his fire and recover his spent enthusiasm. It is like grafting new limbs on to a finished trunk without disturbing the balance of the original.

Better known as a great orator and rhetorician, **Quintilian**②(about 35-95 AD)(originally Marcus Fabius Quintilianus) is another great translator after Cicero and Horace. Quintilian studied in Rome in his early years and finally settled down in Rome where he enjoyed a good reputation as a teacher of rhetoric. His views on translation are found in his book *Elements of Rhetorics*, a founding document of Western rhetoric, educational theory, and literary criticism. Quintilian followed the tradition of Cicero and Horace and summarized in a rigorous manner Cicero's unsystematic thoughts on translation for foreign language teaching.

In summary, Quintilian maintained that to translate Greek orations the translators should use the very best words and invent new verbal figures because the Roman tongue differs from that of the Greeks. The best has already been said by the Greek, Quintilian said, but the translator should not despair of finding a better possibility because the language has the potential of speaking well on a subject in more than one way. By *paraphrase*, Quintilian meant not an interpretation, but an effort to vie with the original in the expression of the same thought. The translator, therefore, has the right to add rhetorical force, supply what has been omitted and give compactness to the diffuse idea.

Further Readings

Barnstone, Willis. *The Poetics of Translation: History, Theory, Practice*. New Haven and

① 小普林尼:古罗马执政官和作家,是老普林尼的外甥。他的书信提供了有关古罗马人生活的珍贵信息。老普林尼(公元 23 ~ 79 年)是古罗马学者和博物学家,他写了三十七卷的《自然史》。

② 昆体良:古罗马时期的著名律师、教育家和皇室委任的第一个修辞学教授。

London: Yale University Press, 1993.

Bassnnet, Susan. *Translation Studies*. Shanghai: Shanghai Foreign Language Education Press, 2004.

Lefevere, Andre. *Translation, Rewriting and the Manipulation of Literary Fame*. Shanghai: Shanghai Foreign Language Education Press, 2004b.

Plautus. Encyclop dia Britannica. Encyclop dia Britannica Inc. 2012-03-16. http://www.britannica.com/EBchecked/topic/464334/Plautus.

Robinson, Douglas. *Western Translation Theory: From Herodotus to Nietzsche*. Shanghai: Foreign Language Teaching and Research Press, 2006.

Shuttleworth, Mark & Moira Cowie. *Dictionary of Translation Studies*. Shanghai: Shanghai Foreign Language Education Press, 2004.

Wilss, Wolfram. *The Science of Translation: Problems and Methods*. Shanghai: Shanghai Foreign Language Education Press, 2001.

谭载喜:《西方翻译简史》,商务印书馆 2004 年版。

Topics for Discussion

1. What type of text is most translated during the Roman translation of Greek culture? What are the general translation strategies? Illustrate the translation strategies with one example and account for them from socio-cultural perspective.

2. What are the popular notions of translation during Roman translation of Greek culture? Cite two instances to illustrate them.

3. Why was Cicero considered the first translation theorist? What is the topic and mode of his discussion?

1.3 *Bible* Translators in Late Ancient Rome

Translation Terms

Retranslation 重译,复译

1. A later translation of the very original text as against the first translation.
2. An indirect translation that is translated via a text that is already a translation. Jerome's *Old Testament* is a later translation of the very original Hebrew text, the first translation being the *Septuagint*. A text is retranslated because the earlier translations are either defective or obsolete in the language or the idea.

Direct translation 直接翻译,顺向翻译(see "inverse translation" on page 1)

A translation that is made directly from the very original text, rather than via another intermediate language. St. Jerome retranslated the *Old Testament* directly from the very original Hebrew language into the Latin language, rather than via the Septuagint, which is a translation itself. Direct translation is a generally approved-of translation method because it is free from interference of previous interpretations and is therefore more accurate.

1.3.1 Socio-cultural Background

The Roman Empire was characterized by an autocratic form of government and large territorial holdings around the Mediterranean in Europe, Africa, and Asia. It was a remarkably multicultural and multilingual society, which encompasses diverse peoples within its political system over a long span of time. The official language of the Roman Empire was Latin, but many Romans studied Greek as a literary language, and most men of the governing classes could speak Greek. In eastern Roman Empire, laws and official documents were regularly translated into Greek from Latin. The everyday interpretation of the two languages is indicated by bilingual inscriptions, which sometimes even switch back and forth between Greek and Latin[①]. In addition to Greek and Latin, various local languages were also used in the Roman Empire.

After the massive translation movement during the Roman Republic, most of the important Greek works (philosophy and literature) were translated into the Latin language. In the second period of the Roman Empire, literary production was on the decline and so was literary translation. In the meantime, *the New Testament*, the holy scripture of Christianity, came out originally in Greek between the 1st and 2nd century AD with the rapid spreading of Christianity among the poor of the Empire. Starting in the 3rd century, the Roman Empire underwent a series of crisis that threatened its existence, but was reunified and stabilized. Towards the end of the Roman Empire, the political crisis deepened. The Roman rulers began to use religion to consolidate and perpetuate its rule. Christianity was no longer viewed as a sinister threat to the Empire. It was proclaimed legal in 313 and made the official religion of Rome towards the end of the 4th century. Religious translating was in its full swing. This massive translation of the *Bible* constitutes the second tidal wave in Western translation history. The great translators and translation theorists during this era are, among others, Jerome and Augustine.

Bible consists of *the Old Testament* and *the New Testament*. *The Old Testament* was written mainly in the Hebrew language and was the holy book of Judaism. *The New Testament*, which is concerned with the lives and teachings of Jesus Christ and his apostles, incorporated many elements of *the Old Testament* and was the holy scripture of Christianity. Translations of *the New Testament* were made very early in history into a number of different languages, i. e. , Syriac and Latin, to be followed by Coptic (several dialects), Ethiopic, Gothic, Gregorian and Armenian. As Christian church had long been a strong force in Western politics, translation of

---

① Roman_Empire. From Wikipedia, the free encyclopedia. 2012-05-16. http://en. wikipedia. org/wiki/Roman_Empire.

the *Bible*, from the antiquity onwards, was made under auspices and control of the church authorities and was interwoven with the conflict between competing denominations.

1.3.2 Philo

The first influential *Bible* translator is **Philo Judaeus** (10/15 BC-45/50 AD), a Greek-speaking Jewish philosopher, the most important representative of Hellenistic[①] Judaism. He occupied a unique position in the history of philosophy as the first one to synthesize revealed faith and philosophic reason, contending that the *Bible* reflected Greek wisdom and attempted to bring it in line with Platonism[②] and the Stoics. His writings provide the clearest view of the development of Judaism in the Diaspora[③]. His valuable commentaries on Jewish law were much quoted until the Middle Ages. He translated portions of the *Bible*, but was far more renowned for his theorization on *Bible* translation.

With Philo, *Bible* translation is a sacred undertaking and a translator, without divine inspiration, could not translate the holy book on the strength of his mastery of the two languages. Philo used the *Septuagint* as an example to show that only constant believers could produce sacred version and only those away from worldly impunities and leading a holy religious life is entitled to the sacred task. Philo was the first person who suggested divine illumination, i. e., the 72 scholars who produced the same versions simultaneously in isolation from one another were inspired by God, while in the *Letter of Aristeas* the translators actually consulted each other on the versions. He described the 72 translators in this way:

> *Sitting here in seclusion with none present save the elements of nature, earth, water, air, heaven, the genesis of which was to be the first of their sacred revelation, for the laws begin with the story of the world's creation, they became as it were possessed, and under inspiration, wrote, not each several scribe something different, but the same word for word, as though dictated to each by an invisible prompter. — For, just as in geometry and logic, so it seems to me, the sense indicated does not admit of variety in the expression which remains unchanged in its original form, so these writers, as it clearly appears, arrived at a wording which corresponds with the matter, and alone, or better than any other, would bring out clearly what was meant.* (quoted in Robinson, 2006: 14)

"Divine illumination" is up against many difficulties because it deprived the translator of his initiative in the process of translating, relegating the translator to a machine doing God's dictation. In his time, nevertheless, Philo's theory was held in high esteem as the only sensible criterion of *Bible* translation. Many *Bible* translations were made under this policy, i. e., word

---

① 希腊化时期:指公元前4世纪末至公元1世纪初希腊文化向东方传播以及与东方文化交流的时期,又称"泛希腊时期"。这一时期的希腊化促进了东西方宗教的融合及世界宗教和中东文明圈的形成。

② 柏拉图哲学:宣称理念是绝对的和永恒的实在,而世界中的现象却是理念的不完美的、暂时的反映。

③ (犹太人)离散:泛指历史上犹太民族从自己的家乡犹太地和后来的以色列地被驱逐出去,流亡异乡的历程。此处主要指犹太人先后在埃及被奴役、在新巴比伦遭囚禁,后又被罗马帝国征服的苦难历程。

for word under divine illumination. At about 130 AD, for example, Aquila[①] translated the Hebrew *Bible* into Greek with slavish literalness. He "attempted to reproduce the most minute detail of the original, even to the extent of coining derivations from Greek roots to correspond to Hebrew usage"[②]. It was towards the late 2nd century that Symmachus the Ebionite[③] made bold to render the target text with the purity and idiomatic elegance of Greek and the translation became more intelligible. His influence was small despite the superior elegance of his work. Jerome utilized Symmachus for his *Vulgate*, saying that "Unlike Aquila, who translated literally, he gave the sense of the scripture" (quoted in Nida, 2004: 12).

1.3.3 Jerome

Saint Jerome[④] (347? -420) is a Latin Christian priest, confessor, theologian and historian, who also became a Doctor of the Church. He was the son of Eusebius[⑤] (260-339), of the city of Stridon, Roman empire. He approved Greek theologian Origen's idea[⑥] and translated his 14 sermons. Besides, he translated church historian Eusebius's *Chronicle of the Church* and adapted some other works. He is best known as the translator of the Latin *Vulgate*[⑦] and his commentaries on the *Gospel of the Hebrews*.

Up to the 4th century, Latin began to replace Greek as a world language of culture and religion. With the spread of Christianity, several Latin translations of the Greek *New Testament* appeared. These earlier translations were fragmentary and uneven, oftentimes contradicting each other and confusing the readers. Partly to end the confusion, Jerome was commissioned by Pope Damasus[⑧] in 382 to revise the Latin *New Testament* with reference to the best Greek manuscripts.

Jerome collated many different translation works, compared them with Greek originals and removed crude or parochial language and dubious interpretations. He introduced bold changes into revised version of the *Four Gospels* of *the New Testament*. The revision was finished by 384. Soon afterwards, he started to translate, among others, *Psalter*[⑨] and *Job*[⑩] from the *Septuagint*. In the course of translating, he was increasingly dissatisfied with the way *Septuagint* was made, insisting that the *Old Testament* be retranslated out of the Hebrew original. At about

① 阿奎拉:公元2世纪的圣经翻译家。

② Biblical literature. Encyclop dia Britannica. Encyclop dia Britannica Inc. 2012-03-16. http://www.britannica.com/EBchecked/topic/64496/biblical-literature.

③ 西玛库斯:公元2世纪的圣经译者,曾将《旧约》译为希腊文。

④ 译为哲罗姆。

⑤ 凯撒利亚的优西比乌:西方历史上第一个教会史家,著有《教会史》。

⑥ 奥瑞金:公元3世纪亚历山大城最知名的神学家和圣经学者。

⑦ 译为《通俗拉丁文圣经》。

⑧ 达玛斯主教。

⑨ 祈祷用的《圣经诗集》。

⑩ 《约伯记》:《旧约》中记述的约伯故事,约伯一个诚实正直的人物,历经危难,仍坚信上帝。

405, Jerome produced, in cooperation with his assistants, a Latin version of the Hebrew *Old Testament*. Jerome's **retranslation** of the *Old Testament* and revision of the *New Testament* were collectively called the Latin *Vulgate* (meaning vulgar or common).

Jerome's *Vulgate* did not put an end to the protracted confusion in the existing renderings of the *Bible*, yet it provided the Latin readers with a comparatively "standard" rendering of the Scriptures in full. As Hebrew and Greek grew more distant and archaic to the Western intellectual world in the Middle Ages, the Latin *Vulgate* remained for many believers the only reliable access to the words of God. Later, it won the approval of the Roman Catholic Church and practically replaced its Hebrew and Greek originals as the source texts from which latter *Bible* translations were made into new European languages. The *Vulgate* dominated Biblical scholarship until the Reformation① and is only now being displaced by more recent versions. The *Vulgate* is a remarkable effort considering the magnitude of the work and the opposition his project provoked. In honor of his contribution to the profession, St Jerome's birthday (30 September) is designated as International Translation Day when Jerome is commemorated with a memorial. He is recognized as a saint by the Catholic Church②, the Eastern Orthodox Church③, the Lutheran Church④, and the Church of England⑤.

When revising the *New Testament*, Jerome did not rely on the traditional interpretations. Likewise, in retranslating the *Old Testament* he oftentimes varied from the old renderings in the *Septuagint*, which was held inviolable at that time. Jerome anticipated that his choice might incur severe criticism from the opposing denomination. His worry was well-founded. Upon the publication of the translation a storm of abuse followed him for the rest of his life because of his "sacrilegious" departure from the old interpretation and further differences from the earlier renderings. Augustine⑥, for example, wrote to Jerome in 403, accusing him of causing further confusions in his translation and requesting him to put the controversial texts, original and translated, side by side in the footnote of the translation for the readers to compare and study.

Jerome was a systematic and disciplined translator who translated under well-conceived and consistent principles. At first, he conceived that the 72 translators of the *Old Testament* indeed translated at the God's call. As he continued with his own translation, however, he felt that on

---

① 宗教改革运动:16 世纪西欧旨在改革罗马天主教某些教义和做法的改革运动,最终导致新教的建立。

② 罗马天主教会:天主教是与东正教、新教并列的基督教三大宗教派别之一,亦称"公教",是基督教最大宗派。天主教主导了整个欧洲中世纪的思想潮流,深刻影响了西欧社会的政治、经济、文化和艺术等各个领域。

③ 东正教:又称"正教会"或"正统教会",是基督教的主要宗派之一,是由东罗马帝国所流传下来的基督教传统的教会。它是与天主教、新教并立的基督教三大派别之一,信徒主要分布在东欧国家。与天主教不同,正教由一些被称为"自主教会"或"自治教会"的地方教会组成,这些教会彼此独立,但却有着共同的信仰。

④ 路德宗:是以马丁·路德的宗教思想之统称,因其教义核心为"因信称义",故又称"信义宗"。它是德意志宗教改革运动的产物,由马丁·路德于 1529 年创立于德国。这一新的宗派的建立,标志着基督教新教的诞生。

⑤ 安立甘宗:是基督教新教主要宗派之一,与信义宗、归正宗合称"新教三大流派",中国常称"圣公会"。该宗在英格兰为国教,称"英国国教会"。

⑥ 奥古斯丁:早期基督教教父及哲学家。著有自传体作品《忏悔录》及长篇作品《上帝之城》。参见第 21 页。

such matters like comprehending and rendering of the *Holy Scriptures* there was no divine revelation at all. He held that the translator should use his own judgment and knowledge, linguistic and encyclopedic, in order to arrive at a right interpretation of the original, and then translate accordingly in conformity with the usage of the target language. He proclaimed his translation principle and defended it with veracity, as was scattered in his letters and prefaces to the translations. In the preface to *Job*, he said that "About this point I have no doubt, that I can only translate what I comprehended" (quoted in Robinson, 2006: 29). In another preface he stated that the translator should use his knowledge of the two languages to understand and translate a sentence. He went further to accuse the first person of telling the lie of the 72 Jewish scholars.

Although translating a religious text Jerome followed Cicero's advice on academic translation, arguing for translating "sense for sense" instead of "word for word". According to Jerome, languages are different from each other in diction, sentence structure and word meaning, which render literal translation impossible. Translation, therefore, should not aim at word for word correspondence; it should regard the sense. One example he cited was the Biblical story in which Jesus brought a dead girl back to life. There is a sentence "And he took the damsel by the hand, and said unto her, *Talitha cumi*, an Aramaic expression meaning literally 'Damsel, arise'". Gospel writer Mark rendered it in Greek expression which meant "Damsel, I say to you, arise." Jerome praised the addition *I say to you* as translating the spirit of the original, despite the fact that it was absent in the original. And this addition was largely retained in later versions of the *New Testament*. He also praised the manner in which the *New Testament* writers freely quoted or adapted the Hebrew *Old Testament* and the *Septuagint*.

> *For all the examples, it should be apparent that the Apostles and the Evangelists in quoting from Old Testament sources have tried to communicate the meaning rather than the literal words, and that they have not cared greatly to preserve exact phrases and sentence constructions, so long as they could clearly present the substance of their subject to men's understanding.* (quoted in Robinson, 2006: 29)

To lend further authority to the idea, he quoted a preface from a biography of St. Antony of Egypt①: "Although my version is hardly literal, I have preserved the sense. Others may chase after syllables and exact duplicate words, I have only regarded the substance." (quoted in Robinson, 2006: 26) In his letter to Pammachius②, he insisted on "transferring the meaning into one's own language by right of conquest" (quoted in Kelly, 1979: 44).

Jerome was inconsistent in his defense of sense for sense translation, though. In a letter written at the end of 395, Jerome explained that he himself mainly used sense for sense translation except when he translated the *Bible*, where "even the syntax contains a mystery"

① 圣安东尼:是来自埃及的基督教圣徒,旷野教父的著名领袖,许多教派都有宗教节日来纪念他。

② 帕玛丘:生平不详,哲罗姆有关翻译的大部分论述都集中在写给帕玛丘的信中。

(quoted in Robinson, 2006: 25). He is hinting that different translation methods should be used for different text types and that *Bible* should be translated with more regard to the wording.

This self-contradictory stance may be accounted for by his theological controversy with Tyrannius Rufinus①, one of the renowned theologians in favor of freer translation than Jerome was willing to accept. The other contributing factor might be the translators' traditional anxiety about translation of sacred texts and the general notion that only a word-for-word translation could make a translation more accurate. Still a more miraculous explanation was his famous dream from 375, where the Lord called him and accused him of following Cicero rather than being a Christian. It was believed that this dream worked a first major self-contradictory claim in Western translation theory, for afterwards Jerome began to argue that *Bible* translator should also regard the word and strive for accuracy. Yet elsewhere he seemed to contradict himself by saying that "in dealing with the *Bible* one must consider the substance and not the literal words" (quoted in Robinson, 2006: 29).

Jerome admitted frankly that he sometimes translated word for word and some other times sense for sense. And he justified himself on the grounds of the complexity of translation per se. A better explanation is that Jerome, realizing the complexity of translation, held a dialectic view on translation method. It is generally accepted today that the two basic translation methods complement as well as modify each other and the relationship between them is complementary rather than mutually exclusive. Jerome's self-contradiction brought the sense versus word dichotomy under spotlight in *Bible* translation theory.

Jerome's translation principles and methods were also a far-reaching influence on later translators and translation scholars. The Medieval *Bibles* were translated into emerging national European languages under his policies. Jerome also had corps of followers among secular translators, who insisted on style as an indispensable part of the original message. In the later antiquity, however, it was Augustine's theory that gained more ground among *Bible* translators.

1.3.4 Augustine

St. Augustine (354-430) was born to a pagan father and Christian mother in today's Algeria, about 60 miles from Bona (ancient Hippo-Regius). He became interested in Manichaeism②, Neo-Platonism③, and Platonism before he finally immersed himself in the *New Testament*. Augustine later served (396-430) as the bishop of Hippo. He was an early Christian church father and philosopher whose summary of Plato and the *New Testament*

---

① 鲁斐努斯:罗马神学家和牧师,把希腊神学著作译为拉丁语。

② 摩尼教:又称作"牟尼教""明教",源自古代波斯袄教,为公元3世纪中叶波斯人摩尼(Mani)所创立。

③ 新柏拉图主义:公元3世纪在埃及亚历山大城发展起来的一种哲学体系,流行于公元3~5世纪。它以柏拉图学说为基础,带有神秘主义色彩,糅合了一些犹太教和基督教概念。新柏拉图主义是古希腊文化末期最重要的哲学流派,对西方中世纪中的基督教神学产生了重大影响。

produced an enormous influence upon the western world. He wrote, among others, the autobiographical *Confessions*①(397), the voluminous *City of God*②(413-426) and *On Christian Doctrine*③(428), all world classics. His methodological innovations inspired Descartes④(1596-1650), Galileo and Saussure⑤(1857-1913). Augustine's influence is felt in language theory, translation studies, and particularly the 14th century theological debate. His sign theory has been regarded as the common property of philosophy and linguistics and is still in circulation today.

Augustine proofread portions of Latin *Bible*. His insightful views on translation were mainly collected in *On Christian Doctrine*. Although the book confessedly aimed at guiding the Christians to understand and study the *Bible*, many issues discussed in it touched on, directly or indirectly, the general issues of language and translation.

Augustine required that the translator should have the following qualifications. 1. knowledge of the two languages involved; 2. knowledge of the subject matter being translated; 3. some skill in comparative critique of the Scriptural texts; 4. care for accuracy. He considers translating as consisting of two stages: reading the original message and writing it out in Latin. These ideas remained current until the 20th century. (quoted in Kelly, 1979: 35)

At the start of the discussion Augustine considered the relationship between the sign, what the sign represents and the translator's judgment, which is a further development of Aristotle's sign theory. Augustine was mainly concerned about verbal signs, or words. As these verbal signs were not common to all peoples, the words of God were translated into various languages so that different peoples would understand them exactly as God wished. In this connection, he posited *Bible* translation under a more general framework of sign theory.

Augustine held that the difficult and confusing points in the *Bible* arose from unknown or ambiguous signs. To understand unknown words, we need to develop our knowledge of languages. Ambiguous words are largely figurative, and to understand them we need to use our judgment. When caught in the ambiguity of words, the codices⑥ are to be emended. In face of many, and sometimes, uneven versions of the *New Testament*, the translator must proofread the earlier translations against the Greek original so as to determine the intended meaning of an ambiguous word. Since the meaning conveyed is not clear enough and since only the very

① 《忏悔录》:描写早期奥古斯丁归信时的内心挣扎及转变经历。

② 《上帝之城》:奥古斯丁的晚期著作,意在说明,按照灵性生活的人组成的"上帝之城",是上帝的"选民"即预定得救的基督徒的社会,这是一座永恒之城。在对比"尘世之城"和"上帝之城"的起源和结局的过程中,他建构了基督教的历史观,融会了他一生中的主要宗教思想。

③ 《论基督教义》:是奥古斯丁的神学著作,教人如何理解和讲授圣经。

④ 笛卡儿:著名的法国哲学家、科学家和数学家,是西方现代哲学思想的奠基人。

⑤ 索绪尔:瑞士语言学家,结构主义语言的创始人。

⑥ codex 的复数形式,指《圣经》等古籍的抄本。

learned translators could avoid mistakes, the translator must consult word for word translations or seek knowledge of those languages in which God's words were originally written. "Yet, as I have said before, a comparison with those translators who adhered more closely to the words of the original is not without use in explaining their meaning." (quoted in Robinson, 2006: 34) Augustine believed a comparison and weighing of varied translations was useful when ambiguity arose.

In Augustine's theory, language, sign and word are used interchangeably. On some occasions Augustine insisted that basic **translation unit** should be as large as possible, yet on some other occasions he argued that the Greek prefixes and bound morphemes should be translated as independent signs. Generally speaking, Augustine came out in more support of literal translation of the *Bible* than Jerome, for he openly approved literal method of translating the *Septuagint*.

Augustine observed that different languages have similar ability of expression. He acknowledged that as some Hebrew words have no correspondents in the Latin language, these words might be imported straight into Latin. Words of mood like interjections are largely untranslatable, too, because they signify the motion of spirit rather than any rational concept. Some other Hebrew words were indeed left untranslated, like *Amen*, not because they could not be translated, but because they had been preserved from antiquity on account of their holier authority.

Augustine held that the distinction must be made between three kinds of style: plain, elegant and majestic, on the basis of the different needs of the target readers. If the translation is mainly made to illuminate general readers, a plain style is preferable; when the translation is to sing the God's glory to the educated Christians, an elegant style is more desirable; where the translation targets at all readers, general and educated, with the purpose of scriptural instruction, a majestic style would be appropriate. Furthermore, the translator has the right to blend the three styles together as he thinks proper. This trichotomy of style based on the different readership is not entirely new, though. In *On the Orator*, Cicero also mentioned the orator in relation to his audience, but Augustine developed it with more perspicuity. Augustine held that whatever the style, the ultimate purpose is definite, i.e., to teach the ecclesiastic truth to the audience in intelligible terms. Translating would fail if the target readers' response is different from what the writer expected of his original readers.

Augustine maintained that *Bible* translation must be done under divine illumination. The translator should have "faith, hope and love" for God. On this point, Augustine was with Philo about three hundred years ago. In fact, Augustine went further than Philo in this respect, emphasizing that only divinely inspired translators were entitled to translating the *Bible*. He believed every word in the *Letter of Aristeas* and insisted that not a word of the *Septuagint* should be changed. "But even if they (the 72 Jewish translators) conferred and arrived at a single opinion on the basis of common judgment and consent, it is not right or proper for any man, no matter how learned, to seek to emend the consensus of so many older and more learned men." (quoted in Robinson, 2006: 34) Augustine admitted that there existed differences between Hebrew original and the *Septuagint*, but these differences, he explained, could be ascribed to the Holy Spirit who made the later translator speak differently from their prophets (the original Hebrew authors). "It may be that the Holy Spirit judged that they should translate in a manner befitting the people whom they addressed and they should speak as if with one voice." (quoted in Robinson, 2006: 34)

Augustine overstated the effect of divine inspiration and further mystified religious translation. He put the privilege of interpreting the Scriptures into the hands of a few church fathers, depriving the common people, ordinary Christians included, of their first-hand access into the *Bible*. As he honored the Greek *Septuagint* most, Augustine insisted that the Latin versions should never take the place of the *Septuagint* as source text. He wrote Jerome several times for fear that Jerome's *Vulgate* might leave the Latin readers in confusion because Jerome's *Old Testament*, a direct translation from the Hebrew original, departed from the *Septuagint* in many places. To set his mind at ease and also to help the Latin readers understand the *Vulgate*, he wrote his 28th letter to Jerome, requesting the latter to add in the footnotes the quoted Hebrew originals alongside controversial Greek translations for the Latin readers' judgment. This was not accepted by Jerome, but was widely employed by later *Bible* translators.

Of the same age with Jerome and Augustine was another influential translator **Tyrannius Rufinus** (345-416), who was known for his quarrel with Jerome. After study at Rome, where he met Jerome, Rufinus entered a monastery at Aquileia. Jerome often visited the monastery, and the two became close friends. Rufinus later turned back on Jerome because of theological contention. Rufinus was an authority on Greek religious literature and translated numerous Biblical commentaries and homilies by Origen①, an Apologia for Origen by the learned teacher and martyr Pamphilus②, sermons by Saints Basil③ and Gregory of Nazianzus④, and the history of the early church by Eusebius⑤; none of these works survive in complete texts. In theory, Rufinus was against Cicero and Jerome. In practice, however, the difference between them is not as big as has often been implied. Whenever he suspected that the works he was translating had been altered by unorthodox theologians, Rufinus did not hesitate to shorten or paraphrase the original text. Rufinus approved a freer method, adding as well as removing and altering the original as he thought proper. In his own words, he loved to add something to the translation to make it more intelligible. "What I did was to give back to the author what he told me." (quoted in Kelly, 1979: 60)

---

① 奥瑞金:公元3世纪亚历山大城最知名的神学家和圣经学者。
② 帕斐鲁斯:凯撒利亚的长老,当时天主教圣经学者中的领袖。
③ 巴兹尔:公元4世纪的神学家,维护基督教正统,反对阿里乌斯派信徒。
④ 格雷戈里:公元4世纪的神学家,维护三位一体教理和基督教正统,抵制阿里乌斯派信徒。
⑤ 凯撒利亚的优西比乌:西方历史上第一个教会史家,著有《教会史》。

Further Readings

Baker, Mona. *Routledge Encyclopedia of Translation Studies*. London & New York: Routledge, 1998.

Bassnnet, Susan. *Translation Studies*. Shanghai: Shanghai Foreign Language Education Press, 2004.

Biblical literature. Encyclop dia Britannica. Encyclop dia Britannica Inc. 2012-03-16. http://www.britannica.com/EBchecked/topic/64496/biblical-literature.

Kelly, Louis. G. *The True Interpreter: A History of Translation Theory and Practice in the West*. New York: St. Martin's Press, 1979.

Roman Empire. From Wikipedia, the free encyclopedia. 2012-05-16. http://en.wikipedia.org/wiki/Roman_Empire.

Robinson, Douglas. *Western Translation Theory: From Herodotus to Nietzsche*. Shanghai: Foreign Language Teaching and Research Press, 2006.

Shuttleworth, Mark & Moira Cowie. *Dictionary of Translation Studies*. Shanghai: Shanghai Foreign Language Education Press, 2004.

谭载喜:《西方翻译简史》,商务印书馆2004年版。

Topics for Discussion

1. Compared to non-religious translation, what is the general method of translating the *Bible*? Illustrate the difference between *Bible* translation theory and secular translation theory with examples.

2. Do you believe in divine illumination in religious translation? Do you think only strong believer of God is entitled to translating the *Bible*? Is religious devotion an essential qualification for *Bible* translators?

3. In what way Augustine is original as a translation theorist? What is sign theory to his discussion of translation? What points he raised impress you most?

1.4 Chapter Summary

The earliest recorded complete translation in the West is the *Septuagint*, a Greek translation of the Hebrew *Old Testament*. The making of the translation is documented in the mysterious book *Letter of Aristeas*. Today, the *Septuagint* is still used by the Greek Church, and serves as the basis for translation into many other languages of the Mediterranean world.

During the early ancient Rome, the Greek literature, particularly the epic poetry and theater, and Greek philosophy were introduced into Rome with free imitation and loose adaptation. Translations made during this period constituted the first climax in Western translation history. Cicero is the first translator who discussed the process and methods of translation. And his dichotomy of translator "as an interpreter or orator" largely defined the debate over literal versus free translation for the next two thousand years. His regard for the original idea and the target language expression have won approval from a multitude of later translators, among them Horace, Quintilian, Pliny the younger, etc.

In late Roman Empire, *Bible* translations were made under the control and patronage of the church authorities, constituting the second tidal wave of translation in the West. Generally speaking, the *Bible* was translated with more accuracy and less freedom than non-religious texts. *Bible* translation theory was on the side of literal translation heavily shadowed by theological thinking. Philo openly praised the literal translation of the *Septuagint* and insisted on the divine illumination in *Bible* translation. Augustine was one of the most systematic *Bible* translation theorists of ancient times. He discussed *Bible* translation within the framework of sign theory, touching on the translator's qualifications, translation process, three different styles for different readers, translation of Hebrew mood words that had no equivalent in Latin, and translation of figurative, ambiguous words in the *Bible*, etc. Jerome was caught between regard for the word or the sense in *Bible* translation.

It needs to be pointed out that throughout the entire antiquity the discussion on translation in general was unsystematic and sporadic. Earliest discourses on translation were mostly found in random talks on issues other than translation, in prefaces to translated works, or in private letters to some important people of the time.

Chapter Two
Cultural Dissemination during the Middle Ages

2.1 Translators in Early Middle Ages

Translation Terms

Indirect translation 间接翻译(see "direct translation" on page 15 and "retranslation" on page 15)

Also intermediate translation, mediated translation, retransaltion or second-hand translation. (Shuttleworth & Cowie, 2004: 76) It is a translation that is based on a source text that is itself a translation. It is used when 1) the source text is unavailable in the original language; 2) the translator with required source language competence is unavailable. Indirect translation is generally considered undesirable because it tends to deviate further from the very original source text. But it flourished in some places in translation history and is still tolerated today.

Semantic Borrowing 语义借用

Also known as semantic loan, semantic borrowing is a process in which a word in the target language borrows a meaning (rather than lexical items) from the source language. In this case, the complete word in the target language already exists before the borrowing took place; after the borrowing the existing word in the target language takes on a new meaning from the source language. The only thing borrowed is this new meaning. Calques, loanwords and semantic borrowing are often grouped roughly under the phrase "borrowing", although there is minor difference between them.

2.1.1 Socio-cultural Background

The Middle Ages in general sense refers to the period in European history between antiquity and the Renaissance, often dated from 476, the year of the collapse of the Western

Roman Empire, to 1453, the year of Ottoman conquest of the city of Constantinople①. Throughout the Middle Ages, the Roman Catholic Church was not only a religious authority over the whole Europe, but also a major political and economic force. Many clergy held posts in government and education, and the church collected enormous wealth from land holdings and taxation. The Church opposed both science (which could undermine theology) and liberalism (which would give people freedom to denounce the Church). Critical thought was supplanted with blind acceptance of Church doctrine and secular scholarship was largely abandoned.

With increased understanding of the accomplishments of the Middle Ages in the 19th century, the characterization of the entire period as one of darkness under the dominance of Christianity was challenged. As a matter of fact, ancient learning was never entirely absent from European society; academic and religious translation flourished in some period of the Middle Ages. Following the general division of European history, the Middle Ages in translation history can be roughly divided into three periods: the Early Middle Ages, with Boethius as the central figure, the School of Bagdad and the School of Toledo during the High Middle Ages and the translations between national European languages in the late Middle Ages.

From the 5th century European culture was in essence bilingual, or even multilingual. Early in the Middle Ages, the barbarian invaders, including various Germanic peoples, formed new kingdoms in what remained of the Western Roman Empire. But most of these emerging kingdoms lacked a mature national language. Meanwhile, the Byzantine Empire survived as a major power in the east and used Greek as the only language of administration and government from the 7th century. Latin was extensively used not only as a medium of scholarly exchange and administration but also as the liturgical language of the medieval Roman Catholic Church. The learned scholars chose to write in Latin, instead of their own language, simply because they wished to be taken seriously by their time. All those cultural elite, ecclesiastics or literati, knew Latin, their native languages, and, in many cases, one or two additional languages. Obviously, in such a culture, translations were made as literary apprenticeship or pedagogical exercises. Towards the end of the Early Middle Ages, *Bible* and Greek culture were translated into national languages through Latin or the Greek language.

Bible dominated the scene of translation in Europe towards the end of the Western Roman Empire. It the Early Middle Ages, *Bible* was translated with literalism into stiff Latin. Meanwhile, secular literary classics rose to the attention of the feudal landlords who needed political as well as philosophical inspirations from ancient Greek works. Thus for quite a long period in the Early Middle Ages, secular translation went in parallel with religious translation,

---

① 古罗马帝国于公元395年分裂,形成东西两个罗马中的东罗马帝国,又称“拜占庭帝国”(Byzantine Empire)。西罗马帝国崩溃后,东罗马帝国继续存在了上千年,是古代和中世纪欧洲最悠久的君主制国家。东罗马帝国信奉东正教,继承了希腊的语言和文化,但其居民却以正统罗马人自居,到7世纪为止官方语言是拉丁语。1453年,其都城君士坦丁堡被奥斯曼帝国攻入而灭亡。

which was still in its full swing under strong auspices of the feudal church authorities. Translations of the same text happened at the same time in different places partly because communications between translators became difficult as the Roman ruins fell into disrepair and the decline of centralized rule resulted in the development of small petty principalities. Another possible explanation for this simultaneous translation of the same text was literary rivalry, i. e., translators vied with each other for greater literary fame, as that between Andronicus and Naevius in ancient Rome. Most of the translations were anonymous and some were indirect. The great translators included, among others, Cassiodorus, Gregory I, Boethius, King Alfred the Great and Aelfric.

Flavius Magnus Aurelius Cassiodorus Senator① (about 490-585), better known as **Cassiodorus**, was born in Southern Italy. He was a Roman writer and statesman. During Cassiodorus's lifetime, theological and classical studies were on the general decline. Cassiodorus wrote King Theodoric's② biography in Latin and took important positions in the Ostrogoth Dynasty③ until 540. Not long after his retirement from office, he founded Vivarium Monastery, where he organized corps of monks to collect, copy, translate and study the ancient manuscripts, theological as well as secular, in the hope of preserving and spreading ancient culture. Vivarium Monastery was an unofficial center for translation and academic research, an example that was followed elsewhere in later centuries. Most of the translations made at Vivarium Monastery were anonymous. The best known of the translators was probably Dionysius Exiguus④ (died in 556), a Scythian⑤ Christian. Cassiodorus himself was neither a good writer nor a great scholar, but his importance in the history of Western culture can hardly be overestimated, for many ancient authors' writings were preserved due to his efforts.

Cassiodorus left behind *Institutions of Divine and Secular Learning*, an extremely influential work which were excerpted and copied in monasteries throughout the Latin Middle Ages. The *Institutions* was composed primarily as a guide for the study of divinity, while "secular" writings were encouraged merely as aids to it.

Another official translation organization was founded by liberal-minded pope Gregory I⑥ (540-604), also called Saint Gregory the Great. He was born into a wealthy noble Roman

---

① 卡西奥多罗斯:罗马作家和政治家。Senator(塞纳特)是他的姓氏,不是职衔。

② 狄奥多里克:东哥特国王(493~526年在位)。

③ 东哥特王朝,是日耳曼民族的一支——东哥特人建立的国家。随着东哥特人在西罗马帝国灭亡后迁入意大利,东哥特王国的势力约在意大利半岛及附近地区。

④ 伊希格斯:基督教神学家,他拒绝采用当时以罗马皇帝戴克里先(Diocletian)统治期为基准的纪元,而改以耶稣降世为基准的新纪元方式。

⑤ 西徐亚人:又称"赛西亚人",具有伊朗血统的一支游牧民族,公元前8~前7世纪以现今克里米亚为中心建立过富裕而强大的帝国,至公元前4~前2世纪被萨尔马特人(Sarmatian)征服而衰落。

⑥ 圣格里高利一世:第64任罗马教皇,中世纪教皇之父。他广建修道院,强制实施了宗教教规,又允许修士从事经济活动,扩大教会资产,极大地提高了罗马教皇的地位。其神学思想主要遵循奥古斯丁的学说,创制了公众礼拜仪式和格里高利赞美圣咏。

family with close connections to the church. Gregory is a Doctor of the Church and one of the Latin Fathers. He is considered a saint in the Roman Catholic Church①, Eastern Orthodox Church②, Anglican Communion③, and some Lutheran churches④. He was the first pope to transform the papacy into the imperial power as we associate it with today. He was renowned in the Middle Ages for his *Pastoral Care*⑤(591), a spiritual and practical guide for bishops. Coming to his pope position in 590, Gregory I set about a series of religious, social and government reforms and founded a translation organization around his settlement. The organization came under the church library and was mainly engaged in translating religious texts and government documents between Eastern and Western European languages. The organization was probably among the first official organizations to deal with day-to-day government translation. Gregory I, trained in rhetoric, protested the literal translation method of his contemporaries. He dogmatically insisted on sense-for-sense translation rather than the ancient tradition of strict literalism. He thought that when close attention was paid to words, the sense was lost.

2.1.2 Boethius

The central figure in early Middle Ages was **Severinus Boethius**⑥(480? -524).

Boethius is a Roman statesman and philosopher, often styled as "the last of the Romans" and called by Roger Bacon⑦"the first translator". Descended from a consular father, he was left an orphan at an early age and was educated in Christian faith by the pious and noble-minded Memmius Symmachus⑧. He for a long time enjoyed the confidence of the King Theodoric, and became the consul of Rome himself in 510. As a patrician of Rome he was entrusted with many important positions and looked up by the nobility of the Rome. At about the climax of his life he lost royal favor and was cast into prison, condemned unheard, and executed by order of Theodoric under the charges of sacrilege (his practice of astrology) and conspiracy. During his one-year imprisonment, he reflected on the instability of the royal favor and looked for consolations in the mind. And the result of his reflections is his best-known

① 罗马天主教会:天主教是与东正教、新教并列的基督教三大宗教派别之一,亦称"公教",是基督教最大宗派。天主教主导了整个欧洲中世纪的思想潮流,深刻影响了西欧社会的政治、经济、文化和艺术等各个领域。

② 东正教:又称"正教会"或"正统教会",是基督教的主要宗派之一,是由东罗马帝国所流传下来的基督教传统的教会。它是与天主教、新教并立的基督教三大派别之一,信徒主要分布在东欧国家。与天主教不同,正教由一些被称为"自主教会"或"自治教会"的地方教会组成,这些教会彼此独立,但却有着共同的信仰。

③ 安立甘宗:是基督教新教主要宗派之一,与信义宗、归正宗合称"新教三大流派",中国常称"圣公会"。该宗在英格兰为国教,称"英国国教会"。

④ 路德宗:是以马丁·路德的宗教思想之统称,因其教义核心为"因信称义",故又称信义宗。它是德意志宗教改革运动的产物,由马丁·路德于1529年创立于德国。这一新的宗派的建立,标志着基督新教的诞生。

⑤《司牧训话》:圣格里高利一世的作品,是教区牧师手册。

⑥ 波伊提乌:也译为波爱修斯,古罗马晚期的政治家、哲学家,著有《哲学的慰藉》。

⑦ 罗吉尔·培根:13世纪英国唯物主义思想家、科学家,著有《大著作》等。

⑧ 西马库斯:6世纪罗马政治家,波伊提乌的养父和岳父,后来以叛国罪和波伊提乌一同被处死。

philosophical work written during his imprisonment, *The Consolation of Philosophy*, which by far has been regarded the most interesting example of prison literature the world has ever seen. The work touches on the nature of good and evil, of fortune, chance, or freedom, and of divine foreknowledge. It introduces Platonism to medieval readers with a charming prose and verse style. The book is considered second only to Jerome's *Vulgate* and translated into many European languages. Its influence may be found, among others, in *Beowulf*① and in Chaucer②, in the first specimens of Italian verse, as well as in the *Divine Comedy*③ by Dante.

Although born into a Christian family and educated in Christian faith, Boethius held Neo-Platonist credo. He questioned some basic Biblical teachings from the viewpoint of the rising feudal class and turned to Greek philosophy for spiritual consolation. He intended to translate all the works of both Plato and Aristotle in the Latin language in the hopes of harmonizing the two philosophies. This dream of his, unfortunately, was broken when he was put to death. Still, he managed to translate Aristotle's *On Category*④, six volumes of his *Organon*⑤, and Porphyry's⑥ *Isagoge* (a 3rd-century Greek introduction to Aristotle's logic) with two commentaries, all of which were widely used throughout the Middle Ages. Up to the 12th century his writings and translations were known collectively as the *Logica vetus* (meaning the old logic) in Europe. His translations introduced Aristotelian wisdom into West Europe, triggering a wave of study on Aristotelian philosophy and producing lasting influence on medieval scholarship.

Boethius used the most literal translation method and tried to translate each letter of the Greek philosophy. He declared his translation policy in his commentary on the translation of Porphyry's *Eisagoge*.

> *I fear that I shall commit the fault of the faithful interpreter when I render each word by a word corresponding to it. The reason for this approach is that, in the writings in which knowledge of the subject matter is sought, it is not the charm of limpid speech but the unsullied truth that has to be expressed. Therefore I feel I have been most useful if, in composing books of philosophy in the Latin language, not a single letter of the Greek is to be found missing.* (quoted in Robinson, 2006: 35)

Boethius also felt the dilemma between translating the sense and translating the word. But with Boethius, the truth comes in conflict with the charm of speech; devotion to the charm of speech results in disloyalty to the truth; translating a text with the purpose of disseminating knowledge means translating the truth as it is with no regard for the art of good writing. And to

① 《贝奥武夫》:创作于公元 8 世纪早期的英国古老英雄史诗。

② 乔叟:14 世纪英国著名诗人,其最为杰出的作品是叙事长诗《坎特伯雷故事集》。

③ 《神曲》:意大利诗人但丁的长诗。

④ 《范畴篇》:古希腊哲学家亚里士多德创作的逻辑学书籍。

⑤ 《工具论》:古希腊哲学家亚里士多德的著作,主要论述了演绎法,为形式逻辑奠定了基础。

⑥ 波菲利: 古罗马唯心主义哲学家,新柏拉图主义者,著有《亚里士多德〈范畴篇〉导论》。

convey the "truth", the translator should translate word-for-word even at the risk of committing the fault of the faithful interpreter. Like Philo in ancient times, he argued for rigid formal correspondence and strived for accuracy to the letter. This view may be traced back to Jerome who emphasized truth, but was also influenced by the medical translators of Cicero's time. Again, "faithful interpretation" is misused in the sense of *word-for-word translation* and associated with the fault of an interpreter.

Like Cicero, Boethius coined a set of Lain philosophical vocabulary through translation. In his translation of Aristotle's *Organon*, Boethius attempted to reproduce the original idea with accurate philosophical terms. He was not eager to import a Greek term straight into Roman philosophy. Rather, he found an existing Latin word that partly corresponded to the original term and used it in this correspondent sense consistently throughout his translation. In this way he gave the Latin word a new meaning similar to that of the Greek original. His method might be described as ***semantic borrowing*** in today's terms.

Boethius was more concerned with translation practice for its own sake, arguing that a good translation came out of hard practice and had little to do with theoretical guidance. And this worked a shift in translation history in the West: the theories and principles advanced jointly by Augustine and others were largely forgotten and the ensuing five to six hundred years' witnessed strict utilitarianism. The situation did not change until the end of the Middle Ages when theoretical discussion on translation attracted scholarly attention again. Translation research between the two periods was scanty or else full of repetition of the old theories.

With the rise of the Eastern Roman Empire, church authorities were stepping up its intellectual control over the emerging European states. They persecuted the scholars engaged in the study of classics at Constantinople and sent missionaries to the new nation states. With these missionaries came Christianity and the Latin *Bible*. Up to then, Latin became the language only of the highly educated and the common people could not understand the Church's liturgy or Scripture written in it. The church attempted to prevent translation of the Latin *Bible* into new languages so that they could interpret the *Bible* in the best interest of the church. And this caused discontent among the common people, who demanded a first-hand access to the words of God.

2.1.3 Translations into Visigoth (Bishop Ulfila)

Ulfila[①] (311-382), meaning *little wolf*, was born probably within today's Romania. He is a bishop, missionary, and *Bible* translator. At thirty, he worked as a lector, or reader, during religious services. This job required a grasp of the *Bible* and prepared him for his later work as

① 乌斐拉:西哥特的主教,《圣经》翻译家。

a *Bible* translator. He was consecrated bishop of the Visigoths① in 341. To spread Arianism② to the Visigoths, Ulfila translated *the New Testament* and part of *the Old Testament* mostly from Greek into the Gothic language. Although considered heretic by the Roman Church, the *Bible* remained current among Arian Christians and active for several centuries, especially in Visigothic Spain③. The monumental work took him 40 years of his bishop career and in the course of his translation evolved a Gothic alphabet.

Prior to this undertaking, Gothic had been strictly a spoken language. Ulfila translated strictly after the Greek word order, sentence structure, transcribing Gothic sounds with Greek and Latin characters and adding some letters from ancient Germanic and Scandinavian alphabets. His alphabet consisted of 27 characters and was different from the German script known as Gothic, a graphic transcription of the Latin alphabet. (quoted in Delisle & Woodsworth, 1995: 9) He coined a Germanic Christian terminology, some of which is still in use today. Ulfila used Gothic word *fastan*, meaning originally *to hold out*, in the religious sense of "to fast", which is still widely used in today's English and many Germanic languages. Similar elements Ulfila invented were largely retained in contemporary Germanic idioms. Ulfila's *Bible* translation was the first major document of Germanic literature. For his contributions to the formation of the Gothic language, Ulfila was styled the "father of Gothic literature" (Delisle & Woodsworth, 1995: 9).

Ulfila's translations largely got lost and only fragments of his Gothic *Bible* remained. Much of his Gothic translations of the *Gospels* and *Pauline Letters*④ survive, together with fragments of his *Book of Nehemiah*⑤. Ulfila did not translate the *Book of Kings*⑥ for fear that the depiction of numerous battles in it may arouse the passion for warfare in the Goths, a belligerent nation.

2.1.4 Translations into the Old English Language (Alfred the Great and Aelfric)

From 43 to 409 Britain was a province of the Roman Empire, today known as Roman Britain. Christianity was introduced into Britain following the Roman conquest of the native Britons. After the Roman Emperor Constantine⑦ granted Christians freedom of worship in 313, Christianity became widespread in England during the 4th century. The Romano-British

---

① 西哥特人:东日耳曼部落的两个主要分支之一,另一个分支是东哥特人。公元4世纪西哥特人兴起于巴尔干地区,后加入对罗马帝国的战争,410年在首领阿拉里克率领下攻陷并洗劫罗马。

② 阿里乌斯教:亚历山大神学家阿里乌斯(Arius)的教义,认为耶稣不是神,但比凡人高超,被罗马教会视为异端。

③ 西哥特人统治下的西班牙:5世纪至8世纪,原罗马帝国高卢行省和西班牙属于西哥特王国。

④ 《保罗书信》:使徒保罗写给各地主教以及普通信众关于教义的回信,信中解释了许多有关基督教教义的疑难问题,阐明了教理原则,被视为基督教教理的重要文献,后被编入《圣经》。

⑤ 《尼希米记》:《旧约》第13部,以第一人称追述了波斯宫廷重臣尼希米重修耶路撒冷城墙,全城人民谨守上帝律法的故事。

⑥ 《列王纪》:《旧约》之一部,叙述了自所罗门王登基直到犹大国灭亡前后400余年以色列国的历史。

⑦ 君士坦丁大帝:第42代罗马皇帝,是世界史上第一位尊崇基督教的罗马皇帝。他于公元313年颁布米兰敕令(Edict of Milan),承认基督教为合法宗教,基督教此后成为欧洲占统治地位的宗教。

population after the withdrawal of the Roman legions was mostly Christian. The Anglo-Saxons, the inhabitants of England, converted to Christianity in the 7th century. The language they spoke, Anglo-Saxon (better known as Old English today), was used together with some other local dialects. Old English translations of the *Bible* were made at the turn of the 7th century. The earliest translations, unfortunately, were either lost or passed on in duplicates, whose identity was therefore questionable and whose influence was limited. A copy of translation preserved at Paris during the 11th century shows that an English churchman named Aldhem① (640-709) translated *Psalms* into Old English. In 735, Venerable Bede②(673-735), Anglo-Saxon theologian and historian, translated St. John's *Gospels* into Old English. These earliest Old English translations, however, were of mere historical significance.

A good majority of earliest Anglo-Saxon literary creation was based on borrowed, foreign materials. Almost from the very start, there was not a clear dividing line between translation, compilation, and adaptation. Works of Caedmon③ and Cynewulf④, although original in many respects, were actually taking hints from existing foreign literatures. Bede once remarked on Caedmon: "all that he could learn by hearing meditated with himself, and, as a clean animal ruminating, turned into the sweetest verse." (Amos, 1920: 6) Cynewulf, an early 9th century Anglo-Saxon poet, wrote some works using the old stories of foreign literatures. He even acknowledged with honesty in *Elene*⑤ that there was the same material already written in another literature. And this was not uncommon in earlier English translations and continued well after the Norman Conquest. From the 13th century, the translations in England showed gradations from close renderings to original reproduction, with many more subtle translation types in between. A retelling of a story in another literature often came out as if it were original production. Until the late 16th century, the term translated was used very loosely, sometimes synonymously with *compiled* and *made*.

There are many reasons behind this phenomenon. One possible explanation is that translators then worked under unscrupulous principle, that is, without a proper notion of translation. Another reason might be a pressing socio-cultural demand for foreign matters and literatures, which justified whatever means to the end. It could also be ascribed to the translator's desire to take advantage of the author's reputation for his own purpose. From time to time translations were made to achieve various purposes in particular social-cultural contexts. These well-motivated translation programs normally deviated from the original in words or even thoughts but still enjoyed a high reputation. These earliest Old English translations, together with some medieval English translations, were comparatively isolated from translations in later

① 译为奥尔德赫姆。
② 比德:公元7~8世纪英国历史学家及神学家。
③ 凯德蒙:公元7世纪盎格鲁-撒克逊基督教诗人。
④ 辛尼武夫:公元9世纪盎格鲁-撒克逊诗人,其诗稿有《埃琳娜》《使徒们的命运》《基督升天》和《朱莉安娜》等。
⑤ 《埃琳娜》:盎格鲁-撒克逊诗人辛尼武夫的诗歌作品。

period. Important Old English translators include King Alfred the Great and Aelfric.

King Alfred the Great① (849-899) was King of Wessex (871-899), scholar, and lawmaker who repelled the Dancs and hclpcd consolidate England into a unified kingdom. When he came to the throne the intellectual life in England was on the general decline. He worked through his reign to redress the problem. To encourage scholarly activities, he established monasteries, attracted scholars and teachers from Wales, Mercia② and the European continent. His real contribution lied in that he used Old English, rather than Latin, as the language of education of his people. He ordered all wealthy young men to read and write English. He commissioned the writing of the Anglo-Saxon Chronicle, which continued two centuries after his death. He promoted national solidarity by appealing to "a sense of Englishness, conveyed by the language" (quoted in Delisle & Woodsworth, 1995: 27).

With the aid of the scholars he launched a grand translation program, translating a series of religious and philosophical texts from Latin to make them more widely available in Old English. He learned Latin approaching his 40 so that he could translate himself or monitor the translation. Remarkably, Alfred translated four works himself: Gregory the Great's *Pastoral Care*③, Boethius's *Consolation of Philosophy*, St. Augustine's *Soliloquies*④, the first fifty psalms of the *Psalter*⑤ and probably excerpts from the Vulgate Book of *Exodus*⑥. The translation program continued up to the last moment of his life. Translations promoted by him became "a medium for rescuing the English language, creating a sense of national unity and laying the foundations for English prose" (quoted in Delisle & Woodsworth, 1995: 28).

Alfred's first translation was *Pastoral Care*, which he meant as a manual for bishops in the instruction of their flocks. In the preface to the translation, he explained why he chose to translate this works from Latin into English. He also stated that he translated sometimes word for word some other times in paraphrase. But he actually kept very close to his original.

In translating Boethius' *Consolation of Philosophy*, Alfred adopted a much freer method and introduced many additions into the original, although it was proposed that many of the additions to the original text are to be ascribed to the glosses and commentaries which he used. He added contemporary conditions, and sometimes revealed his views on the social order and the duties of kingship. In Preface to the *Consolation of Philosophy* he stated that "Sometimes he set word by word, sometimes meaning of meaning, as he the most plainly and most clearly could explain it" (quoted in Robinson, 2006: 37).

---

① 阿尔弗雷德大帝:英格兰韦塞克斯王国国王、学者及立法者,曾击败了丹麦人的侵略并使英格兰成为统一的王国。

② 墨西亚:古代英格兰中部和南部的一个盎格鲁-撒克逊王国。

③ 《司牧训话》:圣格里高利一世的作品,教区牧师手册。

④ 《独白》:圣奥古斯丁的著作。

⑤ 祈祷用的圣经诗集。

⑥ 《出埃及记》:《旧约》的第二部,主要是讲述摩西带领受到迫害的以色列人离开埃及的故事。

In his rendering of *Soliloquies* of St. Augustine, he used a freer strategy. He added materials from other works of the Church Fathers, compared with contemporary conditions, and discussed problems concerning faith, reason and the nature of eternal life from his own point of view. He was casual with the subject under the belief that the translator should be entirely on his own as to what to retain and what to remove in translation. His exact words are

> *I gather for myself cudgels, and stud shafts and horizontal shafts, and helves, for each of the tools that I could work with, and bow-timbers and bolt-timbers for every work that I could perform, the comeliest trees, as many as I could carry. Neither came I with a burden home, for it did not please me to bring all the wood back, even if I could bear it. In each tree I saw something that I needed at home, therefore I advise each one who can, and has many wains, that he direct his steps to the same wood that I cut the stud shafts. Let him fetch more for himself, and load his wains with fair beams, that he may wind many a neat wall, and erect many a rare house, and build a fair town, and therein may dwell merrily and softly both winter and summer, as I have not yet done.* (Amos, 1920: 4)

It can be inferred from above statement that Alfred held a utilitarian attitude towards translation, i. e., he takes what he wants and leaves whatever he does not need, all for his own convenience. In his translation he selects, combines, and deletes wherever he thinks fit. This attitude can partly be ascribed to the old tradition in Anglo-Saxon literary creation that is based on borrowed, foreign materials.

Aelfric① (955-1010?) is Anglo-Saxon abbot of Eynsham, writer and grammarian, another famous translator and translation theorist after Alfred the Great. Little is known of his life. Like King Alfred he was also concerned about the general decline of learning in England and was translating and writing with the similar purpose, i. e., providing in English a summary of the knowledge essential to faith. He translated and adapted parts of the *Old Testament*, including *Genesis*, *Catholic Homilies*② (990-992) and the *Lives of the Saints*③ (993-998). Among his other works are *A Treatise on the Old and New Testaments*; the *Heptateuch*④, an abridged translation of the first seven books of the *Old Testament*; he also wrote a Latin grammar and glossary in Old English for his students with a simple method of interpretation; and the *Colloquy*, a primer with a parallel Old English/Latin text designed to teach pupils to speak Latin correctly. His writings were copied throughout the Middle Ages and were among the first Old English works to be printed. These translations and writings displayed Aelfric's stylistic excellence in Old English. Unlike Alfred the Great, he translated for the simple faithful English readers. His views on translation were mostly presented in Latin in *A Treatise on the Old and New Testaments*, the only exception being the *Preface to Genesis*, which is written in English.

---

① 译为阿尔弗里克。
② 《天主教布道辞》。
③ 《圣徒传》。
④ 《旧约》的开首七卷。

Aelfric noted that different texts should be translated with different methods and styles for different readers. As he was translating for the common English readers, Aelfric insisted on an easily accessible, idiomatic translation. Aelfric repeatedly declared that he translated sense for sense more often than word for word. He cared to be clear and simple rather than adorn his translation with rhetorical ornaments. To this end, he avoided obscure expressions and used "the pure and open words of the language of this people" (Amos, 1920: 4), and had a particular regard for brevity. Even in *Bible* translation he insisted that the Latin idiom should give way to English idiom. As *Catholic Homilies* was meant for simple people, it was put in simple English with the purpose of popularization. This division of translation for the cultural elite and for the masses continued into later translations. In the preface to Book I of *Catholic Homilies* (989), he said

> *I have nevertheless formed this book out of Latin writers and from Holy Scripture, translating into our ordinary speech, for the edification of the simple, who know only his language both for reading and for hearing; and for that reason I have used no difficult words, but only plain English*—(quoted in Robinson, 2006: 39)

He sometimes went too far in the direction of popularization: he abbreviated both the Homilies and the *Lives of the Saints*. Aelfric noticed translation theories brought up by other translators. The Anglo-Saxon preface to *Genesis* (997) seems to imply that he had a greater concern about faithfulness of *Bible* translation and that before advancing his own theories on translation he had studied Jerome's theories about the unusual faithfulness of translating the *Bible*. He highlighted idiomatic rendering in the English language and took into account the readability of the translated text, but he made a point of the most faithful translation of the original facts and wording.

> *We say in advance that this book has a very profound spiritual signification, and we undertake to do nothing more than relate the naked facts. The uneducated will think that all the meaning is included in the simple narrative, while such is by no means the case. We dare write no more in English than the Latin has, nor change the order except so far as English idiom demands. Whoever translates or teaches from Latin into English must always arrange it so that the English is idiomatic.* (quoted in Robinson, 2006: 40)

Further Readings

Amos, Flora Ross. *Early Theories of Translation*. New York: Columbia University Press, 1920.

Delisle, Jean & Judith Woodsworth. *Translators through History*. Amsterdam: John Benjamins Publishing Company, 1995.

Robinson, Douglas. *Western Translation Theory: From Herodotus to Nietzsche*. Shanghai: Foreign Language Teaching and Research Press, 2006.

Shuttleworth, Mark & Moira Cowie. *Dictionary of Translation Studies*. Shanghai: Shanghai Foreign Language Education Press, 2004.

谭载喜:《西方翻译简史》,商务印书馆2004年版。

Topics for Discussion

1. What are the advantages and disadvantages of indirect translation? List as many reasons for indirect translation as possible.

2. Comment on retranslation of world classics (reasons, advantages and disadvantages, actual effects, etc.).

3. Account for the relationship between Visigoth bishop Ulfila's *Bible* translation and the invention of the Gothic language.

4. Boethius coined a set of Latin philosophical vocabulary through semantic borrowing. Is this method still used today? Give an example.

2.2 Schools of Translation in High Middle Ages

Translation Terms

Transliteration 音译

A method of translation in which the graphological features of the source term are transcribed in the target language. As it aims at preserving the form rather than the meaning, transliteration is normally used to translate culturally specific words or technical terms that have no equivalents in the target language.

Arabization 阿拉伯化(see Latinization or Romanization on page 7)

At the school of Bagdad, the world civilizations, particularly Greek culture, were absorbed into Arab framework through cultural assimilation and ideological adaptation. It is a target-oriented translation strategy that strives for the acceptability of the translation, often at the cost of stylistic faithfulness and cultural transmission.

2.2.1 Socio-cultural Background

The contact started early between Arabic and Western cultures in the form of massive translation enterprise in the Middle Ages. In the 7th century, the Arab world spoke Arabic in everyday talk and used a variety of other languages for trade and learning. With the rise of Islam, the Arab people began to raid the neighboring states. At the height of its military expansion, the Islamic Empire stretched from present-day Pakistan to Spain. One of the most important achievements of its military expansion was the growth of the Arabic language from an oral tradition into a written lingua franca. Compared with the highly developed Greek and

Indian civilizations, however, the Arabs were still culturally backward and had a great deal to learn from advanced cultures. The period from the 8th to 11th centuries and beyond witnessed an unrivalled level of translation campaign from advanced languages into Arabic.

With the fall of the Western Roman Empire, knowledge of Greek declined in the west, so did knowledge of the Greek texts. Many ancient Greek texts from classical antiquity①, with the exception to the *Bible*, had remained without a Latin translation and been unavailable to the Europeans. However, in the Middle East (then the southern provinces of the Greek-speaking Byzantine Empire) many of these Greek texts (such as Aristotle) were translated from Greek into Syriac② during the 6th and 7th centuries. After Islamic conquest of southern portions of the Byzantine Empire, these Syriac translations of Greek works fell to Muslim hands and were taken back to the city of Bagdad. When the 2nd Abassid③ Caliph Al-Mansur④ moved the capital from Damascus to Baghdad, he found both Greek classical texts as well as texts from ancient India. Al-Mansur ordered that these rich funds of world literature be translated into Arabic. Under Al-Mansur, translations were made from Greek, Syriac, and Persian into Arabic, the Syriac and Persian books being themselves translations from Greek or Sanskrit. Meanwhile, Abassid philosophers spread the idea that Islam had from the very beginning stressed the gathering of knowledge as important to the religion. These new lines of thinking contributed to an unprecedented scene of prosperity in translation of Greek ideas into Arabic.

2.2.2 Arabization at the School of Translation of Bagdad

In the 9th century, the city of **Bagdad** grew into a cosmopolitan city with a portion of non-Arab population such as Persians, Assyrians, and Greeks. The city became the center of ambitious translation enterprise, which was based in *Bayt al-Hikmah*, or the House of Wisdom⑤. The "House of Wisdom" was a library as well as a translation institute founded by Abbasid caliphs Harun al-Rashid⑥(764-809) and his son al-Ma'mun⑦. It was dedicated to the

① 古典时期:是对以地中海为中心,包括古希腊和古罗马等一系列文明的泛称。一般认为,古典时代起始于公元前8~7世纪荷马史诗时期,一直延伸至基督教出现和罗马帝国的衰落。在这一时期,古希腊文明和古罗马文明十分繁荣,对欧洲、北非、中东等地产生了巨大的影响。

② 古叙利亚语:公元2世纪后中东地区基督教使用的一种语言,是罗马帝国东部仅次于希腊语的重要语言,也是把希腊文明传播到阿拉伯地区的重要媒介。伊斯兰教兴起后,才让位于阿拉伯语。8世纪以前,古叙利亚语用于礼拜仪式。现在,古叙利亚语仍是中东若干教派的礼拜语言。

③ 阿拔斯王朝:阿拉伯帝国的第二个世袭王朝(750~1258)。因阿拔斯王朝旗帜尚黑,故中国史书称该王朝为"黑衣大食",阿拔斯王朝时期是阿拉伯的黄金时代。

④ 曼苏尔:阿拔斯王朝第二任哈里发,公元754~775年在位。

⑤ 智慧宫或智慧馆:是中世纪阿拉伯阿拔斯王朝在巴格达建立的全国性的综合学术机构。亦称"益智宫""哲理大学",由翻译局、科学院和图书馆等机构组成。

⑥ 哈伦·拉希德:阿拉伯帝国阿拔斯王朝最著名的哈里发,因与法兰克的查理曼大帝结盟而蜚声西方,更因世界名著《一千零一夜》生动地渲染了他的许多奇闻轶事而为众人所知。在他统治的23年间,国势强盛,首都巴格达成了阿拉伯帝国的政治、经济、文化中心和文人学士的荟萃之地。

⑦ 马蒙:阿巴斯王朝哈里发,公元813~833年在位。

translation of texts containing both Greek works as well as ancient Indian works primarily through Syriac and Persian languages. It was a key establishment of the translation movement and considered to have been a major intellectual center of the Islamic Golden Age, or the Islamic Renaissance①. Many of the most learned scholars headed to Baghdad from all over the Abbasid Empire and introduced Greek and Indian sciences into the Islamic world. By the middle of the 9th century, the House of Wisdom was the largest repository of books in the world.

The Arab people were exclusively interested in the transmission of ancient Greek culture alone, despite the old English convention in which Greek and Latin cultures were grouped together. At first only practical works, such as those on medicine and technology were sought after, but eventually works on philosophy became popular. The scientists who wrote on medicine, astronomy, mathematics, and philosophy influenced the oriental world most.

Some of these translations were made directly from Greek into Arabic, if the Greek originals were available and the translator was equipped with necessary language competence. As few translators met the requirements in the earlier period of the movement, a large quantity of Greek texts were translated second-hand through other languages. Syriac was one of the most popular intermediary languages, which carried the Greek culture during the Arabic conquest of the Hellenistic world② in the 7th and 8th centuries. (quoted in Delisle & Woodsworth, 1995: 113) Another notable phenomenon was the frequent use of **transliteration**, probably because the Arabic language in its inception was not sufficient to accommodate new and foreign concepts and had to settle down to a sound or form transcription. Thirdly, the translations were accompanied with commentaries, summaries and explanatory notes. The purpose of these additions was to make the literal translation more intelligible. This method was not uncommon among medieval translators and had been followed by Syrian translators of Greek philosophy in the 7th and 8th centuries. The translations sometimes targeted a learned readership and sometimes general readers. Translation methods varied accordingly with different readers and translation purposes, the general purpose of the translation movement being **Arabization** of ancient civilizations.

The translation movement was distinguishable from previous endeavors in three respects: 1. the source texts ranged from Greek, Persian, Aramaic, Syriac, and Sanskrit to other smaller languages; 2. The general attitude towards translation was utilitarian: the Arabs translated, among others, mathematics, astrology, philosophy, logic, medicine, chemistry and politics; the first type of text being translated into Arabic was administrative, partly because the Arabs were in need of knowledge on government of a vast Islamic empire. Next in translation volume were scientific texts. Surprisingly, however, literature received less attention from translators.

---

① 伊斯兰黄金时代：又称“伊斯兰教复兴”，习惯上指公元8～13世纪伊斯兰世界的学术繁荣及社会发展。

② 希腊化世界：一般指马其顿亚历山大征服后的北非、西亚、中亚和希腊世界。

Greek poets, historians, dramatists, or orators did not influence the oriental world very much since they were viewed as serving political ends which were not wanted in Arab states. Another plausible explanation was that world secular classics included some factors that conflicted with Islamic teachings. Also neglected in the massive translation movement was the *Bible*, the most translated texts in world translation history. And the reason was self-evident: the general purpose of the translation movement was **Arabization** of ancient civilizations, i. e., to absorb the world civilizations into an Islamic framework, which run contrary to Christian precepts.

3. The translation movement was highly organized and institutionalized. The translations were usually made with the help of individual patrons or the government, or under the administration and regulation of specific institutions or translation chambers. The "House of Wisdom" was such an institution which involved many of the most learned Muslim scholars into this excellent intellectual and educational project. And the translators were respected and well paid.

The translators from Syriac into Arabic were mostly Nestorian① and Jacobite② Christians, the most important translator of this group being the Nestorian physician **Hunayn Ibn Ishaq**③ (809-873), known to the Latins as Joannitius. Hunayn Ibn Ishaq was the most productive translator of Greek medical and scientific treatises in his day. He mastered four languages: Arabic, Syriac, Greek and Persian. He studied Greek and became known among the Arabs as the "Sheikh of the translators". In his lifetime, Ibn Ishaq translated 116 works, including Plato's *Timaeus*④, Aristotle's *Metaphysics*⑤, and the *Old Testament*. Among the most translated scientific works were Hippocratic⑥ and Galenic⑦ corpus, together with some seminal works as Euclid's⑧ *Elements* and Ptolemy's⑨ *Almagest*.

In his efforts to translate as much Greek material as possible, Hunayn Ibn Ishaq was assisted by his son and his nephew. Hunayn Ibn Ishaq translated Greek material into Syriac, and had his nephew finish by translating the text from Syriac to Arabic. Hunayn Ibn Ishaq corrected his partners' errors while translating Greek and Syriac writings into Arabic. Unlike other translators in the Abbasid period, Hunayn Ibn Ishaq opposed translating texts word for word. Instead, he would attempt to attain the meaning of the subject and the sentences, and

---

① 聂斯脱利派:基督教的一派,起源于公元5世纪时小亚细亚与叙利亚,强调基督的神人二性各自独立。在阿拉伯征服波斯后,聂斯脱利派的学者在阿拉伯文化的形成中发挥了重要作用。

② 雅各比派:公元6世纪叙利亚僧侣,叙利亚基督一性论派的信徒。

③ 侯奈因:阿拔斯王朝著名学者、翻译家,巴格达智慧馆馆长。

④ 《蒂迈欧篇》:古希腊哲学家柏拉图的晚期著作,是关于宇宙论和自然科学的一篇对话。

⑤ 《形而上学》:古希腊哲学家亚里士多德的重要哲学著作,该书考察了人类知识的形成,进而提出关于普遍知识的理论,从根本上奠定了西方哲学思想的基本概念和问题。

⑥ 希波克拉底:(约公元前460~前377年)古希腊著名医生,使医学摆脱了迷信、巫术及哲学,发展成为专业学科,被西方尊为"医学之父"。

⑦ 盖伦:古罗马时期最著名最有影响的医学大师,他被认为是仅次于希波克拉底的第二个医学权威。

⑧ 欧几里得:古希腊数学家,被称为"几何之父"。著有《几何原本》。

⑨ 托勒密:又译"托勒玫",古希腊天文学家、地理学家和光学家。著有《大综合论》。

then in a new manuscript, rewrite the piece of knowledge in Syriac or Arabic. Hunayn Ibn Ishaq noted the difference in the target readers and used different styles accordingly. He regarded intelligibility and clarity when translating texts for his students. He sometimes added an explanation to difficult passages in a Syriac translation of a commentary on the *Hippocratic Oath*①. Some other times he aimed for a style that could be understood by someone "who was not a specialist, or who was unacquainted with philosophy" (quoted in Delisle & Woodsworth, 1995: 115). He also corrected texts by collecting different set of books on a subject and by finalizing the meaning of the subject②.

Persian translator Al-Kindi (Alkindus)③ is another prominent figure in the House of Wisdom. He is unanimously hailed as the "father of Islamic or Arabic philosophy" for his synthesis, adaptation and promotion of Greek and Hellenistic philosophy in the Muslim world. His greatest contribution to the development of Islamic philosophy was his efforts to make Greek thought both accessible and acceptable to a Muslim audience. Al-Kindi's philosophical writings were mostly concerned about the compatibility between Greek philosophy and other "orthodox" Islamic sciences, particularly theology. Whenever he ran into an impasse, he would abandon the Greek ideas in favor of the Islamic faith. He successfully incorporated Aristotelian and (especially) neo-Platonist thought into an Islamic philosophical framework. Much of what was to become standard Arabic philosophical vocabulary originated with Al-Kindi.

Turkish philosopher and scientist Al-Farabi④ (870-950) was known to the Arabs as the "Second Master" (after Aristotle). He introduced Aristotle and Plato's works to the Muslim world with his own original commentaries, elaborations and explanations that were acceptable to the Muslims. In one of his most notable theorization on an ideal state as in Plato's *The Republic*⑤, Al-Farabi represented religion as a symbolic rendering of truth, and, like Plato, saw it as the duty of the philosopher to provide guidance to the state. While incorporating the Platonic view, Al-Farabi also **Arabized** Plato by drawing a parallel from within the Islamic context, i. e., he regarded the ideal state to be ruled by the prophet-imam, instead of the philosopher-king envisaged by Plato. Al-Farabi argued that the ideal state was the city-state of Medina governed by the prophet Muhammad, as he was in direct communion with Allah whose

① 《希波克拉底誓言》:古希腊医学家希波克拉底向医学界发出的职业道德倡议书,是从医人员入学的第一课,其高度的职业道德自律成为社会各行各业的典范。

② Hunayn Ibn Ishaq, From Wikipedia, the free encyclopedia. 2014-03-26. http://en.wikipedia.org/wiki/Hunayn_ibn_Ishaq.

③ 金迪:公元9世纪著名的阿拉伯学者,他对希腊哲学的诠释被犹太思想家及基督教思想家采用,对西方近代欧洲哲学产生了影响。

④ 法拉比:公元10世纪突厥民族著名的科学家、哲学家,中世纪哲学的代表人物之一,被尊为伊斯兰哲学仅次于亚里士多德的"第二导师"。

⑤ 《理想国》:古希腊著名哲学家柏拉图的著作。柏拉图以苏格拉底与其他人对话的方式设计了一个真、善、美相统一的政体,即理想国。在他的理想国里,统治者必须是哲学家,最高尚、最有学识的人,而这种贤人统治下的贤人政体就是最好的政体。

law was revealed to him.

The translation movement exerted a profound influence upon the scientific and philosophical thoughts in the Muslim world. For a time, Bagdad became the center of the scholarly research for the Arabic and was entitled "School of Translation" or "College of Translation". Many episodes of translation were recorded in *A Thousand and One Nights* or Arab chronicles. In this translation movement, the Western knowledge was disseminated in a creative way, i. e., in the ingenious comments and explanations, which inspired new thinking, generated new concepts, and ultimately were incorporated into a Islamic system of thought. The founding of the "House of Wisdom" facilitated the Arab assimilation of the cultural treasures of China, India, Persia, and above all, Greece, furthering the development of science before passing it on to the Western world. (quoted in Delisle & Woodsworth, 1995: 115)

2.2.3 Christianization at the School of Translation of Toledo

While Greek ideas gradually permeated the Islamic world, Muslim conquests extended to the European continent. Arabic translations and commentaries on the Greek ideas followed their forces to Spain and Sicily, which later became the main points of transmission of Islamic knowledge to Europe. Up to the 12th century, Toledo①, Spain, succeeded Bagdad as the "school of translation" and the center of learning of Europe.

Located in the middle of Spain, Toledo became the religious and cultural center of Western Europe very early in history. It fell to Roman hands in 192 BC and later became the capital of the Visigoth Kingdom② (534-712). In 711, the Muslims conquered the Christian Iberian Peninsula and established a Muslim kingdom. From the year of Islamic invasion, the Christian Iberian kingdoms started recovering the lost kingdoms, a process that continued on and off until the last Islamic state on the peninsula fell in 1492. This period of approximately 781 years in the history of the Iberian Peninsula is known as the Christian Re-conquest of Islamic Spain. It is part of the Crusade③, the military campaigns sanctioned by the Roman Catholic Church during the High Middle Ages with the stated goal to recover Jerusalem, the holy land to Christianity, Islam and Judaism. Because of its central location in the Iberian Peninsula, Toledo was involved in the struggles between the Muslim and Christian kingdoms. Dating from 761 to 857, Toledo was the center of numerous insurrections and military clashes. As a matter of fact, it was the first great Muslim city of the Islamic kingdom that was recovered by Christianity.

Toledo after the Re-conquest was a culturally diverse and vibrant city which hosted at least three distinctive cultural traditions: Jewish, Christian and Muslim. It was a cosmopolitan city

① 托莱多:西班牙中部的历史文化名城。

② 西哥特王国:公元5~8世纪初西哥特人在原西罗马帝国境内高卢西南部和西班牙建立的日耳曼国家。

③ 十字军东征:罗马天主教教皇发起的针对地中海东岸的伊斯兰国家的宗教侵略性战争,持续了近200年。

that spoke a variety of languages. In addition to Castilian[①], several other minority languages were also spoken in Spain at the time. Collectively called Romance (derived from Latin), these languages were spoken side by side with Arabic, Hebrew, and Latin. As a linguistic and cultural borderland, it provided fertile ground for translators, since so many of its citizens wrote daily in both Arabic and Latin-based languages.

The scene of translation was intensely complicated in Spain, a multi-cultural city between Christian and Islamic worlds. Translators were mostly Jews, Conversos (Jews publicly converted to Christianity) or Mozarabs (Catholics who lived under Islamic rule and their descendents). Collectively called "the Toledo School of Translators", these Christian scholars were now able to work in "friendly" religious territory, translating many of the philosophical and scientific works from Arabic, Greek, and ancient Hebrew. Many early printed editions of the translations, however, omitted the name of the translator.

In terms of the target language and translation methodology, the School went through two distinct periods with a transitional period of decline in between.

The first period was headed by Archbishop Raymond[②] of Toledo in the 12th century, who promoted the translation of philosophical and religious works, mainly from Arabic into Latin. Translations were made in a well-organized teamwork, that is, at first a native speaker of Arabic language (generally a Jew or a Mozarab) orally communicated the contents of the books to a scholar; after that the scholar (normally a bilingual of Arabic and Latin) would dictate its Latin equivalent to a scribe (usually a native speaker of Latin), who wrote down the translated text.

No evidence shows that Archbishop Raymond actually founded any school of translation, but the quest for scientific knowledge through translation and education continued into successive archbishops of Toledo, which later acquired the name of "Toledo School of Translation". As a matter of fact, many of the translators worked outside Toledo or after Raymond's episcopacy and the Toledo School of translation actually included Barcelona[③] and Tarazona[④] regions as well, although Toledo was the most important place of all.

The 12th century translators of Toledo showed more interest in new scientific and philosophical information, less in religious texts and still less in literary pieces. Regular scientific translation from Arabic into Latin started in early 12th century and was strengthened by Peter the Venerable[⑤] (1092-1156), the French abbot of Cluny. The Greek Church Fathers

① 卡斯提尔语:以卡斯蒂利亚方言为基础的纯正西班牙语。

② 雷蒙:12 世纪西班牙基督教会大主教,曾大力资助托莱多翻译院的翻译活动,对欧洲中世纪的学术进步作出过积极贡献。

③ 巴塞罗那:西班牙东北部地中海沿岸城市。

④ 塔拉索纳:西班牙城市。

⑤ 可敬的彼得:12 世纪法国克吕尼修道院院长,著述丰厚,组织翻译了第一部拉丁文《古兰经》,促进了伊斯兰教和基督教的交流。

and Jewish teachings were translated into Latin; a large number of Greek works were translated into Latin by way of intermediate languages such as Syriac and Arabic. Significantly, some Arabic literature and Islamic religious texts were also rendered into Latin.

Peter the Venerable organized the first Latin translation of Koran and its commentary documents from 1141 to 1143. This first Latin Koran, entitled "The law of Mahomet the false prophet", was evidently biased against Islam. According to modern scholars, the translation "tended to exaggerate harmless text to give it a nasty or licentious sting" and "preferred improbable and unpleasant meanings over likely and decent ones"[①]. As a matter of fact, the first Latin Koran was part of the Christian propaganda campaign in justification of the Crusade. Despite religious prejudices, this Latin Koran was republished in 1543 in three editions and used as the source text for many later European translations of the Koran. As a result, the errors and distortions in the first Latin Koran were largely retained in the early European translations.

Domingo Gundisalvo[②] is considered to be the first appointed director of the Toledo School of Translators. At first, Gundisalvo only translated from Greek into Latin or Castilian, as he did not have sufficient knowledge of Arabic. He collaborated with linguists versed in Arabic, especially John of Seville[③], in making Latin translations of Arabic philosophical treatises. Later Gundisalvo mastered Arabic sufficiently to translate it by himself. Unlike his colleagues, he focused exclusively on philosophy, translating Greek and Arabic works and the commentaries of earlier Muslim philosophers, among them works by Avicenna[④] (980-1037). He is known for frequently eliminating passages and adding his own commentaries, rather than being scrupulously faithful to the originals[⑤].

The most prolific translator **Gerard of Cremona**[⑥] (1114-1187) translated, with the help of others, some 87 books, most of them scientific and philosophical texts. He even made a sabbatical trip of Toledo in search of the *Almagest*. There, he found a massive stock of Arabic books on every subject and embarked on thoroughly learning the Arabic language. Gerard's notable Arabic translation was Ptolemy's *Almagest* (finished in 1175). Among other Greek authors translated from Arabic versions by Gerard are Aristotle, Euclid, and Galen. Translations of original Arabic texts attributed to him include works on medicine—notably the Canon of Avicenna—mathematics, astronomy, astrology, and alchemy.

---

① Quran translations. From Wikipedia, the free encyclopedia. 2013-09-10. http://en.wikipedia.org/wiki/Quran_translations.

② 译为岗狄萨尔维。

③ 塞维利亚的约翰:塞维利亚为西班牙西南部古城。

④ 阿维森那:中世纪穆斯林哲学家。

⑤ Toledo School of Translators. From Wikipedia, the free encyclopedia. 2013-09-21. http://en.wikipedia.org/wiki/Toledo_School_of_Translators.

⑥ 杰拉德:意大利克雷默那的翻译家。

Another important translator was **John of Seville**. His three translations were all medical texts, intermixed with alchemy in the hispano-Arabic tradition. John of Seville translated the Arabic astrological work "Book of Birth" into Latin in 1153. Overall, he's known for his intelligent syntheses, combined with his own observations and interpretations, particularly in astrology.

After Archbishop Raymond's death in 1151, the translation activities in Toledo for some time fell into a decline.

Under **King Alfonso X**① (1221-1284) of Castile during the 13th century, Toledo rose even higher in importance as a center for translating as well as writing of original scholarly works. But translation movement in this period was different in both languages and methodology of translation. The translators translated into a revised version of Castilian in stead of Latin, gradually establishing Castilian as both a scientific and literary language. A new translation methodology evolved in the 13th century as well. Usually several persons were involved in the same translation in collaboration with each other. Under the new methodology, a translator, with a good command of several languages, dictated from the source language and translated into Spanish for the scribe, who wrote down the Spanish version. The scribe's work was later reviewed by one or several editors, the King himself one of them. The Castilian Crown paid for most of their work, and sometimes hired the most able translators from other parts of Spain and Europe to join the school at Toledo②.

As the patron king of the translation movement, Alfonso X prescribed an updated vernacular variety of Castilian, instead of Latin, as the target language for the translations. By insisting that the texts translated be "easy to understand", he ensured that the texts would reach a much wider audience, both in Spain and other European nations. As one of the most prominent editors of the translation, the King effectively managed and selected each of the translators, reviewed some of their work, and encouraged intellectual debate. The King also commissioned the translation into Castilian of several Hindi fables and tales out of Arabic sources.

Under Alfonso X's lead, Sephardic③ Jewish scientists and translators acquired a prominent role in the School. They were highly valued by the King because of their intellectual skills and mastery of the two languages mostly used in the translations: Arabic and Castilian. Alfonso X's nephew Juan Manuel wrote that the King was so impressed with the intellectual level of the Jewish scholars that he commissioned the translation of the Talmud④, the law of the Jews, as

---

① 阿尔丰沙十世:西班牙君主,提倡学术研究,创建学校并倡议制定法规。

② Toledo School of Translators. From Wikipedia, the free encyclopedia. 2013-09-21. http://en.wikipedia.org/wiki/Toledo_School_of_Translators.

③ 塞法迪:西班牙系犹太人的。

④ 亦称《塔木德》。

well as the Kabbalah①.

Yehuda ben Moshe Cohen② was one of the most notable Jewish translators during this period. Among his most notable translations is the *Lapidario*, a book about the medical properties of various rocks and gems he translated from Arabic into the Castilian language under Alfonso X's command. Besides, he translated the *Picatrix*, a composite work of ancient treatises on magic and astrology. He also translated Ptolemy's works, 15 treatises on astrology (effects of stars on man and properties of 360 stones with which to ward off negative astral influences), and others. Yehuda ben Moshe Cohen also collaborated in the translation of the famous Alfonsine tables③. Thanks to their endeavors under Alfonso X's auspices, the Alfonsine tables became the most popular astronomical tables in Europe with updated versions being regularly reprinted for over three hundred years④.

Isaac Ibn Sid⑤ was a Spanish-Jewish astronomer favored by the King on account of his knowledge of astronomy, astrology, architecture and mathematics. Isaac Ibn Sid took a leading part in the compilation of the Alfonsine Tables. He translated several scientific treatises typically used by astrologers. At the King's direction, he produced a translation that was simple and easy to understand, so that "any man could readily use it".

Mark of Toledo, a Spanish physician, translated the Koran and various medical works. **John of Toledo** is believed to have translated into Latin several medical treatises which dealt with practical medicine. **Hermannus Alemannus**⑥ worked in Toledo from 1240 to 1256. He translated, among others, most of Aristotle's *Rhetoric*, interspersed with portions of commentary by Averroes⑦ and short fragments from Avicenna⑧ and Al-Farabi⑨. Aristotle was among the most translated of Greek philosophy. Although the works of Aristotle and Arab philosophers were banned at some European learning centers, such as the University of Paris in the early 13th century, the Toledo translations were accepted, due to their physical and cosmological nature. The translations of different sciences, such as astronomy, astrology, algebra, medicine, etc., attracted numerous scholars from all over Europe to Toledo in search of all those books that had been out of reach to Europeans for many centuries.

---

① 卡巴拉:犹太教内部的神秘教派的修行教材,解释永恒而神秘的造物主与短暂而有限的宇宙之间的关系,为众多犹太教派所吸收。

② 科恩:13 世纪杰出的犹太天文学家、托莱多翻译院的翻译家、作家。

③ 阿尔丰沙行星表:被证明是中世纪最佳的行星表,此后三百年都一直没能被取代。

④ Toledo School of Translators. From Wikipedia, the free encyclopedia. 2013-09-21. http://en.wikipedia.org/wiki/Toledo_School_of_Translators.

⑤ 艾萨克·伊本·希德。

⑥ 阿列曼诺斯。

⑦ 阿维罗斯:阿拉伯哲学家,评注亚里士多德著作,具有唯物主义和泛神论思想,遭巴黎大学和梵蒂冈谴责。

⑧ 阿维森那:中世纪穆斯林哲学家。

⑨ 法拉比:10 世纪突厥民族著名的科学家、哲学家,中世纪哲学的代表人物之一,被尊为伊斯兰哲学仅次于亚里士多德的"第二导师"。

Despite the two distinct periods of translation, translation undertaking at the School of Toledo is distinguishable in the following respects. 1. It received strong assistance from church authorities and secular governments. Translators in the first period enlisted support from Archbishop Raymond of Toledo. Afterwards, Alfonso X became the best-known patron king of translation activities of Toledo. 2. Translations were largely indirect. Translations during this period were made not directly out of the original Greek but via a tertiary language, primarily Arabic or Syriac, which carried the Greek cultural heritage and represented the most advanced level of culture in the world. This situation did not improve until the 13th century, when Greek originals were carried to Toledo and the scholars, with first-hand access to the Greek original, began to translate directly from the Greek works. 3. Translation methods varied considerably, ranging from literal to liberal and influenced by the translator's relation with the patron, the physical working conditions and also the target readership. Many of the translations were very literal and transliterations were used to introduce unknown and unintelligible words. These strategies produced very opaque texts which had to be understood with the help of marginal notes, glosses and extended commentaries. On the other hand, formal changes were made in accordance with the target language convention; adaptations and deletions were not uncommon; certain Arabic historical and geographical terms were considered irrelevant and removed; semantic borrowings were also used to assign specific scientific meanings to existing terms in the target languages. 4. Translators worked under strict ideological restraints. Under Christian Reconquest, Toledo was dominated by the Church and the classical authors and theologians. Translators translated on behalf of the Church, absorbing the ancient Greek and Arabic works into a Latin framework. As a matter of fact, the Toledo translators avoided any references they considered unorthodox so as not to offend their Christian readers. For these purposes, omissions and transformations were used to **Christianize** some texts that run contrary to traditional Christian values. 5. Discussion on translation was sporadic and translators translated under some self-defined principles.

In general history study, School of Toledo was a topic that can not afford to be ignored. First, it signals large-scale friendly and scholarly contact between Islamic and Christian cultures and is considered the third climax in the Western translation history. Second, the School of Toledo disseminated Greek culture, nourished by Islamic commentaries, and promoted the development of Western civilization. Thanks to this group of scholars and writers, the knowledge acquired from the Arabic, Greek and Hebrew texts found its way into the heart of the universities in Europe. Third, as many scholar-translators taught at Toledo, the city ultimately evolved into the first comprehensive university in the middle and western parts of Spain. In 1986 the city of Toledo was declared a World Heritage Site by UNESCO for the coexistence of Christian, Jewish, and Moorish cultures. Lastly, translation at the school of Toledo gave birth to the variety of the Castilian language that incorporated a large amount of scientific and technical vocabulary, streamlined its syntax in order to be understood by people from all walks of life, and was made suitable for higher expressions of thought. The contributions of all the scholars under the tutelage and direction of Alfonso X established the foundations of the modern supranational Spanish language.

The School of Toledo did not last long, yet its significance reached far and wide and its socio-cultural influence has always been felt. Albertus Magnus① (1200-1280) based his systematization of Aristotelian philosophy, and much of his writings on astronomy, astrology, mineralogy, chemistry, zoology, physiology, and phrenology upon those translations made in Toledo. His pupil, Thomas Aquinas② (1225-1274) also used many of the translated work to bring Aristotle into his philosophical and theological treatises. Roger Bacon③ relied on many of the Arabic translations to make important contributions in the fields of optics, astronomy, the natural sciences, chemistry and mathematics. In general, most disciplines in the field of medicine in Europe greatly benefited from the translations made out of works that reflected the advanced state of medicine in medieval Islam and some Asian countries. Nicolaus Copernicus④ (1473-1543), the first scientist to formulate a comprehensive heliocentric cosmology, studied the translation of Ptolemy's astronomical *Almagest*. He also used the data for astronomical computing contained in the Alfonsine tables. Other translated works of astronomical nature were used as an introductory text in astronomy by European students all through the 15th century⑤.

Further Readings

Delisle, Jean & Judith Woodsworth. *Translators through History*. Amsterdam: John Benjamins Publishing Company, 1995.

House of Wisdom. From Wikipedia, the free encyclopedia. 2013-09-22. http://en.wikipedia.org/wiki/House_of_Wisdom.

Hunayn ibn Ishaq, From Wikipedia, the free encyclopedia. 2014-03-26. http://en.wikipedia.org/wiki/Hunayn_ibn_Ishaq.

Quran translations. From Wikipedia, the free encyclopedia. 2013-09-21. http://en.wikipedia.org/wiki/Quran_translations.

Shuttleworth, Mark & Moira Cowie. *Dictionary of Translation Studies*. Shanghai: Shanghai Foreign Language Education Press, 2004.

Toledo School of Translators. From Wikipedia, the free encyclopedia. 2012-03-16. http://en.wikipedia.org/wiki/Toledo_School_of_Translators.

① 大阿尔伯特:中世纪欧洲重要的哲学家和神学家,提倡神学与科学和平并存,首次将亚里士多德的学说与基督教哲学综合到一起。罗马天主教认可的33位圣师之一。

② 阿奎纳:中世纪经院哲学家和神学家,著有《神学大全》,是天主教教会认可的33位教会圣师之一。

③ 罗吉尔·培根:英国13世纪唯物主义思想家、伟大的科学家,他最知名作品是《大著作》。

④ 哥白尼:波兰天文学家,他提出日心说,推翻了托勒密的天文学理论即地心体系。

⑤ Toledo School of Translators. From Wikipedia, the free encyclopedia. 2013-09-21. http://en.wikipedia.org/wiki/Toledo_School_of_Translators.

谭载喜:《西方翻译简史》,商务印书馆2004年版。

Topics for Discussion

1. List as many factors as possible that influence the translation method.

2. Compare Roman translation of Greek culture with Arab translation of Greek culture. List the similarities and differences.

3. Comment on the first Latin Koran. Are the distortions and errors accidental or well-motivated? Account for its translation strategy from socio-cultural perspective.

4. In what way could a patron of translation influence translation activity? Illustrate your point with an example.

5. What translation movement is considered the third climax in the Western translation history? In what ways is it different from the previous translation movements? What influence did it produce?

6. China has made systematic efforts to introduce Chinese culture into the West, but met with little success, despite the fact that their translations were generally more accurate than those made by foreign translators. Account for the phenomenon with translational facts from Western translation history. Apart from the quality of translation itself, what factors make a translation or a translation movement a success?

2.3 Translators in Late Middle Ages

Translation Terms

Untranslatability 不可译性

A term used to discuss the impossibility of translating from one language to another. Its opposite is translatability, which means the extent of possibility of translating from one language into another. It is now generally agreed that translation is still possible, but the degree of translatability is limited by linguistic and cultural differences.

Pseudo Translation 伪翻译

Pseudo Translation is a translation without an identifiable original and its identity is therefore dubious. In ancient and medieval times the relationship is very complicated between the source and target texts because of frequent use of anonymous translation, indirect translation and retranslation. The situation was further complicated by simultaneous translations of the same text, the self-contradictory manuscripts as well as inaccurate hand copies of ancient texts.

2.3.1 Socio-cultural Background

In the Late Middle Ages, prosperity and growth in Europe came to a halt. The population of Europe was reduced in half by a series of famines and plagues, such as the Great Famine of 1315-1317 and the Black Death of 1348 and 1350. With the rise of strong and royalty-based nation states (England, France and the Christian kingdoms of the Iberian Peninsula), serious conflicts cropped up between the popes and the national monarchs. The situation was worsened by disunity within the Catholic Church. These events, political, religious and economic, were collectively called the Crises of the 14th century.

Despite these crises, the 14th century Europe witnessed great progress within the arts and sciences. The intellectual revival in the 12th century marked by the emergence of universities and rediscovery and translation of the Arabic and Greek texts continued into the Late Middle Ages. Gothic style and Christianity still dominated late medieval art and architecture, but the rise of the cities, establishment of universities, increased trade and growth of bourgeois art patrons contributed to the secular motifs of intellectual life. Latin was still used in creation and translation, but a variety of national languages evolved in response to general demand for national independence. Replacement of Latin with the vernacular national languages and introduction of classical ideas were the most important changes in late medieval literature. Translations happened from ancient languages into more recent national languages and indirect translations were gradually being replaced by direct translations. Under the strict censorship of the church, scientific translations were scanty. The most translated texts were religious and literary, particularly poetical. The translation practice and discussion reflected the tension between cultural supremacy represented by Latin and the growing confidence in the potential of the vernacular national language.

Italy first entered the period of the Renaissance—a cultural movement marked by revival of ideas from classical antiquity which spread throughout Europe by the end of the Late Middle Ages. The pioneers of Renaissance humanist literature and promoters of the vernacular languages were Dante Alighieri, Francesco Petrarch, Giovanni Boccaccio and Geoffrey Chaucer.

2.3.2 Italian Translation Tradition (Dante and Bruni)

In the Late Middle Ages, the Italian peninsula was not a nation state. It was dominated by the city-states (Florence, Milan, Venice, Genoa) competing with each other for supremacy. The Italian language did not gain its independence from Latin until the 16th century. Prior to that, a variety of dialects, all derived from the Vulgar Latin, had been spoken in Italy, each with distinctive phonetic and lexical features. The earliest translation happened from Latin into these vernacular varieties.

The first wave of systematic translation occurred in the middle of the 13th century in the

Law Schools of Bologna[①] and Florence[②]. Cicero was the first important Latin author that was translated, with strict literality, for the purpose of improving the regional dialects. Many other rhetoric works and philosophical texts were translated with the same accuracy and literalism. The translators, mostly prominent teachers of law and rhetoric, were authored. Concurrently, some French texts, primarily of entertainment literature, were also translated into Italian, among them the Arthurian legends[③] and other narrative tales. Translators of the entertainment literature were largely anonymous, though. Theoretical discussion among the scholar-translators at the universities, although sporadic and crude, emerged.

Translation played an important role in establishing Italian poetical tradition. **Jacopo Da Lentini**, also called **Giacomo Da Lentini**[④], one of the earliest Italian poets, is traditionally credited with the invention of the sonnet through his translation of Folquet de Marseille,[⑤] who is known primarily for his love songs. Da Lentini adapted the themes, style, and language of Provencal poetry to Italian, infusing it with his own aristocratic tastes. His works in that form remain the earliest known and its influence lasted for over a century. Most poetic translators were unknown, however, for the focus was the work for its own sake and the translator's existence was always overlooked.

In the 14th and 15th centuries, religious translation appeared. A remarkable effort is a series of translations of the *Bible* in central Italian vernacular made by anonymous monks in the 14th century. The translation was among the most popular devotional works to be printed in the late 15th century translated from the Latin *Vulgate*.

Translations in the 14th and 15th centuries were made in the faith of translating the meaning rather than the words. The first important translator, among others, was **Dante Alighieri**[⑥] (1265-1321), the author of *Devine Comedy* and one of the greatest poets of world literature.

Dante was born into Florence, a city-state harassed by the internal conflict, which led to his death sentence in 1302. To flee the execution Dante spent the rest of his life in exile. Dante wrote three great works in Italian: *Convivio*[⑦] (1304-1307), *The New Life* (1293) and *the Devine Comedy* (1308-1321). *Book I* of *Convivio*, meaning the Banquet, is largely a stirring and systematic defense of the Italian vernacular, where Dante openly defended the

① 波罗尼亚:今意大利中北部城市,公元前2世纪成为罗马的殖民地。

② 佛罗伦萨:今意大利中部城市,文艺复兴时期的艺术中心。

③ 亚瑟王的故事:英国公元5世纪左右亚瑟王和他的圆桌武士们的传奇故事。中世纪作家,特别是法国作家,对亚瑟王的故事有不同的描述。

④ 达伦蒂尼:13世纪的意大利“西西里诗派”诗人,最早用十四行诗体进行创作。

⑤ 福柯斯:又称 Foulques De Toulouse,普罗旺斯13世纪初游吟诗人,在普罗旺斯和阿拉贡地区享有盛誉。主要创作爱情诗、十字军东征诗歌和宗教诗歌。

⑥ 但丁:中世纪意大利诗人,著有《神曲》等,被视为文艺复兴的先声。

⑦ 《飨宴》:但丁通过诠释自己的一些诗歌,把当时各方面的知识通俗地介绍给一般读者,作为精神食粮,故名《飨宴》。书中盛赞俗语的优点,批判封建等级观念,阐明真正的高贵在于道德品质的人文主义思想。

comprehensibility and intelligibility of the Italian vernacular as compared to Latin as a language of commentary. Dante himself fervently encouraged its use and in the final sentence of *Book I* he predicted its glorious future in metaphorical terms:

> *This shall be the new light, the new sun, which shall rise when the worn-out one shall set, and shall give light to them who are in shadow and in darkness because of the old sun, which does not enlighten them.* ①

The revolution Dante described was the uncertain struggle between the predominantly clerical Latin culture and the emergence of a secular, vernacular urban literacy. The Italian literature, Danti predicted, was soon to become the leading literature and Italian the leading literary language of Europe for more than three centuries to come.

His views on translation were also collected in *Convivio*. He strongly asserted the impossibility of translating poetry. He observed that "the verses of *Psalter* lack musical sweetness and harmony, for they have been translated from Hebrew to Greek, and from Greek to Latin, and in the first translation all this sweetness perished" (quoted in Robinson, 2006: 48). On the basis of the observation he advanced his famous theory that poetical works in general are untranslatable. "Let all observe that nothing harmonized by the laws of Muses can be changed from its own tongue to another one without destroying all its sweetness and harmony." (quoted in Baker, 1998: 475)

Dante's discourse on untranslatability of poetical texts formed part of the earliest Italian translation legacy. The theory was later extended to bear on literary text in general, which is also composed with the laws of Muses. In later theoretical discussions on literary translation, Dante was frequently quoted to shed light on the translation that lost sight of the original form and rhythm. Despite his strong assertion that poetical texts are untranslatable, Dante went on undauntedly with translating Latin and Provencal poems into Italian. Thanks to his endeavors, the Italian language grew into a lingua franca for the next several centuries.

The Italian writer-translators of the time also include **Petrarch**② and **Boccaccio**③.

Francesco Petrarca (1304-1374), known in English as **Petrarch**, was an Italian scholar, poet, and one of the earliest Renaissance humanists. Petrarch was made to study law at his father's wish but his real interest was writing and Latin literature. With his first large scale work *Africa*, an epic in Latin about a great Roman general, Petrarch emerged as a European celebrity. On April 8, 1341, he became the first poet laureate since antiquity and was crowned

---

① Dante Encyclop dia Britannica. Encyclop dia Britannica Inc. 2012-03-26. http://www.britannica.com/EBchecked/topic/151164/Dante.

② 彼特拉克：意大利诗人、学者和人文主义者，曾用十四行诗创作了著名的爱情抒情诗集《抒情歌谣集》。

③ 薄伽丘：意大利诗人和作家，代表作有《十日谈》。

on the holy grounds of Rome's Capitol. During his extensive trip of Europe, he collected Latin manuscripts and was an active initiator of the recovery of knowledge from writers of Rome and Greece. He is also known for being the first to develop the concept of the "Dark Ages".

Petrarch was an enthusiastic Latin scholar and did most of his writing in the Latin language, among them scholarly works, introspective essays, letters, and poetry. His literary models included works by Cicero, Virgil, and Seneca. Petrarch is best known for his Italian poetry, notably the *Songbook*, in which he polished and perfected the sonnet form inherited from Giacomo Da Lentini①. Petrarch's sonnets were admired and imitated throughout Europe during the Renaissance and became a model for lyrical poetry. He encouraged and advised Leontius Pilatus'② translation of Homer, a bald and almost word for word rendering into Latin prose, although he was severely critical of the result. Homer, Petrarch said, "was dumb to him, while he was deaf to Homer"③.

Boccaccio (1313-1375) was an Italian author and poet, a friend and correspondent of Petrarch, and an important Renaissance humanist. His most notable works include *On Famous Women*, the *Decameron*④, and his poetry in the Italian vernacular. From Naples⑤, the young Boccaccio brought with him a store of literary work. Two works are noteworthy with themes derived from medieval romances: *Filocolo*⑥(*The Love Afflicted*), a prose work in five books on the loves and adventures of Floire and Blanchefleur, based on a very popular French romance *Florio e Biancifiore*. It is considered to be the first novel of Italian literature written in prose. And the other was *filostrato* (*The Love Struck*), a short poem in ottava rima⑦, a stanza form composed of eight 11-syllable lines telling the story of Troilus and the faithless Criseida. Boccaccio enriched the familiar themes of chivalry and love with his own acute observation of real life, presenting them by a display of learning and rhetorical ornament, so as to make his Italian comparable with the classics of Latin literature. Boccaccio elevated the literary status of ottava rima, the verse metre of the popular minstrels, which was eventually to become the characteristic vehicle for Italian verse.

Boccaccio's early works had an immediate effect outside Italy: Geoffrey Chaucer drew inspiration from *filostrato* for his own *Troilus and Criseyde* (as William Shakespeare was later to do for *Troilus and Cressida*) and Boccaccio's Teseida was the source of inspiration for the "Knight's Tale" in *The Canterbury Tales*. From 1350, Boccaccio became closely involved with

① 达伦蒂尼:13 世纪的意大利"西西里诗派"诗人,最早用十四行诗体进行创作。

② 彼拉图斯:14 世纪意大利的人文主义学者。

③ Petrarch. From Wikipedia, the free encyclopedia. 2013/9/23. http://en.wikipedia.org/wiki/Petrarch.

④ 《十日谈》:薄伽丘代表作,收集了以逃避黑死病为背景的 100 个故事。

⑤ 那不勒斯:意大利南部城市。

⑥ 《菲洛柯洛》:薄伽丘第一部比较成熟的长篇小说。

⑦ 八行诗:一种意大利诗体。

Italian humanism and also with the Florentine[①] government. He promoted the study of Greek, receiving Barlaam of Calabria[②] at his house and encouraging his tentative translations of works by Homer, Euripides and Aristotle. Boccaccio was a man of the Renaissance and humanism, because he not only indulged in classical studies and attempted to rediscover and reinterpret ancient texts, but also aimed to raise literature in the modern languages to the level of the classical by setting standards for it and then conforming to those standards. Without Boccaccio, the literary culmination of the Italian Renaissance would be historically incomprehensible. In October 1350 he met Petrarch as he entered Florence and ever since then the two men became best friends. Together, through the exchange of books, news, and ideas, the two men laid the foundations for the humanist re-conquest of classical antiquity.

Another great Italian translator and translation theorist towards the end of the Middle Ages was **Leonardo Bruni Aretino**[③] (1369-1444). In his lifetime Bruni enjoyed international reputation as a scholar, author and statesman, his manuscripts the most voluminous among Renaissance authors. In the power struggle between the pope and the secular state, he helped consolidate the power of Pope. He wrote biographies of Dante, Petrarch and Boccaccio in the Italian language until his death in 1444. Bruni translated, among others, Plato, Aristotle and Petrarch into Latin, but he is best remembered for his Latin translation of Aristotle.

In the preface to Aristotle's *Nicomachean Ethics*[④], he pointed out the mistakes in previous translations. When accused of being too harsh in his criticism he justified himself by saying that he could not bear to see the Greek works, which were full of elegance, delight and beauty, were defiled and disfigured by the worst sort of **translationese**. He continued to discuss, from the translator's mastery of the two languages, what he thinks is the correct way to translate (1424/1426). "In my view, then, the essence of translation is to transfer correctly what is written in one language into another language. But no one can do this correctly who has not a wide and extensive knowledge of both languages." (quoted in Robinson, 2006: 58-59)

Bruni held that the translator must be able to tell the difference between literal meaning of words and the real sense behind them. He cited instances to illustrate the point. For one example, "something is lacking" means that something good is wanted, as in "an orator lacks good diction or an actor lacks good gesture". "*free from* something", however, means free from something bad, as in "doctor is free from ignorance or a lawyer from corruption". Similarly, there is the difference between literal meaning and idiomatic meaning of words. Everybody knows the word "pain" (an unpleasant sensation), but when used in "*take pains*", it has acquired an idiomatic meaning (make great efforts or have great patience), which has little to

① 佛罗伦萨:今意大利中部城市。

② 巴兰:拜占庭人本主义运动的代表人物。

③ 布鲁尼:15 世纪意大利人文主义学者。

④ 《尼各马克伦理学》:亚里士多德关于美德的伦理学作品,由其子尼各马克编辑成书。

do with the literal meaning of "pain". Similar difference exists between the literal meanings of words and the meaning in literary allusions. Aristotle, for example, quoted Homer's "when two go together" to refer to the power and strength of friendship. The translator must translate the sense behind this literary allusion rather than the words. Equally important is his knowledge of the target language. The translator must be able to tell the nuances between words like "be fond of" and "love" and thousands of similar target language words. When he translates these expressions he should imitate them and avoid verbal and grammatical novelties, especially those that are imprecise and barbarous.

The translator should also possess a sound ear so that his translation does not disturb and destroy the fullness and rhythmical qualities of the original. He should be able to perceive the nicety of a language so as to preserve the original integrity and rhythm. The translator should imitate the original style as much as possible and translate in the target language in the way Aristotle wrote in Greek original. (quoted in Robinson, 2006: 58)

> *For every writer has his proper style: Cicero his sonority and richness, Sallust his dry and succinct expression, Livy his rough grandeur. So the good translator in translating each will conform himself to them in such a way that he follows the style of each one. —This is then the best way to translate: to preserve the style of the original as well as possible, so that polish and elegance be not lacking in the words, and the words be not lacking in meaning.* (Robinson, 2006: 59, my ellipsis)

He concluded that difficult as it is, effective translation is still possible provided the translator is equipped adequately with this language knowledge. As he attached importance to the translator's language competence, rather than divine inspiration, in his argument for translatability, Bruni was considered a humanist translator.

2.3.3 Translations into Middle English (Chaucer, Caxton and Wycliffe)

For much of the Middle English period (1100-1500), two vernaculars were spoken in English society: Anglo-Norman and Anglo-Saxon. The Anglo-Norman language is traditionally used to refer to the variety of French used in medieval England following the Norman Conquest in 1066. Relatively speaking, Anglo-Norman was considered a prestigious language as it was mainly spoken by the Norman rulers, while Anglo-Saxon English was still thought to be the language of the "savages". In addition, Latin, the language of religion and culture, was still an important source language of translation. Translations in late medieval England primarily happened from Latin into either of the two vernaculars or between the two vernaculars themselves. French, a prominent language of Norman rulers, became an important source language of translation, too. With the growth of national consciousness, there came a strong cry for translation into native English. The translation practice and discussion reflected the tension between cultural supremacy represented by Latin and French and the growing confidence in the potential of the English language.

The general socio-cultural climate was unfavorable to the enterprise of translation. First, in a trilingual society where translation and interpretation happened on a day-to-day basis, translating was a low job and the translator was not respected. Second, compared with Latin, English was underdeveloped and still in want of a standard form and had "no savor before a clerk" (Amos, 1920: 9). English was still considered the low language intended for the uneducated peasants without taste for artistic work, while the readers with higher cultural attainment normally turned to Latin or French sources. Indeed there was little stimulus for the English translators except the feelings of patriotism. Third, for much of the medieval times, literary texts existed in sporadic manuscripts and obtaining them normally involved long distance travels only the rich and free scholars could afford. Under this circumstance, what texts to translate was normally a matter of chance and most translators had no choice but settle down with the texts they could have on hand. Thus the source texts were not necessarily to the translator's liking. Fourth, in late medieval England, the translators translated under the auspices of his patron, who provided funds and prescribed the source text and even dictated the method of translation. The quality of translation suffered as a result.

As the translators were mostly unnamed in medieval England, many translations were dubious, i. e., it is difficult to determine whether it is translation or original composition. This gave rise to the problem of "**pseudo translation**" or "fictitious translation", i. e., translation without an identifiable original. Some other social factors aggravated the problem. The inconvenience of transportation and communication was an important reason for simultaneous translations of the same text. When similar texts appeared in several languages or in the same language, the precise relationship between them became unclear unless the source text was a world classic. The situation was further complicated by the self-contradictory manuscripts as well as by the hand copies which were inaccurate to the original. "Prior to the advent of printing culture, translators regularly worked with hand copies at one or more removes from their originals." (quoted in France, 2000: 40) As most of the Middle English translations were made before the appearance of the printing industry, the manuscripts and the hand copies differed from one another to varying degrees. The relationship between the source text and the translated text became intensely complicated.

Indirect translation only complicated the situation. Many English translations were made not directly out of the original text, but via its French translation or other tertiary text. The English translator often "was engaged in translating something that was already a translation. More frequently, it was a French version of a Latin original, but sometimes its ancestry was complicated by the existence or the tradition of Greek or Hebrew sources" (Amos, 1920: 13). As a result, many second-hand, or even third-hand, translations were produced. The omissions, errors and even added comments in the first-hand translation were largely retained in the derived versions, to be complicated by additions and more mistakes made in the new renderings. "What at first seemed to be the English translator's comment on his own treatment of source is frequently only a literal rendering of a comment already present in his original." (Amos, 1920: 14)

Also, the sources from the prefaces to Middle English translations seem to imply that the translator was not working with a written manuscript or even a copy of the manuscript, but on the basis of what they had read, heard or memorized some time earlier. Contemporary evidence shows that literature was very often transmitted by word of mouth. "—one can not ignore the possibility that occasionally, a 'translated' saint's life or romance may have been the result of hearing a French or Latin narrative read or recited." (Amos, 1920: 22, my ellipsis)

All these factors made it hard to account for the discrepancies between original and translated texts, i. e., whether they occurred in the inaccurate original, were influenced by the patron, or wrought by the translator. Translation thus became a very flexible concept that ranged from original composition to strict interlinear glosses, with compilation and commentary in between the two extremes. At one end of the scale, paragraph after paragraph were deleted without qualm and additions were made at random; at the other extreme of the scale, word-for-word translation was not uncommon; the original sense was altered at the translator's will to the extent that translation bordered very much on original creation. It is therefore suggested that the original text needs not be taken as the standard against which the translation is assessed. Instead, it should merely be regarded as a point of departure of translation, or as the first step in the process of textual transmission.

Despite all these unfavorable conditions, English translators translated a flood of works into Middle English. As the English language then was still in its infancy, many Latin manners of expressions, which were full of beauty and grace, were defiled during the transferring process. This led to the conclusion that English, compared with more developed languages, was still tragically deficient in its ability of expression. The situation began to improve, though, through a grand enterprise of translation in late medieval England, which enriched the English language with embellishments from a variety of languages. "The English language is the sea which receives tributaries from every region under heaven", said American poet Ralph Waldo Emerson. (quoted in Delisle & Woodsworth, 1995: 26) Indeed the English language is a hybrid language that incorporates elements of several branches of the Indo-European language family, a process that depended heavily on translation. Translations into English vernacular helped consolidate national consciousness and establish national self-confidence until "By the 14th century the English language began to replace French as the official language. It was introduced into schools in 1350, into the court in 1362 and into parliament in 1399" (quoted in Delisle & Woodsworth, 1995: 29).

The most remarkable translators, among others, were Roger Bacon①, Richard Rolle②

① 罗吉尔·培根:英国13世纪唯物主义思想家、伟大的科学家,他最知名作品是《大著作》。

② 罗尔:13世纪英格兰最著名的隐修士,最多产的作家之一。

Geoffrey Chaucer[①], William Caxton and John Wycliffe.

Roger Bacon (1220-1292) is a celebrated philosopher and scientist of the 13th century England. In his *Opus Maius* (*Great Work*) he discussed the importance of teaching grammar, which he understands as grammars of Hebrew, Greek and Arabic, the foreign languages that carried the wisdom of the world. In the discussion he argued against translation on three grounds. 1. As languages are so widely different, an excellent piece of work in one language cannot be transferred into another without losing its peculiar qualities; all translations, therefore, are unreliable; 2. The lack of knowledge of target language and of the subject matter makes translations incomprehensible; 3. With a few notable exceptions, a great majority of translators were tragically unqualified for the task and produced translations that are not only self-contradictory, but also impossible to read. As pointed out by Robinson, his is not a translation theorist, but anti-translation theorist who insisted on untranslatability between languages. (quoted in Robinson, 2006: 46)

Richard Rolle (1300-1349) translated the *Psalter* into Middle English with painful literality, which exerted an important influence on the later translations of the *Bible*. For the following century the translation was read to the public from the pulpit and became the backbone for Lollard[②] translation. He classified translation into translation proper and extensive commentary. He stated that "In the translation I follow the letter as much as I am able to, and where I cannot find an exactly equivalent English word, I follow the sense, so that those who are going to read it need have no fear of not understanding" (quoted in Robinson, 2006: 49-50).

Geoffrey Chaucer (1343-1400), known as the Father of English literature, is widely considered the greatest English poet of medieval times and was the first poet to have been buried in the Poet's Corner of Westminster Abbey. Chaucer is a central figure in promoting the prestige of the vernacular Middle English, at a time when the dominant literary languages in England were French and Latin. During his service in the royal court, Chaucer made extensive tours of Italy and France, whose literatures became sources of inspiration to his own literary production. Among his many works, he is best known for *The Canterbury Tales*[③]. Many of his works, however, are very loose translations of, or simply based on, works from continental Europe. Some of allegedly original works by Geoffrey Chaucer are later found to be translations. Chaucer's works might be divided into three periods: a French period (1360-1372), an Italian period (1372-1386) and an English period (1385-1400), as Chaucer was influenced by those literatures in turn.

---

① 乔叟:英国诗人,中世纪英国最伟大的文学家,作品包括《悼公爵夫人》《特洛伊拉斯和克莱希斯》以及《坎特伯雷故事集》等。

② 罗拉德教派:英格兰宗教改革派一个分支的成员,也称为"威克利夫派"。

③ 《坎特伯雷故事集》:乔叟最知名的诗体短篇小说集。

During the French period, Chaucer translated such allegorical French poetry as *The Romance of the Rose*①. This is a partial translation, as Chaucer confessed in one of his works. He translated part of the poem from French sources and wrote the rest himself. For this translation he earned the honorific title of "grant translateur", meaning grand translator, from his French contemporary Eustache Deschamps②(1346-1406). *The Book of the Duchess*③ is indebted to French poetry, too.

In the Italian period, he wrote a long poem *Troilus and Criseyde*④ in 1381, a book that shows evident reliance on Boccaccio and on the Latin philosopher Boethius. It uses a new Italian poetry form which was little known in England at the time but familiar to Chaucer during his frequent trips abroad on court business. *The Legend of Good Women*⑤ is a series of narratives based on writings of Ovid and Virgil. *The Parliament of Fowles*⑥, a depiction of a dream vision in rhyme royal stanza, was also influenced by Italian Renaissance.

Although he borrowed abundantly from French and Italian poetry, Chaucer insisted on writing poetry in London dialect, an English vernacular. Even in his *Treatise on the Astrolabe*⑦, a scientific text, he made the point of translating into English rather than Latin. During the English period in which he wrote about English subjects mostly in London dialect, the influences from other sources were evident though. The representative work from the English period is *The Canterbury Tales*, which is more similar to Boccaccio's *Decameron* than any other works. Like the *Decameron*, *The Canterbury Tales* presents a number of narrators who tell stories along a journey. Like the *Decameron*, it ends with an apology in which Chaucer asks for forgiveness for the vulgar and unworthy parts of this and other past works, and seeks absolution for his sins. A quarter of the tales in *The Canterbury Tales* are similar to a tale in the *Decameron*, although most of them have closer parallels in other works. These works include poetry by Ovid, the *Bible* in one of the many vulgate versions available at the time, and the works of Petrarch and Dante. *The Clerk's Tale*⑧ was a version of Petrarch's retelling of the last story in Boccaccio's *Decameron*, supplemented by an intermediate French version. The influence of Boethius' *Consolation of Philosophy* is seen in several tales by Chaucer. Chaucer also seems to have borrowed from John Gower⑨(1330-1408), numerous religious encyclopedias

---

① 《玫瑰传奇》:13 世纪法国寓言长诗。
② 厄斯塔什:法国中世纪诗人。
③ 《悼公爵夫人》:乔叟早期的诗歌作品。
④ 《特洛伊罗斯与克丽西达》:特洛伊王子特洛伊罗斯和他的爱人克丽西达的悲剧故事。
⑤ 《好女人的故事》或《贤妇传》。
⑥ 《百鸟会议》:乔叟的诗歌作品。
⑦ 《论星盘》:乔叟关于星盘的专题文章。
⑧ 《小职员的故事》:《坎特伯雷故事集》第四部分的第一个故事。
⑨ 高尔:与乔叟同时代的英国诗人,乔叟的朋友。

and liturgical writings[①]. *The Man of Law's Tale*[②] was primarily translated from an episode in the Anglo-Norman chronicle, a long universal history, completed sometime around 1334 by Nicholas Trevet[③] (1257-1334). The major theme in the tale, of an exiled princess Constaunce uncorrupted by her suffering, was common in the literature of the time. Chaucer altered Trevet's form and content. Trevet's chronicle was written in prose, while Chaucer's translation came out in rhyme royal. According to the research by Rose, Trevet presented his Constaunce as intelligent, capable and politically powerful, whereas Chaucer had deprived his heroine of these stalwart, erudite and bold qualities, highlighting her utter powerlessness and female passiveness and rendering her more reliant upon the power of God for her authority and her worldly fortune[④].

Some other works of Chaucer's also show reliance on the existing works. Chaucer's *Boece*[⑤] (1380?) is surprisingly similar to the *Consolation of Philosophy* by Boethius. But it is difficult to define it as a translation because the *Consolation of Philosophy* came to Chaucer in its French version with a variety of explanatory notes, marginal glosses and extensive commentaries. All these became the sources of inspiration to Chaucer's *Boece*.

In his literary career, Chaucer translated a wide range of literary genres, i. e., courtly romance, moral allegory, scientific handbook, and classical literature. He sometimes kept close to the original, sometimes merely took over the idea and reworked the original at his free will. Many new literary genres, such as ballad[⑥], romance[⑦], fabliau[⑧] were introduced into English literature through his translation. He was the first English poet to use iambic pentameter, in the seven-line stanza rhyming *ababbcc* called "rhyme royal". He was also the first English poet to introduce a verse unit consisting of two rhymed lines in iambic pentameter later known as the heroic couplet. Chaucer's translation opened out great potential for translation into Middle English, making indelible contributions to the establishment of the English literary tradition. Chaucer demonstrated to the world the artistic legitimacy of the vernacular English language, and was styled the father of English literature.

John Lydgate[⑨] (1370? -1449) worked with strong support from royalty and wealthy commoners. Commissioned by the Prince of Wales, and later Henry V, Lydgate made an

---

① The Canterbury Tales. From Wikipedia, the free encyclopedia. 2013-09-25. http://en.wikipedia.org/wiki/The_Canterbury_Tales.

② 《律师的故事》:《坎特伯雷故事集》的第五个故事。

③ 瑞维特:中世纪英国编年史家。

④ The Canterbury Tales. From Wikipedia, the free encyclopedia. 2013-09-25. http://en.wikipedia.org/wiki/The_Canterbury_Tales。

⑤ 《波切尔》:乔叟的《哲学的慰藉》英译本。

⑥ 民谣:常是源于民歌并适于演唱的叙事诗歌,由简单诗节组成,通常有循环叠句。

⑦ 传奇故事:中世纪重要的文学体裁,讲述英雄和不寻常的或神秘事件的长篇虚构故事。

⑧ 故事诗:中世纪的韵文故事,取材于日常生活中滑稽、粗俗的主题。

⑨ 利德盖特:15 世纪英国作家,主要创作道德训诫和宗教作品。

amplified translation of *Troy Book* (1412-1420) of Guido delle Colonne[①]. The purpose of the translation was to ensure that the great epic about the Trojan War would be known in English. The *Troy Book* is less an epic than a compendium of political and moral counsel, which linked England with Troy by the myth of origins. It primarily followed Chaucer's iambic pentameter, often varied by the so-called "broken-backed line"[②] and Lydgate's "signature" line characterized by the omitted unaccented syllable after the medial caesura. In 1420, Lydgate began the *Siege of Thebes*[③], another moralizing history that begins with a prologue in which Lydgate imitates and extends the opening of Chaucer's *The Canterbury Tales* as Lydgate projects himself into the story as the new pilgrim-narrator[④]. The main story is drawn from a lost French romance, embellished by features from Boccaccio. In 1431 Lydgate was commissioned to translate *The Fall of Prince*[⑤] into Chaucerian rhyme royal from a French version of Boccaccio's work. The result is a universal encyclopedia of history and mythology, somewhat ponderous in tone and exhaustively fleshed out with moral teaching[⑥].

John Trevisa or **John of Trevisa** (1342? -1402?) translated, at the request of his patron Lord Berkeley, the Latin *Polychronicon* of Ranulf Higden[⑦] in 1378.

Originally composed in Latin, *Polychronicon* is a chronicle of the world from the Creation to 1357. This translation was made in the late medieval period when there was an increasing general interest in history, and Trevisa's version was just one of several standard vernacular histories available in English. His translation was interesting for the additional comments he made to update the original text. Where Higden, for example, discussed the fact that children learned their lessons in French, Trevisa commented that the situation had changed up to the time he was writing, and that lessons were now conducted in English. He acknowledged that the children may learn faster in English, but pointed out rather disapprovingly that now children "know no more French than their left heel, and that is harmful for them if they should pass the sea and work in strange lands"[⑧]. He translated poetry with a prose style that was plain and forceful and prefaced it with *Dialogue between a Lord and a Clerk upon Translation*. Trevisa translated the words as much as possible, but sometimes supplied an explanation or changed the wording so as to make sure the sense was not changed.

---

① 圭多:13 世纪意大利作家,著有拉丁文作品《特洛伊故事》。

② 断背诗:指诗行中间删节的诗体,特指利德盖特的诗歌作品中的形式特征,即很多诗行只有 9 音节,在诗行中间停顿处缺少一个轻读音节。

③ 《围攻底比斯》:利德盖特于 1420 年前后创作的诗歌。

④ Claire Sponslor. John Lydgate. 2008-04-11. <I:\Literary Encyclopedia John Lydgate. mht>

⑤ 《王子的堕落》。

⑥ MS Hunter. The World of Chaucer: Medieval Books and Manuscripts. 2008-04-11. http://special. lib. gla. ac. uk/exhibns/chaucer/contemporaries. html.

⑦ 希格登:14 世纪英国作家,《编年史》是其拉丁文作品。

⑧ MS Hunter. The World of Chaucer: Medieval Books and Manuscripts. 2008-04-11. http://special. lib. gla. ac. uk/exhibns/chaucer/contemporaries. html.

In the same vein he made various other translations, among them *On the Properties of Things* (1389) by Bartholomaeus Anglicus①, a medieval forerunner of the encyclopedia of natural science. Printed about 1495, it was highly influential in Tudor England. He also translated a number of books of the *Bible* into French, including a version of the *Book of Revelation* by his patron. Trevisa may well have been one of the contributors to the Early Version of Wycliffe's *Bible*. The preface to the *King James Version of 1611*② singles him out as a translator amongst others at that time.

In *Dialogue between a Lord and a Clerk upon Translation* (1387), Trevisa addressed some issues of translation in the form of a dialogue between the translator's patron and the translator. It is an interesting illustration of the patron's dominant status in the translating activity. The lord decided almost everything from the expected function of the translation in the target culture to the specific issue of translating the chronicle in rhyme or prose. The Lord dictated that the function of translation should be to educate the English people in the knowledge of world history to the benefits of the target culture. When the Clerk meekly asked if the chronicle should be translated in rhyme or in prose, the Lord's answer is unequivocal: "In prose, for commonly prose is more clear than rhyme, more easy and more plain to know and understand." (quoted in Robinson, 2006: 52)

William Caxton (1422-1491) was the first English printer and a prolific translator after Chaucer.

During his travel to Cologne③, Caxton observed, and was well impressed by, German printing. He wasted no time in setting up a printing press in Bruges④, where he printed the first English book in 1475: *Recuyell of the Historyes of Troye*⑤, a translation from French by Caxton himself. Up to his death in 1491, he had printed about 100 books, 29 of which he translated himself. He translated *Charles the Great*⑥, *Blanchardyn and Eglantine*⑦, *Eneydos*⑧, *Faytte of Arms*⑨, *Mirror of the World*⑩, etc. Caxton's translation of the *Golden Legend*⑪ (1483) and *The Book of the Knight in the Tower*⑫ (1484) contain perhaps the earliest verses of the

---

① 巴塞洛缪:圣芳济会的百科全书编纂者,因编著《物体属性》而知名。

② 《钦定本圣经》:又称《詹姆斯王译本》。是在英王詹姆斯一世的支持下,由多位学者经七载之久,于 1611 年完成出版的权威译本。宗教观念上调和了天主教和新教,语言优美,在英译本圣经中具有举足轻重的地位,对英语语言和文学产生了深远的影响。

③ 科隆:今德国城市,位于莱茵河上波恩北部。

④ 布鲁日:位于今比利时西北部的文化古城。

⑤ 《特洛伊历史故事集》。

⑥ 《查理大帝》。

⑦ 《勃兰夏丁和伊格兰丁》。

⑧ 《伊尼德斯》。

⑨ 《用武的绝技》。

⑩ 《世界明镜》。

⑪ 《金色传奇》。

⑫ 《塔中骑士》。

Bible to be printed in English.

The English language was changing rapidly in Caxton's time and the works came to him in a variety of styles and dialects. The common English language, particularly the spoken form, was so diverse from one region to another that one dialect may sound a foreign language to a speaker of another dialect. Amid linguistic diversity in spoken dialects, however, the London standard of English was gaining increasing popularity in writing in most parts of the country by the time Caxton established his press. Caxton made a crucial decision to reproduce the English, particularly its spelling, of London and the Southeast in his prosperous printing enterprise. Thus Caxton is credited with standardizing the English language (that is, homogenizing regional dialects) through printing, which has stimulated the development of English vocabulary, inflection, syntax and consequently led to the widening gap between the spoken and the written language. His printing industry was one of the most decisive factors that established English as the official language of England over French and Latin. And the works he printed marked the end of the Middle English and the beginning of Early Modern English. It is said that Caxton was "as important for the language, in his own way as Geoffrey Chaucer, whose work he printed" (quoted in Delisle & Woodsworth, 1995: 31).

Caxton was up against strong criticism from merchant class of the time, who felt anxiety and unease about the consequence of the printed book. As printing facilitated the spread of learning and knowledge, the poor, they were afraid, might then become aware and enlightened of their circumstances and dissatisfied and aggrieved, which might give rise to social unrest and civil disturbance. To this criticism, Caxton announced: "If tis wrong I do, then tis a fine and noble wrong"①. He played a decisive role in popularizing and disseminating knowledge among the common people.

In the preface to *The Recuyell of the Histories of the Troy*, Caxton discussed the problem of diversity of dialect in the course of translation. Caxton believed that what dialect to use depends on the readers for which the translation is made: "For this book is not for every rude and unconning (ignorant) man to see, but to clerks and very gentlemen that understands gentlemenness (gentility) and science." (quoted in Robinson, 2006: 61)

In a similar way, he made various other translations with exclusive regard to the target language, thinking that, as the readers of the translation are Englishmen who know not the character of the French language, it is unnecessary to imitate the French style. In the preface to *Blanchardyn and Eglantine*, he admitted frankly that he knew little about rhetoric or much of popular melodious phraseology and that his only wish was to make his translation intelligible to his English readers.

① William Caxton. From Wikipedia, the free encyclopedia. 2008-04-12. http://en.wikipedia.org/wiki/William_Caxton.

Osbern Bokenam[①] translated many saints' legends, and was very interested in the development of literary expression. He translated "plainly, after the language of southfolk speech" (Amos, 1920: 40). Bokenam's style was striking in two respects: he writes "compendiously" and tried to avoid "gay speech" (Amos, 1920: 43). He repeatedly went against wordiness and rhetorical embellishments. He was unable to emulate the earlier rhetoricians—Gower, Chaucer and Lydgate—for they have already gathered "the most fresh flowers" (Amos, 1920: 44). He thought that an embellished style would not suit him, for it is dotage for as old a man as him to affect such a language style.

Another important translation of this period was a collaborative translation project of English *Bible* initiated by John Wycliffe.

John Wycliffe[②] (1320? -1384) is the well-known theologian and philosopher, an early dissident in the Roman Catholic Church in the 14th century England. He and his followers preached anticlerical and Biblically-centered reforms, a movement generally considered a precursor to the Protestant Reformation. For this reason, Wycliffe is sometimes called "The Morning Star of the Reformation".

In Medieval England, the Roman Catholic Church was the established state church of England. The only *Bibles* available were the Latin *Vulgate*, an official *Bible* of the Roman Church. Only clergy had access to copies of the Latin *Bible*, and common Englishmen were unable to read them. For these reasons, all the countrymen were dependent on their local priests for the reading of Scripture. Most Christian people mainly heard the *Bible* read out to them at church since they did not know how to read the Latin and the *Bible* was costly before the appearance of the printing press. Unauthorized translation of the *Bible* into the common language was forbidden by the Roman Catholic Church. The earliest Old English translations of the *Bible* ended with the Norman Conquest of England in 1066, which marked the beginning of the Middle English with profound changes in its vocabulary. As Old English was beginning to change into Middle English, there were attempts to provide *Bible* translations in that language.

Wycliffe believed that every Christian should study the *Bible* on his own instead of listening to it read and interpreted by the clergy. For every Christian to have a personal relationship with God, Wycliffe believed that *Bible* should be available to them in their own language. Starting in 1382, Wycliffe defied the clergy by translating, in collaboration with his assistants, the Latin *Vulgate* into English on behalf of the dissident common people. Involved in the massive project were well-known translators of the time as John Wycliffe, John Purvey[③] (1354-1421), Nicholas Hereford[④], John Trevisa, etc. The work took about 13 years. Wycliffe initiated the project,

---

① 博克南姆:15 世纪英国作家和修道士,作品以圣徒传记为主。

② 威克利夫:14 世纪英国著名神学家和学者。

③ 帕维:英国威克利夫教派信徒和翻译家,和威克利夫合作翻译了第一部完整的英文《圣经》。

④ 赫里福德:14 世纪英国神学家,和威克利夫合作翻译了第一部完整英文《圣经》。

but it is unclear how much of the *Bible* he translated himself.

Wycliffe *Bibles* survive in two versions. The earlier version, allegedly copied by Hereford, is a rigid and literal translation which often leads to confusion or meaninglessness. It was intended for the less learned clergymen and the lay man. The later translation, presumably prepared by John Purvey, aimed towards all literates. It was an improvement on Hereford's version, attending more to the English usage and enjoying a larger readership. Wycliffe and his associates were credited with introducing over 1,000 words of Latin origin into the English language. Many of these words have technical endings like *-able*, *-ible*, *-ent*, *-live*, *- al*, which are now common suffixes of the modern English language. (quoted in Delisle & Woodsworth, 1995: 33)

Bible appealed to clergy, who cared for theological details, as well as lay people, whose concern was their spiritual welfare. The best standard for *Bible* translation, naturally, must combine theological fidelity with practical intelligibility. Purvey expounded his translation methods and principles in the general preface to his translation. He emphasized the importance of the use of the national English language and insisted that Latin-English translation should translate not only words but also sentences.

> *First it is to know that the best translating out of Latin into English is to translate after the sentence, and not only after the words, so that the sentence be as open or opener in English as in Latin, and not go far from the letter; and if no appeal may be made to the letter in the translating, let the sentence ever be whole and open, for the words owe to serve to the intent and sentence, and else the words be either superfluous or false.* (quoted in Robinson, 2006: 54)

Purvey elucidated the changes that are allowed in the process of transference, i. e., the Latin absolute ablative, or participle construction, may be translated by *if*, *while* or *and* clauses in English. An example is "the master reading, I stand" may be rendered into "If / While the master reads, I stand". Medieval translator were normally caught in the dilemma that it was hard to confine an English sentence to the same number of words in a Latin sentence and that when, by necessity, they changed the number of words, they feared that they might deviate from the Latin original in meaning. Purvey dispelled their doubts by showing that translation, with additions and deletions, could still be faithful to the original. His translation is an impressive achievement in the medieval England when most *Bible* translations merely paraphrased the Latin texts or were made with strict literalness. The need for brevity, for avoiding superfluous words, was a good quality for its own sake.

The academia lent general support to the *Bible* as well as Wycliffe's ideas on church reformation. And these supporters, called "Lollards"①, were traveling preachers who were dissatisfied with the church authority's insistence on only one correct reading of the *Bible*. The

① 威克利夫派教徒。

church started a massive crackdown on unauthorized *Bible* translation and the clergy attacked with increasing severity Wycliffe's version and his theories on church reformation. From 1407 to 1409, Archbishop of Canterbury imposed a total ban on the translation and use of Wycliffe's *Bibles* and other unauthorized *Bible* translations. Wycliffe's *Bibles*, and later his bones, were burned in public. The prohibition, unfortunately, fell through. Up to the 15th century, Wycliffe's *Bibles* were widely available in England and were actually the only complete versions available in Middle English. And ironically, more *Bible* translations appeared in more earnest and greater variety in the early 15th century. Today about 250 copies of the *Bible* survive, the majority of them copied from 1420-1450.

As in Anglo-Saxon England, England after Norman Conquest is not a very dynamic period for translation theories. And the translation theories merely repeated the old rules proposed by Jerome and adopted by Alfred the Great and Aelfric. There was little originality and explicitness in the translators claims, which were oftentimes self-contradictory. Much of the technical discussion came in the form of random commentaries on translation.

Further Readings

Amos, Flora Ross. *Early Theories of Translation*. New York: Columbia University Press. 1920.

Baker, Mona. *Routledge Encyclopedia of Translation Studies*. London & New York: Routledge, 1998.

Claire Sponslor. John Lydgate. 2008-04-11. I:\Literary Encyclopedia John Lydgate. mht.

Dante Encyclop dia Britannica. Encyclop dia Britannica Inc. 2012-03-26. http://www.britannica. com/EBchecked/topic/151164/Dante.

Delisle, Jean & Judith Woodsworth. *Translators through History*. Amsterdam: John Benjamins Publishing Company, 1995.

France, Peter. *The Oxford Guide to Literature in English Translation*. New York: Oxford University Press, 2000.

MS Hunter. The World of Chaucer: Medieval Books and Manuscripts. 2008-04-11. http://special. lib. gla. ac. uk/exhibns/chaucer/contemporaries. html.

Petrarch. From Wikipedia, the free encyclopedia. 2013/9/23. http://en. wikipedia. org/wiki/Petrarch.

Robinson, Douglas. *Western Translation Theory: From Herodotus to Nietzsche*. Shanghai: Foreign Language Teaching and Research Press, 2006.

Shuttleworth, Mark & Moira Cowie. *Dictionary of Translation Studies*. Shanghai: Shanghai Foreign Language Education Press, 2004.

William Caxton. From Wikipedia, the free encyclopedia. 2008-04-12. http://en. wikipedia. org/wiki/William_Caxton.

The Canterbury Tales. From Wikipedia, the free encyclopedia. 2013-09-25. http://en.

wikipedia. org/wiki/The_Canterbury_Tales.

谭载喜:《西方翻译简史》,商务印书馆 2004 年版。

Topics for Discussion

1. In what ways did Caxton contribute to the English language through his translation and printing?

2. How was English translation practice and theory influenced by the relationship between Latin and English?

3. What caused the problem of pseudo translation?

4. Describe the socio-cultural conditions in late medieval England.

5. Is literary text translatable? Give reasons for your opinion.

6. In what ways did Chaucer contribute to English literature through his translation?

2.4 Chapter Summary

In summary, translation undertaking in medieval West could be divided into three periods: the Early Middle Ages was represented by Boethius, who was engaged in translating Greek philosophy into Latin. In High Middle Ages, particularly in the 9th century, Bagdad became the center of translation, where the wisdom of the ancient civilizations, primarily Greek, were translated into Arabic through Syriac. In the 12th century, Western scholars assembled at Toledo, translating the Greek culture, nourished by ornate and elaborate oriental culture, into Western languages through Arabic and Syriac. Under the lead of Alfonso X in the second period of the Toledo School, translations were made directly into Castilian. In Late Middle Ages, translations were increasingly made from Latin into more recent national languages, such as Italian, French or English, and between these new languages themselves. Indirect translations were being replaced by direct translations. Dante is the first important writer and translator in the vernacular Italian language. Chaucer translated into Middle English a wide range of literary genres, i. e., courtly romance, moral allegory, scientific handbook, and classical literature. Latin continued to be the most important source language of translation. Translations into Latin were normally made for a wider recognition by the elite culture. Bruni, for example, continued to translate Plato, Aristotle and Petrarch into Latin. Greece, with the most brilliant civilization of its own, did not care much for importing knowledge into its own language. Hence there was little translation activity in Greece.

Throughout the middle Ages, Jerome's Latin *Vulgate* was universally accepted by the Catholic Church and for some time there was no more need for translating the *Bible* into Latin language. Translation of the *Bible* was under the regulation and administration of the church and *Bible* translation into national languages was strictly forbidden. But with the rise of national consciousness, the *Bible* was still translated into new national languages, very often without the approval of the church. Wycliffe *Bible* is the first important dissident *Bible* translated from the Latin *Vulgate* into the Middle English language.

Theoretical discussion on translation as a whole was sporadic and unsystematic. Particularly since Boethius aired his pragmatic view on translation, theoretical talk on translation was for a time laid aside, the translators invariably infatuated with the effect of translation for its own sake. This situation did not improve until discussions on translation began to resume its enthusiasm and intensity in England and Italy in Late Middle Ages. Dante openly defended the comprehensibility and intelligibility of the Italian vernacular as compared to Latin which represented the predominantly clerical Latin culture. Dante's discourse on untranslatability of poetical texts formed part of the earliest Italian translation legacy. Bruni discussed the correct way to translate from the translator's mastery of the two languages. Late Medieval translators debated among themselves over the best way to translate in relation to the development of national languages and the merits of the Latin language.

Chapter Three
Translations during the Renaissance

3.1 Socio-cultural Background

Up to the late medieval times, the spirit of freedom was starting to grow, due largely to the rise of the cities, establishment of universities, increased trade and growth of the bourgeois middle class. The Christian dominance was increasingly replaced with the secular motifs of intellectual life. Renaissance scholars searched for realism and human emotion in art, emphasizing practical, pre-professional and scientific studies. Latin was still used in creation and translation, but a variety of national languages evolved in response to general demand for national independence. Replacement of Latin with the vernacular national languages and introduction of classical ideas, which originated in Italian literature, were expanding to other new vernacular languages and literatures.

European overseas expansion starting in late 15th century led to the rise of colonial empires, together with a contact of cultures between the Eastern and Western hemispheres, which represented one of the most significant globalizing events in human history. After the fall of the Eastern Roman Empire① in 1453, many Greek manuscripts, including the Greek *New Testament*, were discovered and brought back to Western Europe, when many Byzantine scholars had to seek refuge in the West, particularly Italy. Availability of paper and the invention of metal movable type accelerated the dissemination of knowledge from the late 15th century. Starting in the early 16th century, ancient texts were accessible to Europeans in comparatively standardized edition and the next forty years would see humanists both translating these classics and adapting them in their native language. Renaissance scholars were engaged in research and study of ancient texts with renewed interest and from fresh perspectives.

The Renaissance started in Italy in the later half of the 14th century, not long after the death of Dante. It spread to the whole Europe, particularly Western European nations, during

① 东罗马帝国:从原罗马帝国分离出来,又称拜占庭帝国(395 ~ 1453),信奉东正教的君主专制国家。拜占庭帝国继承了希腊的语言和文化,但其居民却以正统罗马人自居,到7世纪为止官方语言是拉丁语。

the 15th and 16th centuries. By definition, Renaissance means rebirth or rediscovery of the classical Greek and Latin cultures, which remained buried under layers of dust for centuries. And this is done largely through massive translation movement. Renaissance, therefore, has acquired the title of the "age of translation". Translation history, however, reveals that there was developmental continuity between the medieval times and the Renaissance age and translations of Greek and Latin cultures never really ceased during the Middle Ages. Yet there were notable differences between Renaissance and medieval translations of classical cultures.

First, during the Middle Ages, the primary purpose of translation was to incorporate the Greek and Latin cultures into the new cultural system. From time to time, explanatory notes and commentaries were added to, or else passages were deleted from, the original work, as in the Translation School of Bagdad. Renaissance translators, relatively speaking, held the classical authors in high esteem and insisted on restoring them to their true colors. This is why when the Greek culture was translated into new national languages, the earlier additions were removed and deletions supplied, all to restore the Greek thinking to its original state.

On the other hand, Renaissance translators translated with Renaissance spirit of freedom from the dominance of theological thinking in the Middle Ages. *Bible*, for example, was translated with updated language in warm response to reformation movement. Non-religious texts were chosen with great care and translated with Renaissance spirit of freedom to fill a particular intellectual vacuum in the target culture. Typical of this strategy is an affirmation of the present through the use of contemporary idiom and style as against Latin, the dominant language of the church and education in the Middle Ages. As a result, many ancient texts were modernized and domesticated before they took root in the target culture system.

Third, medieval translations happened mostly through a third or fourth language and deviated much from the original. In consequence, classical culture was distorted and adulterated. Most Renaissance translators, by contrast, abandoned indirect translation. As the classical culture was now available to Renaissance translators in the Greek or Latin originals, the bulk of translation was made directly from Greek or Latin into new national languages.

Lastly, following the invention of printing techniques in the 15th century, the role of translation underwent great changes. Translation played a prominent role in spreading Renaissance spirit and Reformation movement across Europe. It was no longer a secondary activity for literary exercise. It was a primary activity of intellectual life.

During the Renaissance, religious texts were generally translated by monks or priests with the purpose of propagating religious message. Practical and academic translations were largely made by lay people in the hope of disseminating useful knowledge. The sole purpose of practical translation was to make the text easy to understand by common people. Typical of this attitude is a line on the title page of a translated book of mathematics: "—translated for common convenience and usefulness. It is so clear that every average, uninformed and inexpert mind will be able to understand it." (quoted in Baker, 1998: 476, my ellipsis) In the preface to a translated book on agriculture there is a line in similar vein: "—translated into the vernacular, so that those who don't know Latin may benefit, enjoy and gain useful information from this book." (quoted in Baker, 1998: 476, my ellipsis) Literary translation was more difficult to describe because they happened under more diversified conditions.

Up to the 16th century, the Renaissance had reached its climax. At that particular time, the Western world was eager to explore the world. And in translation community, corps of translators went all out to excavate, study, and introduce foreign cultures into their home country.

3.2 Translations in German Language Area

Translation Terms

Interlinear Translation 逐行翻译

In an interlinear translation, a source text is transcribed line after line, with the grammatical units corresponding closely to those of the source text. It is source-oriented translation method that disregards the target language norms. Interlinear translation is used mainly for language teaching or in descriptive linguistics.

Germanize 德国化

In translating the *Bible*, Luther oriented his translation towards the German culture and language, reworking the *Bible* as a German Text. Luther realized that semantic equivalence alone was inadequate and that the text had to be interpreted so as to bridge the gap in time, space and particularly mentality between the source and target texts. The conceptual difference must be taken into account, as well. The historical text was thus updated in the mentality and spirit of his own time. His translation presented the various literary genres in ways which conform to German usage.

3.2.1 Socio-cultural Background

Before the 8th century, a great variety of dialects were used around present-day Germany. In the 8th century the Old High German gradually took shape as a written language through translation of primarily Latin Biblical (the *Vulgate*) and literary texts. Around the early 13th century, the Middle High German had developed into a language on an equal footing with Latin through translation. Ovid's *Metamorphoses*[①], for instance, was translated into two levels of Middle High German to cater to different readers. Thomas Aquinas[②] (1225-1274) was

① 《变形记》:罗马诗人奥维德的作品。

② 阿奎纳:中世纪经院哲学家和神学家,著有拉丁文《神学大全》,是天主教教会认可的33位教会圣师之一。

translated with such efficiency that convinced people of the ability of the Middle High German to express the subtleties of theological and philosophical discourse.

During the German Renaissance there was a renewed interest in classical learning, which was considered an essential part of one's education. The basis of literature and art in this time was references back to times of ancient Greek and Roman societies and mythology. Latin continued as the prestigious language in creation and education. For some time it went in parallel with common German in German language area, Latin aiming at a highly-cultured intellectual elite and German the common people. Poetry was written in Latin for the few cultural elite, whereas the common German was used among the common people and in popular poetry. Translations made in the 14th and 15th centuries reflected this tension between Latin and German: the translations either conformed to the Latin original conventions or attended more to the German usage, trying to be free from the constraints of the Latin usage. After acknowledging latent potential and special qualities of the German language, German translators began to shift their attention away from the source text to the target text and mechanical imitation of the Latin style abated in German translation. Luther strengthened this tendency with his translation of the *Bible* which is oriented towards the target language. (quoted in Baker, 1998: 420)

3.2.2 Humanist *Bible* translator Erasmus

Desiderius Erasmus①, (1467? -1536) known as Erasmus of Rotterdam②, is an influential Dutch humanist and remarkable philosopher in the 16th-century Europe. Erasmus was born into a priest family in Rotterdam, the second illegitimate son of a priest. He wrote *On Free Will*, *The Praise of Folly*, *Handbook of a Christian Knight*, and many other works. During the medieval times, the area of the Dutch language was politically divided, parts of it belonging to France and parts of it owing allegiance to the German Holy Roman Empire③(Germany). So Erasmus will be discussed under German translation tradition, although he translated into Latin instead of the German language.

Erasmus was a cautious translator. Before trying his hands on the *Bible*, he began with translation of secular works, so as to "avoid risking my potter's skill all at once on a great jar, as the Greek adage has it, or rushing into such a large enterprise with feet as yet unwashed, as the saying goes" (quoted in Robinson, 2006: 64). Erasmus translated from Greek into Latin

---

① 伊拉斯谟:荷兰文艺复兴时期学者,罗马天主教神学家。他试图恢复基于《圣经》的朴素的基督教信仰,消除中世纪教会的不当行为。他的作品包括《基督教骑士手册》(1503 年)和《愚人颂》(1509 年)。

② 鹿特丹:荷兰西南部港市。

③ 神圣罗马帝国:962~1806 年西欧和中欧的一个封建帝国。早期是由拥有实际权力的皇帝统治的国家,中世纪时演变成承认皇帝为最高权威的公国、侯国、宗教贵族领地和帝国自由城市的政治联合体。

classical works of Libanius[①] (314-393), Lucian[②] (125-200?), Euripides[③], Isocrates[④] (436-338 BC) and Plutarch[⑤].

In the preface he wrote for three Greek declamations in 1503, Erasmus declared that he followed Cicero's translation methods. "I have followed Cicero's old rule: in translating I thought it my duty to weigh the meaning, not count the words. However, as an apprentice-translator I have preferred to err on the side of accuracy rather than of boldness." (quoted in Robinson, 2006: 63) In the preface to Lucian's work (1506), he made a close analysis of the language style of the two speakers in a dialogue, concluding that the two speakers exhibit two entirely different styles, which reflect their personality: one good-natured, elegant, and humorous as a Greek while the other simple, rude, sober, tough and vigorous like a Scythian[⑥]. Erasmus tried to imitate the two styles in his translation, and deleted the original where he felt the difficulty. It can be seen that he was moving from accuracy to greater degree of freedom as he proceeded with translation of classical works.

In 1506, Erasmus translated two of Euripides' dramas. In the preface to *Hecuba*[⑦], he insisted again that it was difficult to put good Greek into good Latin. The reasons, he maintained, were two. 1. The works were written by a poet of antiquity, who was various, unfamiliar, remarkably succinct, delicate, and exquisite in his style, which resisted translation. 2. Euripides's copied manuscripts were varied and there were not enough commentators on him to consult. There was not a good translation, he concluded, of Euripides and other ancient Greek works, not even a passable translation. Erasmus mainly used literal translation,

> *—especially since I had deliberately added considerably to the other difficulties by my scrupulous accuracy in translation, attempting as far as possible to reproduce the shape and, as it were, the contours of the Greek poets, striving to render verse for verse and almost word for word, and everywhere trying zealously to adapt the force and effect of the meaning to Latin ears, with all fidelity.* (quoted in Robinson, 2006: 64)

The more works he translated, the further he began to move from strict literalness to a more expansive paraphrase. He deleted rather liberally where he failed to translate. "In one respect I have dared in both plays to depart from my author's practice: I have to some extent reduced that metrical diversity and license of the choric parts, hoping that scholars would take

---

① 利班尼乌斯:古希腊诡辩家和修辞学家。

② 卢西恩:又译为琉善,古希腊讽刺作家。著有《神的对话》和《死者的对话》,讽刺了希腊哲学和神话。

③ 欧里庇得斯:古希腊戏剧家,著名作品包括《美狄亚》《希波吕托斯》和《特洛伊妇女》等。

④ 伊索克拉底:古希腊修辞学家,希腊十大演说家之一。

⑤ 普鲁塔克:公元1~2世纪古罗马历史学家,著有《名人传》。

⑥ 塞西亚人:亚洲与欧洲东南部之一古地区的游牧居民,公元前8世纪至公元前4世纪最为强盛。

⑦ 《赫卡柏》:欧里庇得斯公元前424年作品,赫卡柏是特洛伊国王普里阿摩斯的妻子,特洛伊城破后被杀。

my difficulties into account and excuse me for this." (quoted in Robinson, 2006: 65) He actually deleted the choruses of Greek tragedies which were not to his literary taste.

> *For it seems to me that nowhere did the ancients write more foolishly than in choruses of this sort, where, through excessive striving for novelty of utterance, they destroyed clarity of expression, and in the hunt for marvelous verbal effects their sense of reality suffered.* (quoted in Robinson, 2006: 65)

In Erasmus's time, the Roman Catholic Church was corrupted and the authority of the church was increasingly questioned. While critical of the abuses within the Church and calling for reform, Erasmus kept careful distance from Luther and continued to recognize the authority of the pope and attempted to preserve a unified church. He preferred to live the life of an independent scholar. His middle road disappointed not only many Protestants, such as Martin Luther, but also conservative Catholics.

Throughout the whole middle ages, Jerome's *Vulgate*, the official *Bible* of the Roman Catholic Church, was copied by hand from one scribe to another. In the process, the book was partly replaced with some old Latin texts, constantly "improved" and "purified". In one word, Jerome's *Bible* was far from a stable, standardized text during the whole Middle Ages; it was constantly modified, corrected and interpreted anew in the interest of different religious and political groups until it was, to some eyes, totally corrupted. Still, the *Vulgate* gave birth to other vernacular translations in French, German, Italian, Spanish, and English.

The textual differences between different hand copiers of the Vulgate only worsened the deepening church crisis. Erasmus felt called upon to use his learning to revive classical texts from antiquity and restore simple Christian faith based on true Scriptures. Using humanist techniques, Erasmus critically compared and collated early Greek manuscripts of the *New Testament* as well as all the important *Vulgate* manuscripts to establish the most reliable editions of the *New Testament*. On the basis of this close textual criticism he published, in 1516, a Greek *New Testament* in parallel with a new Latin translation. In 1519, the second edition appeared, together with annotations, commentary, an apologia for the Greek and Latin texts and a methodological introduction in which he outlined his aims: to eradicate textual corruptions as a result of scribal errors. And his annotations provided an insight into his methodology and editorial decisions.

He demonstrated the reason for the inclusion of the Greek original in his translation: to permit qualified readers to verify the quality of his Latin version. Whenever he was caught in semantic confusion, he translated one meaning and explained other possible meanings in the notes, leaving the readers to their own judgment. Twice as long as the first edition, the second edition of his *Bible* replaced the Latin *Vulgate* and was later used by Martin Luther in his German *Bible*. There were subsequent editions of the *Bible*, each with additions as well as deletions on the basis of newly discovered manuscripts. Of these later editions, the 3rd edition (1522) produced felt influence on the first English *New Testament* (1526) made by Tyndale as well as on translators of the Geneva *Bible*① and *King James Bible*②. His Latin translation of the *New Testament* was the first new translation accepted by the church since the *Vulgate* over a thousand years before.

By producing two updated versions simultaneously Erasmus "synchronized" or "unified" the Greek and the Latin traditions of the *New Testament*. He worked to resolve the divergences between the two, both being part of canonical scriptures. This is clearly indicated by the fact that he was translating in both directions: at some time his Greek text was the basis for his Latin translation and at others he edited the Greek text on the basis of his Latin version. For instance, in the 4th edition of the *Bible* (1527) he supplied the last six verses of *Revelation*, which were missing from his Greek manuscript, on the basis of the *Vulgate*. Erasmus also translated the Latin text into Greek whenever he was caught in the confusion in the Greek text and its accompanying commentaries, or when he simply preferred the *Vulgate* over the Greek text. He meant the publication as an improvement on, rather than a replacement of, Jerome's Latin *Vulgate*. In a letter to Maarten Lips (1518) he says:

> *He imagines, and assumes as proved, that I publicly correct and alter the Vulgate text whereas I leave that intact and untouched and have turned into Latin what is found in the Greek copies, pointing out as I go along the agreements and disagreements of our own texts; not seldom preferring what is in these copies of ours, correcting anything corrupt, explaining ambiguities, elucidating obscurities, and changing anything that is notably barbarous in expression.* (quoted in Robinson, 2006: 66)

In the preface he stated his translation methods and in the postscripts he explained why he did not use the style of the *Vulgate*. Erasmus set the keynote for Renaissance *Bible* translation with the following ideas: (1) The authority of the theologians should be questioned and the original texts respected; (2) The individual translator had the right and latitude in interpreting and translating the *Bible* relying on his knowledge of the two languages; (3) *Bible* should be translated into all languages.

(1) In the preface to the *Bible* he maintained that it is important to return to the very original, i. e., Hebrew *Old Testament* and Greek *New Testament*. Erasmus pointed out that *Bible* translation and study must be based on the most authoritative source texts. He believed that without first-hand access to Hebrew or Greek scriptures, the theologians in the Middle Ages were unable to understand the ultimate truth in the *Bible*, and their teachings, therefore, might be faulty. The truth in the *Bible*, consequently, was obscured, misread or stereotyped in a bad way. To retrieve the truth, the translators must look to the very original text as the reliable point of departure. In interpreting the *Bible*, likewise, the translator must go back to its

① 《日内瓦圣经》:也称为《宗教改革圣经》,是一部按照新教精神翻译的英语《圣经》。为逃避玛丽王朝对新教徒的清洗,许多新教徒逃亡到日内瓦翻译出版的《圣经》。

② 《钦定版圣经》:《圣经》的诸多英文版本之一,于1611年出版。《钦定版圣经》是在英王詹姆斯一世的支持下翻译出版的。《钦定版圣经》不仅影响了随后的英文《圣经》,对英语语言和文学也产生了深远的影响。

Hebrew or Greek originals for reference, and all interpretations based on Latin translation of the *Bible*, the *Vulgate* included, was ineffective and questionable. The medieval interpretations of the *Bible* were thus seriously questioned under the humanist principle. In the preface to the Latin *New Testament* Erasmus insisted that it was the truth, not the church authority, that should be respected. His *Bible* reflected a modern and familiar approach different from traditional interpretations of the scriptural text. This was notable because in his time *Bible* translation in Europe was in constant confusion about the authenticity of the original and *Bible* translation was still authorized and censored by the church authorities. After Erasmus, however, it is unanimously agreed among humanists that a translation at its best was but a poor substitute of the original, and therefore was not to be used as the reliable basis for another translation. Indirect translation, therefore, was dismissed as undesirable.

(2) In order to interpret the *Bible* correctly, Erasmus said, the translator must be familiar with the original language, literature, and rhetoric, that is, he should be a scientist of language rather than a theologian. Erasmus held that teachers of the *Bible* must explain the meaning of each word and the meaning of a particular word must be derived from the meaning of the whole sentence. He stressed the difference between languages, insisting that, only when equipped with adequate language knowledge, could the translator arrive at a correct understanding and rendering of the *Bible*. Erasmus held that in *Bible* translation there is no divine illumination or absolute authority. With the advance of knowledge on human language, the same original, secular or religious, will be interpreted and translated anew. This is a progressive idea because in his time *Bible* translators still clung to the divine illumination for the understanding of the words of God.

(3) In late medieval times, church authorities held vernacular translations of the *Bible* with suspicion. Unauthorized translation of the *Bible* into the vernacular language was strictly forbidden for fear that some unorthodox interpretations of Biblical texts would challenge the authority and damage the interest of the church. Erasmus thought that *Bible* should be translated into all languages. He was confident that his translation was accurate in diction, more intelligible in wording and therefore made better sense to most ordinary readers.

These humanist views above would be influential in the Protestant Reformation and Catholic Counter-Reformation. As a matter of fact, Martin Luther's movement began in the year following the publication of Erasmus' *New Testament*. Erasmus was accused by the monks against the Reformation that he "had laid the egg, and Luther had hatched it". Erasmus wittily dismissed the charge, claiming that Luther had "hatched a different bird entirely"①.

---

① Desiderius Erasmus From Wikipedia, the free encyclopedia. 2014-07-20. http://en.wikipedia.org/wiki/Desiderius_Erasmus.

3.2.3 Germanization in Luther's *Bible*

Martin Luther[①] (1483-1546) is the founder of German religious reformation[②] and regarded as the father of German literary tradition.

Martin Luther was born into a farmer's family in central Germany. In Luther's time, medieval feudalism was disintegrating and the church was in deep crisis. With the rise of nationalism, the High German had developed into a legitimate form of communication, gradually replacing Latin as the language of literature and science. Under the influence of the earliest attempts at church reform (notably promoted by John Wycliffe and Jan Huss[③]), malpractices and doctrines of the church were being increasingly questioned.

In 1517, Pope Leo X[④] offered indulgences[⑤] for those who gave alms to rebuild St. Peter's Basilica in Rome. Greedy commissaries sought to extract the maximum amount of money for each indulgence. The aggressive marketing practices provoked Martin Luther to write his *Ninety-Five Theses*, condemning what he saw as the purchase and sale of salvation. He elaborated on spiritual and practical effects of the dispensation of indulgence, which triggered a series of heated contests with Papal representatives. These theses won him a multitude of followers among the middle class and the German princes and knights, who wanted to be free from the control of Roman Catholic Church. For the same theses, on the other hand, he was excommunicated (1520) and was put under the ban of the Holy Roman Empire (1521). He was taken into protective custody by his patron at the castle of Wartburg[⑥], where he translated the Greek *New Testament* in hiding (published in 1522).

After that he set about translating the Hebrew *Old Testament* (published in 1534), in collaboration with a few assistants, a project that continued until his death. His *Bible* occupied an important position in Western translation history, enjoying equal status with the *Septuagint*, Andronicus' *Odyssey*, Jerome's *Vulgate* and the *Authorized Version* later. More significantly, Luther's rendering of the scriptures into the language of the common people provided the reformation movement with an ideological framework, that is, with a program. His translation

---

① 马丁·路德:德国神学家、欧洲宗教改革运动的领袖。

② 宗教改革运动:16 世纪西欧旨在改革罗马天主教某些教义和做法的改革运动,最终导致新教的建立。

③ 胡斯:14~15 世纪初捷克宗教思想家、哲学家。受到英国宗教改革家威克利夫的影响,胡斯反对天主教会占有土地,反对教皇兜售赎罪券,抨击教士的奢侈堕落,主张信徒在圣餐中可与教士一样领取圣体血;提倡用捷克语举行宗教仪式,并亲自将《圣经》译为捷克文。因其激进的宗教改革主张,胡斯最终因异端罪名被处死。胡斯之死激起捷克人民义愤,引发了胡斯战争。胡斯著有《论教会》一书。

④ 利奥十世:文艺复兴时期最后一位教皇,出身豪门梅第奇家族。1513~1521 年在位期间通过出售赎罪卷筹款修建圣彼得大教堂,引起路德攻击,宗教该运动由此掀开序幕。

⑤ 赎罪券:教皇乌尔班二世于 1095 年发动第一次十字军东征时,为了激发士气向每一位十字军人发放赎罪券。到了 16 世纪初路德宗教改革时期,赎罪券沦为教会敛财的工具。马丁·路德写成《九十五条论纲》,斥责教皇的无耻行径,并由此引发了具有深远影响的宗教改革运动。

⑥ 瓦尔特堡:位于德国图林根,始建于 1067 年或 1068 年,是目前欧洲保存最完整的中世纪古城堡之一。

was part of the Reformation movement that spread to the rest of Europe. Not long afterwards, the German people began to cite passages from the book in defense of their own interest. Hence it was called "the first *Bible* of the common people". The German Reformation initiated by Martin Luther led to the German Peasants' War in 1524-1525.

Up to Luther's time, the translated Biblical texts had formed an impressive corpus that represented German *Bible* translation culture. Medieval translations of the *Bible* were based on the Latin *Vulgate* produced by St. Jerome in the 5th century instead of Greek and Hebrew originals. Luther's *Bible* was the first complete German *Bible* translated directly from the Hebrew and Greek originals.

Luther's German *Bible* produced far-reaching influence on the evolution of German national language and literary tradition. On the basis of the language used in public writing around Thuringian① and Middle-eastern and Central-southern dialects, Luther created many new words, which were retained in the German language. Through this translation he introduced a standardized German lexicon and the practice of capitalization of nouns, and developed a balanced syntax that had such formal means as verb position and conjunctions. The German grammars ever after were heavily based on Luther's *Bible*. This language remained the medium of written system for centuries and soon developed into a lingua franca. His Biblical style became a yardstick against which later *Bibles* and translations were judged. Clarity, general understandability, simplicity and vividness were the most prominent stylistic features of his *Bible*, and they are still measures of a good piece of writing in general. (quoted in Delisle & Woodsworth, 1995: 51)

In addition to the *Bible*, Luther translated *Aesop's Fables*②. Luther defended his translations in two texts *Circular Letter on Translation* (1530) and *Defense of the Translation of the Psalms* (1531-1533). He wrote them in defense of his own translation and in refutation of the charges against him that he falsified or distorted the Scriptures. The issues discussed are still of theoretical relevance to translation research today, namely, free versus literal translation, naturalization versus foreignization, translation of style and the importance of taking the conceptual framework into account.

Luther advocated the return to the original language of the *Bible*—the Hebrew *Old Testament* and the Greek *New Testament*, with some reference to the Latin *Vulgate*. This new approach challenged the Catholic Church that regarded the *Vulgate* as the authoritative text.

He adhered to the principle that the word should follow the meaning of the text and not the other way around. (quoted in Delisle & Woodsworth, 1995: 47) He was more concerned about moral and situational appropriateness than about verbal accuracy. Luther wrote in reference to *Psalm* 68:

---

① 图林根语:德国中部图林根地区使用的语言。

② 伊索:约公元前6世纪古希腊寓言作家,相传原为奴隶,善讲故事,讽刺权贵,有《伊索寓言》传世。

> *Whoever would speak German must not use Hebrew style. Rather he must see to it—once he understands the Hebrew author* ①*—that he concentrates on the sense of the text, asking himself, 'Pray tell, what do the Germans say in such a situation?' Once he has the German words to serve the purpose, let him drop the Hebrew words and express the meaning freely in the best German he knows.* ②

In relation to his meaning-based translation, Martin held that in order to communicate, a translation must change the linguistic form of the original. Luther raised seven systematic principles for linguistic changes in translation. (1) shifts of word order; (2) employment of modal auxiliaries; (3) essential connectives should be supplied when necessary; (4) original Greek or Hebrew words that have no equivalents in the German language might be removed; (5) single word might be translated with phrasal words; (6) metaphorical usage might be translated into non-metaphorical expression and vice versa; (7) enough attention should be paid to textual variants or editorial differences. Luther's translation techniques were universal guidance for translation between any language pair and his 7th point was particularly useful for translation of voluminous classics that developed textual differences over centuries. His ideas were upheld by William Tyndale of England and Reina③ (1520-1594) and Valera④ (1532-1600) of Spain in their *Bible* translation.

Luther oriented his translation towards the target culture and language, reworking the *Bible* as a German Text. Luther realized that semantic equivalence alone was inadequate and that the text had to be interpreted so as to bridge the gap in time, space and particularly mentality between the source and target texts. The conceptual difference must be taken into account. The historical text was thus updated in the mentality and spirit of his own time. From 1466 to 1522, the year when Luther's *New Testament* met the public, there appeared in Germany 14 versions of German *Bible*, which were invariably full of Latinisms. Luther, however, had Germanized his *Bible*.

He cared for the effect of his translation on his readers and their ability to digest his words. His translation presented the various literary genres in ways which were natural to the receptor language. He said that real translation happened when a foreign language became the translator's native tongue and that translation into German should conform to German usage. One example suffices to illustrate his intention to translate for his people. In *Matthew* 12:34 is a line: "O generation of vipers, how can ye, being evil, speak good things? for out of the abundance of the heart the mouth speaketh." Luther did not translate "Out of the abundance of the heart the mouth speaketh" literally, for no German could say that. Instead, he rendered it

---

① hence the need for a careful exegesis!

② Scott Munger. *Bible*, Babel and Babble: The Foundations of *Bible* Translation Section. 2009-5-15. http://www.ibsstl.org/niv/munger/5-5-4.php.

③ 雷纳:16 世纪西班牙《圣经》翻译家,路德派教徒。他据希伯来文本与希腊文本把《圣经》完整译为西班牙语,后经瓦勒拉修订出版,称为《雷纳 - 瓦勒拉圣经》。

④ 瓦勒拉:16 世纪末负责修订出版雷纳《圣经》译木的西班牙学者、编辑。

into a German proverb meaning "what fills the heart overflows the mouth" because the mother in the home and the common man would say this. When he translated into the German language,

> *He personalizes it, humanizes it, blends it with the vitality of his own sense of self. In so doing, significantly enough, he socializes it: what he internalized is no solipsistic fantasy-system but language as social communication, language as what people like him (members of his class) say to each other in real-life situation.* (quoted in Robinson, 2006: 84)

In *Circular Letter on Translation* he stated the use of the language of the common people,

> *We do not have to inquire of the literal Latin, how we are to speak German, as these asses do. Rather, we must inquire about this of the mother in the home, the children on the street, the common man in the marketplace. We must be guided by their language, and do our translating accordingly. That way they will understand it and recognize that we are speaking German with them.* (Berman, 1992: 25)

Enlightened by Augustine's theory, Luther maintained that the translator should use his language knowledge to arrive at a right reading of the original. But on the other hand he also believed that language knowledge alone could not enable the translator to grasp the essence and spirit of the *Bible* and that something in the *Bible* is unaccountable from linguistic analysis, insinuating that there is mystery about translation of the *Bible*.

Further Readings

Baker, Mona. *Routledge Encyclopedia of Translation Studies*. London & New York: Routledge, 1998.

Berman, Antoine. *The Experience of the Foreign: Culture and Translation in Romantic Germany*. Albany: State University of New York Press, 1992.

Desiderius Erasmus From Wikipedia, the free encyclopedia. 2014-07-20. http://en.wikipedia.org/wiki/Desiderius_Erasmus.

Martin Luther From Wikipedia, the free encyclopedia. 2013-10-05. http://en.wikipedia.org/wiki/Martin_Luther.

Robinson, Douglas. *Western Translation Theory: From Herodotus to Nietzsche*. Shanghai: Foreign Language Teaching and Research Press, 2006.

Scott Munger. *Bible*, Babel and Babble: The Foundations of *Bible* Translation Section. 2009-5-15. http://www.ibsstl.org/niv/munger/5-5-4.php.

Shuttleworth, Mark & Moira Cowie. *Dictionary of Translation Studies*. Shanghai: Shanghai Foreign Language Education Press, 2004.

谭载喜:《西方翻译简史》,商务印书馆 2004 年版。

Topics for Discussion

1. In what way is medieval translation of Greek and Latin classics different from

Renaissance translation?

2. Discuss the influence of German *Bible* on the development of German language.

3. Comment on the seven principles of translation put forward by Luther. Are they applicable to translation between Chinese and English?

4. How is Erasmus' *Bible* different from earlier translations of the *Bible*? What is the purpose of his *Bible*? Why is he considered a humanist *Bible* translator?

3.3 Translations in French Language Area

Translation Terms

Free Imitation 仿译

In the *Defense and Illustration of the French Language*, the manifesto of the Pleiade, Du Bellay argued that French literature should be enlarged and enriched by free imitation rather than through slavish translation. But Du Bellay added that there must be limits to imitation, that is, the imitator should never seek the beauty of words at the cost of the force of the original content. His concept of imitation combines innovation of forms with respect for the real content. Free imitation today is a rather loose adaptation of the source text, a reproduction in the target language based on the foreign themes or style.

Slavish Translation 奴性十足的翻译

In the manifesto of the Pleiade, Du Bellay strongly disapproved "translation", by which he means slavish translation that was constrained by "the limits of the author" and prohibited creativity. "Translation" is misused in the meaning of slavish as against free imitation and innovative recreation.

3.3.1 Socio-cultural Background

For a long time in history, French translation tradition was an integral part of Latin translation heritage: translations in France were made into Latin in monasteries until the Old French was derived from the Vulgar Latin as a new language. Guillaume de Loris's *Roman de la Rose*① (1235) includes translations of Latin texts. Latin chronicles of French history were put into Old French too. But it was during the reign of King Charles V (1337-1380) that translation of classical works into French was actively encouraged.

Translations in the 16th century France were made under diversified and complex linguistic and cultural background. The target languages of translation were primarily two: French

① 洛利思：13世纪法国寓言长诗《玫瑰传奇》上卷的作者，以玫瑰象征贵族妇女，写一个诗人怎样爱上玫瑰而受到环境阻碍的故事。

(called Middle French now) and Latin. In spite of a 1539 royal ordinance that established French as the official language of the state, Latin was still used as a firmly-established language of the church and education until the 18th century. Once again, Latin became the target language of translation and French translation tradition part of Latin translation heritage. Source languages of translation in France were diverse, including Greek, Syriac, Hebrew, German, English and other romance languages like Italian. Indirect translations were still common.

As a result of the spreading of Renaissance and the development of the printing industry, Renaissance translators turned their eyes to the original sources of ancient classics. Under the influence of secularization of knowledge translations were increasingly made into the vernacular French for a rapidly expanding audience. The texts for translation were of two types: literary and scientific. Under the influence of a literary circle known as the Pléiade①, literary texts were translated, or rather, imitated, with much more freedom for the purpose of enriching the French language and literature. Scientific texts, by contrast, were translated with more literalism, almost free from the impact of the Pléiade. It was generally presumed that the purpose of scientific translation was to disseminate useful knowledge to a large audience. General intelligibility became the standard of scientific translation. Pliny, Galen, Hippocrates, among others, were translated. Amplification was used often in translations of this period, which became longer than the original.

Issues on translation were discussed at length and new translation terms emerged out of the discussions, like *traduction* (translation) and *traduceteur* (translator) introduced by humanist translator Dolet②. His five principles on translation were believed the first systematic translation principles in the history of translation in the west. Michel de Montaigne③(1533-1592) made a synthesis of 16th century translation in his *Essays*.

3.3.2 The Pléiade and Du Bellay

The 16th century France was a remarkable period of literary creation. In all literary genres, there was a great interest in love (both physical and Platonic) and in psychological and moral analysis. Around Pierre de Ronsard④, Joachim Du Bellay⑤ and Jean Antoine de Baïf⑥ there formed the Pléiade, a group of radical young noble poets of the court. The members of the Pléiade urged the cultivation of the French language into a literary language of equal status with Latin through creative introduction of foreign literatures. The group aimed to ennoble the

---

① 七星诗社:法国文艺复兴时期的七人诗社,主要有龙萨德、杜贝莱等。也指公元前3世纪亚历山大的七名诗人和悲剧作家。1323年,Pléiade也指14名图卢兹诗人(七男七女)。

② 多雷:法国文艺复兴时期的人文主义学者。

③ 蒙田:法国散文作家,其散文被认为是16世纪法国散文的最佳典范。

④ 龙萨德:法国七星诗社主要作家之一。

⑤ 贝莱:法国七星诗社主要作家之一。

⑥ 巴伊夫:法国七星诗社主要作家之一。

French language by imitating the ancient models and breaking down the constraints of earlier traditions of French poetry. Among the most favored ancient models were Pindar[①], Anacreon[②], Alcaeus[③], as well as Virgil, Horace and Ovid. The dominant poetic forms employed by the group included the Petrarchan[④] sonnet (of an amorous encounter or an idealized woman) and the Horatian/Anacreontic ode (of the "wine, women and song" variety, often making use of the Horatian theme—life is short, seize the day)[⑤]. The translations made by the literary circle combined literalism and innovation, introducing a large number of new terms from Latin and Greek.

Ronsard attempted earlier to translate the Pindaric ode into French and later to write a nationalist verse epic based on Homer and Virgil. He practiced with admirable skill the sonnet very soon after its introduction into France. He was the acknowledged chief of the Pléiade and its most voluminous poet and probably also its best. And de Baïf created an entirely new poetry form in his specific attempt to recapture the ancient Greek and Latin ethical effect of poetry, and in applying the metrical innovations to music. Baïf also meditated reforms in French spelling. He made a free translation of Terence's work. In an imitation of the *Miles Gloriosus*[⑥], also known as "The Swaggering Soldier", he turned the Latin-speaking Greek characters of Plautus into Frenchmen and moved the setting of the action from Ephesus[⑦], a Greek city on the coast of Asia Minor, to Orleans[⑧], a city in central France. While Ronsard and de Baïf were most influenced by Greek models, du Bellay was more inspired by Latin works.

Joachim Du Bellay (1522-1560?) is a French poet-translator and a leading member of the Pléiade. He was born near Lire, France, lost his parents at an early age and was raised by his negligent brother. Du Bellay's greatest poems were a sonnet cycle of remarkable sadness and severity partially inspired by Ovid. His sonnets were evidently indebted to Petrarch. Du Bellay wrote *Defense and Illustration of the French Language* (1549), the manifesto of the Pléiade, at the age of 27. In the manifesto, Du Bellay detailed a program of literary renewal and revolution, maintaining that French, like the Tuscan of Petrarch and Dante, was a worthy language for literary expression. As the name suggests, the essay declares that the French language is able to express all the niceties in the classical language and to introduce innovations into itself. "And whoever will look well at it will find that our French language is not so poor that it cannot render faithfully what it borrows from others; so unproductive that it cannot, of

① 品达:古希腊诗人。
② 阿那克里翁:古希腊诗人,诗歌以歌颂爱情和美酒为主题。
③ 阿卡拉斯:古希腊诗人。
④ 彼特拉克:意大利诗人、学者和人文主义者,曾用十四行诗创作了著名的爱情抒情诗集《抒情歌谣集》。
⑤ La Pléiade, From Wikipedia, the free encyclopedia. 2009-05-23. http://en.wikipedia.org/wiki/La_Pléiade.
⑥ 《吹牛军人》:古罗马喜剧作家普劳图斯的作品。
⑦ 艾菲索斯:目前世上保存的最好、最大的希腊罗马古迹城,位于今土耳其。
⑧ 奥尔良:法国中部城市。

itself, bear a fruit of good invention." (quoted in Robinson, 2006: 103)

Du Bellay recommended creative translation of Greek and Roman poetic forms into French by way of emulation of classical literary models and the creation of new terms from Greek and Latin. To this end Du Bellay strongly disapproved "translation", by which he means literal and slavish translation or the translation that was constrained by "the limits of the author" and prohibited creativity. The pamphlet, therefore, was described as "an anthology of all arguments against translation" (quoted in Baker, 1998: 411). Du Bellay, for example, concluded that translations are not enough to perfect the French Language and that innovations should be introduced into the French language. Du Bellay distinguished poetic and non-poetic texts and considered poetic texts untranslatable due to peculiarities of languages.

> *I will never believe that one can learn all that (way of elocution) from translations, because it is impossible to translate it with the same grace that the author has put into it: because each language has something indefinitely individual only to itself; and if you make an effort to render its innate character into another language, observing the law of translation, so that it is not expanded at all beyond the limits of the author, your diction will be constrained, turgid, and without charm.* (quoted in Robinson, 2006: 103)

Du Bellay had a higher aim for translating classics into French: to improve the French language. He cited Roman translation of Greek literature as the role model that the French translator should take after. Du Bellay argued in the document that French literature should be enlarged and enriched by **imitation**, an idea obviously indebted to Horace's statement on translation and imitation in *The Art of Poetry*, where he insisted that one should imitate freely, rather than translate like a slave. The proper way of translation, Du Bellay argued, was imitation if the translator wanted to improve his target literature.

> *Write himself, then, must he who wishes to enrich his language, write in imitation of the best Greek and Latin authors; at all their best qualities, as at a fair target, direct the aim of his style; for it cannot be doubted that the great part of the art is contained in imitation.* (quoted in Robinson, 2006: 105)

He warned the imitators that it was no easy thing to follow well the excellent qualities of a good author, because translators were easily carried away by the beauty of language rather than the power of content.

> *—there are many in every literature who, without penetrating to the secret, innermost part of an author whom they have approached, adapt themselves solely to first appearances, and spend themselves rather on the beauty of words than on the might of the real content.* (quoted in Robinson, 2006: 105)

Obviously Du Bellay held that there must be limits to imitation, that is, the imitator should never seek the beauty of words at the cost of the force of the original content. His concept of imitation combines innovation of forms with respect for the real content.

He moved on to discuss in detail what poets, genres and topics should be chosen for imitation and what to avoid. He maintained that imitators should devote themselves to the exemplary Greek and Latin poets, to pleasant epigrams, to the imitation of a Martial[①], and plaintive elegies. Du Bellay wished to hear beautiful sonnets, such as by Petrarch and other Italian poets; he hoped to listen to poems, such as after the style of Theocritus[②] and Virgil. Comedies and tragedies should also be imitated in their ancient dignity to the benefit of the French language. And materials for imitation should come from the praises of the gods and of great men, the deathward tread of earthly things and the disquiet of youth, love, the unrestrained rites of wine, and all good cheer. While the vulgar, the epistles should be avoided unless they were improved with care to enrich the French language; the satires should also be avoided unless the evil gossip and vices were censured with moderation in the interest of the French people. All these should be imitated freely, rather than translated slavishly, into the French language. In imitation of ancient poets, he held that

> *Above all, take care that the type of poetry be far away from the vulgar, enriched and made illustrious with proper words and vigorous epithets, adorned with grave sentences and varied with all manner of colorful and poetic ornaments.* (quoted in Robinson, 2006: 105)

Du Bellay's criticism of slavish translation and advocate of free imitation had impact upon literary production at home. Thanks to their efforts, translation into the French language was considered a particular literary genre for its own sake. Poetry rose up as the dominant literary form and many verses were translated during the time. At that point the focus of translation shifted from religious to literary texts. An alexandrine[③], a line of poetic meter comprising 12 syllables, was revived under the influence of Ronsard and other members of the Pléiade.

Despite the effort by the Pléiade and others, the French language was still in its inception, for the whole country was still in want of a unified, standardized language. The culture of the 16th century France remained profoundly oral, which was a central part of the style in such literary genres like the short story, the chivalric novel and Rabelais's[④] works. A majority of translations were "byproducts" that writers made in their spare time of literary creation. Then it came as no surprise that the quality of translation was not high and its impact not far-reaching. The general attitude towards translation in this period, therefore, was negative: translated text was considered an inferior text that was unable to provide the "grace and elegance of the original" (quoted in Baker, 1998: 411).

---

① 马提雅尔:古罗马诗人,以讽刺短诗闻名。

② 忒奥克里托斯:古希腊田园诗人。

③ 亚历山大体:法国诗体的一种,每行 12 个音节。

④ 拉伯雷:文艺复兴时期法国最杰出的人文主义作家之一。

3.3.3 Dolet, Amyot and Pasquier

Etienne Dolet[①] (1509-1546) was a French humanist printer, translator, and scholar. He threw himself in the wave of humanist movement, was involved in many political and scholarly contentions and was for a time engaged in academic warfare with Erasmus. His humanist thinking incurred hatred from the Paris University, which represented the reactionary church elements then. Consequently he was brought to trial on the alleged charge of heresy, tortured and burned at the stake. He is often referred to as the first martyr of the Renaissance, and especially as the first martyred translator.

He had translated a Platonic dialogue *Axiochus*[②], which contained a passage where Socrates seemed to suggest that there is nothing after death. This cast doubt on the immortality of soul and shook the foundation of the Christian belief. Since it was impossible that Plato, the alleged author, was suggesting this, the suspicion fell on Dolet. He was accused of deliberately misinterpreting and falsifying Plato by adding a phrase to the passage, which "doubted the existence of eternal life". Because of alleged blasphemy and heresy that occurred in his translation, the thirty-seven year old humanist Dolet was condemned as a confirmed atheist and burned at stake, together with his thirteen books, translations included.

Dolet was an excellent writer in ancient and modern languages. He translated a few books, but in translation community today he was credited with his brilliant essay *How to Translate Well from One Language into Another* (1540), which was the first essay devoted exclusively to translation. In the essay, he formulated five principles of a good translation in which he rejected word-for-word translation, described the stages of the translation process and put forward the obligations the translator should have toward the work he translated.

Dolet believed that in the first place, the translator must understand perfectly the sense and matter of the author he is translating, for having this understanding he will never be obscure in his translations, and if the author he is translating is difficult in any way he will be able to render him easy and entirely understandable. This principle ensures that meaning be faithfully translated.

The second thing that is required in translating is that the translator should have perfect knowledge of the language of the author he is translating, and be likewise excellent in the language into which he is going to translate. In this way he will not violate or diminish the majesty of the one language or the other.

Thirdly, in translating one must not be servile to the point of rendering word for word. And if someone does that, he is proceeding from poverty and lack of wisdom. Dolet was

① 多雷:法国文艺复兴时期的人文主义学者。

② 《阿克西奥丘斯》:公元前1世纪苏格拉底对话录中的一篇,据称作者为柏拉图。对话中苏格拉底向即将死亡的阿克西奥丘斯宣传生死观,帮助他克服了恐惧心理。

obviously against word-for-word translation and in favor of sense-for-sense translation.

As the fourth rule, he stated that when a translator translates a Latin book into a vernacular national language he should avoid using words too close to Latin and little used in the past and introducing any new terms foolishly out of curiosity. Rather, he should be content with the common tongue. (quoted in Robinson, 2006: 96) Dolet, like all humanists, emphasized the importance of using popular national languages and customary usage.

The fifth rule consists of nothing other than the observation of rhetorical numbers to create the correct tone, that is, "a joining and arranging of terms with such sweetness that not alone the soul is pleased, but also the ear is delighted and never hurt by such harmony of language." (Robinson, 2006: 96) The last of his principles is concerned about the transference of musical quality, which is an essential part of style transference. Language competence alone is far from enough; literary competence, that is, the translator's sensitivity to the beauty of language is equally important. Then a good translation would be delightful not only to the mind but also to the ear of the audience.

The defect, however, is that Dolet was very brief about these principles, which went without systematic elucidation. In terms of the depth and scope of the discussion, Dolet was not entirely original, either. His five principles were a natural development on Bruni and some other translation scholars before him. His reputation as a martyred translator perhaps helped promote his status as a translation theorist.

Jacques Amyot① (1513-1593) is a French Renaissance writer and translator. From 1559-1565, he translated Plutarch's *Lives*② and later seven books of Diodorus Siculus③ (1554), Longus's *Daphnis and Chloe*④ (1559) and Plutarch's Opera *Moralia*⑤ (1572). His translations were criticized later for being too literal, but he actually translated with his French readers in mind, for he introduced glosses and definition into the target text which were not there in the original. His translation of Longus was said to be a better work than the original.

In 1542 Amyot started to translate Plutarch's *Lives* at the command of French king. To clear up verbal ambiguity in the original, he compared different editions of the book and visited Venice and Rome to verify all kinds of historical data. Although unimpressive in volume, the book took him 17 years and won him the reputation of a grand translator. The interest of his books today lies primarily in the style, which is as natural as an original work. As the personal method of Plutarch appealed to a generation addicted to memoirs, Amyot's Plutarch obtained an immense popularity, and exercised great influence over successive generations of English and

---

① 阿米欧:法国文艺复兴时期翻译家。

② 《名人传》:古罗马作家普鲁塔克的历史著作。

③ 西库鲁:约公元前1世纪西西里的希腊语历史学家。

④ 《达夫尼斯和郝洛亚》:公元2世纪古希腊作家郎戈斯的田园爱情小说。

⑤ 《道德论说文集》:普鲁塔克作品。

French writers, among them Shakespeare, Racine① and Montaigne. His vigorous and idiomatic version of *Lives* was later translated into English by Sir Thomas North②.

Amyot believed that "The office of a fit translator consisted not only in the faithful expressing of his author's meaning, but also in a certain resembling and shadowing forth of his own style and manner of his own speaking" (Amos, 1920: XII). Aymot gave fair consideration to both the author's meaning and the translator's style and manner of speaking, regarding the two as complementary.

Concerning the style and manner of translation, he was of the opinion that the translation should be simple and natural and free from any ornaments. He employed both the language of the common people and of the scholar, paying particular attention to the simplicity of the language and rendering the translation an artistic work for its own sake. Simplicity and clarity of expression in his translation became the general standards for successive French translators.

In the process of translation, Amyot borrowed a large number of Greek and Latin words and coined many more neologisms in politics, philosophy, science, literature, music, etc., thus significantly enriching the French language.

Etienne Pasquier③(1529-1615) was known in his day as a lawyer and a historian. He wrote a ten-volume history of France (1560-1621), which provides valuable source of information for the study of people and events of the time period. Pasquier was not remembered for his translation of Cicero, but for his insightful arguments against translation.

In the letter to humanist scholar Jaques Cujas (1576), Pasquier announced that translation is a most unrewarding task and the most important factor that makes translation non-profitable is the change of language, which quickly becomes obsolete and alienates the readers.

> *Nevertheless, the translator's language changes little by little over time, and one day, as if we had given him a new gown, we no longer wish to make use of the old one. That is why, as the old vernacular vanishes, we discard old translations and wish to return to the original books, be they Greek or Latin, that were translated.* (quoted in Robinson, 2006: 112)

The second important factor which makes translation difficult is the differences in the languages,

> *In addition, languages do not correspond to each other in their form of expression, and what is becoming in one language will be awkward when transplanted in another. In this way, just as there are many things in Latin that cannot be duplicated in our French with the same elegance, so are there many in French that even Cicero, should he be reborn, would be unable to render with the same grace in Latin.* (quoted in Robinson, 2006: 113)

---

① 拉辛：法国古典主义时期最伟大的悲剧作家，作品多取材于希腊和罗马的古典主题。

② 诺思：16 世纪英国翻译家，他把阿米欧《名人传》的法语译本译为英文，为莎士比亚戏剧提供了素材。

③ 帕基耶：法国人文主义历史学家和律师。

The third point he mentioned is the considerable change of socio-political environment since Roman times. As a result, the original connotations of Latin words are entirely lost to the modern French readers. "I grant you that, as the Romans lived under a government of the people, while we live under a monarch and his royalty, our regulations and administration have nothing in common with theirs." (quoted in Robinson, 2006: 113) It follows that Latin words on government provide no edification to the French people, not even when they read them in Latin original. If the translator gave a new meaning to a native French word that he believed would correspond to the Latin word, he became unintelligible and the object of mockery. He therefore was pessimistic about the fate of the translators of Latin text who wished to conform to French usage.

Besides these common translation difficulties there are words that are untranslatable at all. He cited examples to illustrate his point. Cicero was called in his day "a great orator" and the defense he wrote for Milo "oration". ① The orator is the noble speaker in the Roman forum who uses all his encyclopedic knowledge with vivid style and good effect to move and persuade his audience to his point of view on an urgent and widely resonant issue, in a way suitable to the place and occasion. In ancient Rome, the orator was someone who pleads or argues for a cause and oration was the art of speaking in public, a professional competence especially cultivated by politicians and lawyers. The French translation for the word orator is *orateur*, which is only used by French bishops and prelates when they address themselves as "their humble *orateur*" in their letters to kings and princes, or is repeated in devotions and prayers. Therefore the French word *orasion* has a different connotation to any Frenchmen in the street from the word oration to Latin readers.

Another translation difficulty is caused by the difference in the target audiences themselves. With examples, Pasquier shows that a translator must choose of two extremes, for he either writes for those who understand the Latin language or for those who do not. If he writes for the people who understand the Latin language he is doing a thankless job for they will soon forsake his work and return to "drink from the water at the fountain's source" (quoted in Robinson, 2006: 114). If he wants to make Cicero understood by the people who know not the Latin language, very often he fails to do this to his own expectations, thus disappointing both the author and his readers. The third group of readers are the curious people who are fewer in number but more difficult to please. The three types of readers are enough to dissuade us from translating.

One more translation difficulty lies in the difference between the source audience and target audience. For the Romans, public speech was their only dedication of life on which their reputation rested. The Romans dealt with a people who delighted in words, were instructed in the art and manner of making public speech. They took great pains to please an audience that

① 公元前52年克洛狄乌斯被杀一案中西塞罗为弥罗辩护。(Robinson, 2006: 113)

was used to all techniques and devices of good rhetoric and that was expected to be aroused by passions, brought over by their argument and excited by various emotions.

> *But in our case, we must ply our trade before solemn judges, obliging us to be more reserved. We expect our speech to have more muscle and less flab. If we took the liberty of cajoling, as did the majority of these ancients, beyond what is normally permitted, we would be providing everyone with comic material.* (quoted in Robinson, 2006: 114)

As the audiences of the orations are different, the ancient manner of speaking has to change. Or else the same material will have undesirable effect on the target audience.

Pasquier's lists of translation difficulties touch on all the important factors, socio-cultural and linguistic, that make translation impossible. He also mentioned the effect of translation on the audience, which becomes the heated topic for discussion in the 20th century translation theories.

In 1569, **Michel Eyquem de Montaigne**①(1533-1592) published a French translation of the 15th-century *Natural Theology* by the Spanish monk Raymond Sebond. In his *Essays* (1580-1588), Montaigne classified languages into different levels, the vernacular being at the bottom and the classical at the top. He also distinguished two text types: informative and aesthetic. Informative texts, he believed, posed less challenges for translators. His idea on the hierarchy of languages produced a far-reaching influence on the 16th century thought that viewed vulgar "vernacular language" as unable to carry and disseminate culture. (quoted in Baker, 1998: 411)

Further Readings

Amos, Flora Ross. *Early Theories of Translation*. New York: Columbia University Press. 1920.

Baker, Mona. *Routledge Encyclopedia of Translation Studies*. London & New York: Routledge, 1998.

Jacques Amyot. From Wikipedia, the free encyclopedia. 2013-10-01. http://en.wikipedia.org/wiki/Jacques_Amyot.

La Pléiade. From Wikipedia, the free encyclopedia. 2009-05-23. http://en.wikipedia.org/wiki/La_Pléiade.

Robinson, Douglas. *Western Translation Theory: From Herodotus to Nietzsche*. Shanghai: Foreign Language Teaching and Research Press, 2006.

谭载喜:《西方翻译简史》,商务印书馆2004年版。

Topics for Discussion

1. How did Aymot influence the French language and literature with his *Parallel Lives*?

---

① 蒙田:法国散文作家,其散文被认为是16世纪法国散文的最佳典范。

Comment on Amyot's translation principle that "The office of a fit translator consisted not only in the faithful expressing of his author's meaning, but also in a certain resembling and shadowing forth of his own style and manner of his own speaking". What does he mean by "his own style" and "his own speaking"? Do you think a translation that represents the translator's style and manner of speaking can still be faithful to the original author?

2. How did Pléiade promote the French language and poetry through their translation? Did du Bellay really argue against translation in general? What kind of translation did he oppose and what kind of translation did he approve?

3. Pasquier's list of translation difficulties touches on many important factors that make translation impossible or difficult. List all the socio-cultural and linguistic factors that he mentioned.

4. How was the rivalry between Latin and French reflected in early modern French translation performance and theory?

5. Are Dolet's five principles of translation entirely original? Compare Dolet with Bruni and point out their differences and similarities.

3.4 Translations in Renaissance England

Translation Terms

Sense-for-Sense Translation 意译

A method of translating a source text sense-for-sense rather than word-for-word. The opposition might be traced back to Cicero, who argued that it was his duty to weigh the meaning, not count the words. Comparatively speaking, sense-for-sense translation retains the idea without trying to reproduce the word.

Word-for-Word Translation 逐字对译

Sometimes called literal translation, is a method of translating a source text word after word. It is used as against sense-for-sense translation. Comparatively speaking, word-for-word translation stays closer to the wording, sometimes at the cost of the smoothness and naturalness of target language. Word-for-word translation is normally considered a fault of an unskilled translator.

3.4.1 Socio-cultural Background

The English Renaissance was a cultural and artistic movement in England dating from the late 15th and early 16th centuries to the early 17th century. The English Renaissance largely coincides with the Tudor Dynasty and the English Protestant Movement. The Elizabethan era, the last monarch of the Tudor House in the second half of the 16th century, is usually regarded as the height of the English Renaissance.

In the early 16th century, Renaissance movement was in its full swing in England. Many factors contributed to the process: the decline of feudalism and the rise of nationalism, the rise of the common law, the invention of the printing press and increased circulation of the *Bible*, the transmission of new knowledge and ideas among scholars, the upper and middle classes and readers in general. Translation in England responded warmly to the Renaissance spirit of freedom, regarding classics as a treasure house of world knowledge and rejected medieval, feudal, and religious restraints. During the Elizabeth's reign (1558-1603), England emerged as a world power and translation enterprise corresponded to a flowering of English Renaissance. It was believed that the number of translations produced during the first decade of the Elizabeth's reign was four times that of the Henry and Mary years. (Barnstone, 1993: 203) Translations happened from ancient Greek, English, and Continental Languages into Latin. Still, 20% of the published works in the country were translations into English from other languages. (quoted in Delisle & Woodsworth, 1995: 201) To the end of the century translation was defended and encouraged almost as a public obligation.

The conditions for translation in this period were more favorable than in earlier times. The printing industry made a large number of books, including Greek and Latin classics, available in England. The English language was being standardized with the increasing sense of Englishness and an essentially monolingual English readership was gradually taking shape. Comparatively speaking, however, English was still a young language inferior to Latin, Italian, French, and Spanish. Many people voiced their opposition against the use of the vernacular English because: "They count it barren, they count it barbarous, they count it unworthy to be accounted of." (Amos, 1920: 93) Indeed Elizabethan English was still weak in resources, limited in vocabulary and vague in sentence structure. (Amos, 1920: 94) Besides, in terms of cultural attainment, England was a pupil not just before the Greeks and Romans, but also before France and Italy, who responded earlier to the spirit of humanism.

The general attitude towards translation was utilitarian: translations were made for the purpose of enriching and improving the English language, importing advanced European cultural properties and educating a rising middle merchant class, who formed a comparatively homogenous readership unschooled in classical education. Translators introduced foreign cultures in the best service of their home country. Holland compared his translation to military exploits. He and North once asked Queen Elizabeth to protect their translations, arguing that world classics, including Plutarch and Livy's works, provided useful guidance to the Queen and her law consultants. The translators also supplied raw materials for literary production at home. Late 16th-century English literature, therefore, reflected the immediate influence of foreign literatures. The importance of translation was publicly recognized, although translation was still held as secondary compared to original composition. The translated texts fell into two types: religious and secular. Religious works in general were translated with more accuracy than non-religious material.

3.4.2 Secular Translations (North, Cheke, Chapman)

The primary sources of secular translation were classical pagan antiquity and works from Renaissance Continent, particularly Italy. Secular translations were commissioned by art patrons or else censored by the authorities from a moral, religious, or political point of view. Consequently, translated classical works in England covered a rather limited range compared with translations on European continent. Unlike *Bible* translation, which was often a collaborative endeavor, secular translators worked independent of each other, with a mass of diverse texts, and under self-defined translation principles. Though translation theory in general marked the influence of the Renaissance respect for the original, the secular translation practice turned in the free and careless direction.

In England, the focus of secular translation was Romans and Greeks living in the Roman Empire. The most favored genres were moral and political philosophy, epic poetry, and history. History was particularly welcome because of its didactic value of individual actions in the past for the study of the present. Biography, a subgenre of history, became popular. The ancient Greek philosophy and ethics conformed to the sensibility and interest of Tudor House and therefore became the favored text of translation, too. The most translated Greek philosophers included, among others, Aristotle, Boethius, Cicero, Seneca, Ovid, Demosthenes①, Lucius Apuleius② and Marcus Aurelius③.

Many translations were second-hand, or even third-hand. When material was available in more than one language, it was the translator's individual choice to determine whether he should return to the Greek or Latin original or content himself with an intermediary text. Translations of Demosthenes, Homer, Isocrates, and Plutarch were largely by way of intermediate source, the most notable example being Thomas North's④ 1579 translation of *Plutarch's Lives* based on Jacques Amyot's French version. Alexander Barclay⑤ (1476-1552) translated Sebastian Brant's⑥ German text *Das Narrenschiff* into *Ship of Fools* (1509) by way of Jacob Locher's⑦ Latin version. John Southern translated Pindar's hymns and Anacreon's odes by way of Ronsard's French text. To many translators, recognition of source was a matter of choice rather than of obligation. William Painter⑧ admitted that he often used the French rendering of Boccaccio because it was written with the same fineness as the original. The claim of the

① 狄摩西尼:希腊演说家,因号召雅典市民反抗马其顿国王腓力二世的一系列演讲《强烈抨击》而知名。
② 阿普列乌斯:公元2世纪罗马哲学家和讽刺作家,代表作为《蜕变》,又称《金驴子》。
③ 奥里利乌斯:罗马皇帝(161~180年在位),斯多葛派哲学家,被誉为聪明的皇帝。
④ 诺斯:16世纪下半叶英国著名翻译家、诗人。
⑤ 巴克雷:16世纪英国翻译家、诗人,据拉丁语译本翻译了《愚人船》。
⑥ 布兰特:生于法国阿尔萨斯地区,16世纪人文主义者、讽刺作家,著有《愚人船》。
⑦ 洛克:15世纪末、16世纪初德国人文主义学者。
⑧ 品特:16世纪英国作家和翻译家。

translation as the work of one's own was not uncommon. Nicholas Grimald called his translation of Cicero as "my work" on the ground that "I call it mine as Plautus and Terence called the comedies theirs which they made out of Greek" (Amos, 1920: 85). The borderline between translation and original composition was thus obscured.

Normally, translation strategies varied with target readers and purpose of translation. As education became the principle objective of England in the late 16th century, translation came to be understood as a core exercise to learn the art of rhetoric from ancient and choicest models. The translator meant his translation as a textbook for the students to learn a language. In the 16th-century England, a merchant middle class was rising rapidly to the attention of the translators. In the preface to *Book of the Courtier* (1561), for example, Sir Thomas Hoby stated that he was addressing a readership extending beyond aristocratic circles to include the gentry and higher merchant class. Similar remarks show that "The translator's conception of his audience encouraged and guided his pen" (Amos, 1920: 90).

As the general readers of translation were ignorant about the source culture, the translators were up against the difficulty of representing the sophisticated, diversified foreign concept in the native English language. And they were constantly caught up in the tension between ideological renewal and traditional morality. The tension, together with the purpose to improve English language, was reflected in the two means of translating cultural words and acquiring new concepts: borrowing from the source words or formation of new words from Anglo-Saxon sources that would express the foreign cultural phenomenon. The latter strategy became increasingly widespread in Elizabethan England, which resulted in the widespread **domesticating translation** of the source texts. (quoted in Delisle & Woodsworth, 1995: 203) Besides, special rearrangements were made at every point to guarantee that the contents are worthwhile, harmless and, above all, useful and vivid for English readers. These devices were diverse and individual, ranging from the addition of maps, illustrations, and commentaries. "The whole book is thoroughly 'Englished' by a kind of multi-media transformation which often included the addition of aids such as maps, engraved illustrations and commentaries." (quoted in France, 2000: 51)

Some example will suffice to illustrate this domesticating method. Plutarch's *Lives* contains gladiatorial combat specific to Roman civilization. Amyot added some explanatory glosses in contemporary neutral terms in his French translation. Although translating from Amyot's French translation, Sir Thomas North modernized the term, replacing the neutral stance in Amyot's text with strong disapproval of the cruel practice, as is reflected in his adjective for the fighting *cruel*. Another example is Sir Thomas Hoby's translation of *The Book of the Courtier*, in which Baldassare Castiglione[①] (1478-1529) addresses the cultivated refinement of a perfect courtier of

① 卡斯蒂利昂:意大利文艺复兴时期的杰出作家和外交官,代表作《朝臣》记载了意大利文艺复兴时期的宫廷生活和宫廷朝臣的完美特质,是16世纪欧洲流传最广的书籍之一。

the Italian courts, which profoundly modified the mental outlook of Renaissance Europe. An ideal Italian courtier has grace through his refined behavior called *Sprezzatura*, the art of "concealing art, and presenting what is done and said as if it was done without effort and virtually without thought". How to express this refined behavior of advanced society to a less cultivated English audience? Thomas Hoby translated this positive word with a rather negative word *recklessness*, which suggests brazen indifference to, or defiant disregard for, consequences, and expresses Puritan disapproval of deceitful behavior. Alexander Barclay used a similar free translation method in his *Ship of Fools*, sometimes adding, sometimes detracting and taking away things that seemed unnecessary and superfine to him. As a result his text gave the fools strong English color, and attacked social evils of his time with unsparing spirit. More interestingly, he added an envoy at the end of each section to reveal the moral more clearly. The concluding poem is written in the ordinary Chaucerian stanza, and in language which is more modern than the common literary English of his day.

Women translators were also involved in translation. As in the Middle Ages, women were allowed to try their hands on pious passages only. The work of a woman translator was understandably anonymous, or circulated in manuscripts within a restricted circle. A powerful women translator was Mary Herbert①, Philip Sidney's② sister and Countess of Pembroke (1561-1621). She translated, among other works of poetry, Petrarch's *Triumph of Death*. But she is better known for her translation of the first secular play ever to be translated into English, namely, Robert Garnier's③ *Antoine*, which presented a positive image of Cleopatra④. Her translation is praised for its stylistic excellence. At about the same time, Jane Lumley⑤(1537-1576) translated the first extant English version of Euripides's *Iphigenia in Aulis*⑥. (quoted in Delisle & Woodsworth, 1995: 150) Margaret More Roper (1505-1544), the daughter of Sir Thomas More, translated Erasmus's *Precatio Dominica* (*Treaties on the Lord's Prayer*) in 1524. Margaret Tyler⑦ was another late 16th-century women translator who distinguished herself with her translation of a Spanish Romance *A Mirrour of Princely Deedes and Knighthood* (1578) as well as her liberalism. More than that, she wrote a preface in vigorous defense of her work and introduced a new profile of women of action. This is a courageous act in Renaissance England, when women were still much confined at home and supposed to be inactive. Thanks to her efforts, chivalry romance came into vogue and continued to be translated from Spanish sources

① 赫伯特:伊丽莎白时期的女翻译家。

② 西德尼:伊丽莎白时期的诗人、学者,当时英国最优秀的散文家,诗歌成就仅次于斯宾塞。

③ 加尼耶:法国悲剧诗人,著有《安东尼》。

④ 克莉奥帕特拉:埃及艳后,曾卷入罗马共和末期的政治旋涡,同凯撒、安东尼关系密切,是文学和艺术作品中的著名人物。

⑤ 拉姆莉:英国文艺复兴时期女翻译家,最早将欧里庇得斯作品译成英文。

⑥ 《奥里斯的伊菲格涅亚》:欧里庇得斯的悲剧。

⑦ 泰勒:16 世纪英国女翻译家。

for the subsequent centuries. Other women translators included the Cooke sisters① and Elizabeth I.

In spite of the large number of translators, the theories were in chaotic motley and some insightful ideas, if any at all, were fragmentary and unsystematic. The comment they made was incidental and only applicable to the particular translation problem on hand. No statement was concerned about what translation should be in general. The translators continued to talk about translation in metaphorical terms. More discussions on translation difficulty centered round vocabulary than sentence structure, which was uncertain and awkward in Renaissance England. The core issue of discussion was the translation and the increase of vocabulary. The general strategies were of two kinds: expand the English word stock by borrowing foreign words or looking for equivalents in the English language. The prejudice against the first means is understandable: foreign words do not conform to the accepted English usage and sound bookish and uncouth. Nevertheless, many of these borrowed words were naturalized and later became part of Modern English vocabulary, e. g., *emotion*, *effort*, *conscientious*, *comfort*, *tarnish*, *regret*. Yet there was also vigorous encouragement for the revival of old English words out of patriotism. Holland says of his translation of Livy: "I framed my pen, not to any affected phrase, but to a mean and popular style. Wherein if I have called again into use some old words, let it be attributed to the love of my country's language." (Amos, 1920: 98)

On the whole, secular translation theory is much less homogeneous and consecutive than *Bible* translation theory. The points of contact between religious and literary translation theories are mainly established by the translation of psalms. In the early 16th century, Sir Thomas Elyot② and Sir Thomas More were considered the authorities on translation. Slightly later Cheke③ was the strongest force in the field of translation. Since the middle 16th century, the active exponent of the new vitality in translation theory is represented by Nicholas Udall④.

Gavin Douglas⑤(1475? -1522) is a well-known Scottish poet and literary translator. He translated Vigil's epic *Aeneid* in the early 16th century. The translation was written in Scottish, the spelling of which was difficult to the modern readers. In his translation he introduced lengthy poetic prologues to the various books. Generally speaking, he meant to be faithful to the essential matter rather than to the letter. Convinced that the Scots is not adequate enough to match the original eloquence, he chose to write in the direct, vernacular style that is reminiscent of Chaucer and alliterative verse in the Middle Ages.

In the preface to volume 1 of the translation Douglas discoursed upon the translator's

---

① 库克姐妹指人文主义学者安东尼·库克爵士的五个女儿,均受过良好的古典教育,其中长女米尔德丽德(Mildred Cooke)最为出色,不仅译笔出众,而且知识渊博,出入宫廷,成为伊丽莎白一世的重要朝臣。

② 埃利奥特:16 世纪上半叶英国外交官和学者。

③ 契克:又译为奇克,16 世纪英国翻译家、学者。

④ 尤德尔:16 世纪英国伊顿公学校长,学者、翻译家。

⑤ 道格拉斯:18 世纪苏格兰翻译家、主教。

responsibility in an odd manner that reminded us of both medieval times and modern England. He criticized the free hand with which Troy story was generally rewritten in medieval times. He particularly rejected the medieval historian's combination of, and selection from, a wide variety of sources for translation. Caxton's *Eneydos*① was an indirect translation of the great poet Virgil on the basis of a French text. He maintained that it was glaringly distant from Virgil's original to the same degree as devil was different from St. Augustine. (Amos, 1920: 107) Douglas himself translated not **word for word, but sense for sense**. He admitted that he had but to deviate from the original when it came to translation of hard word, tricky sentence and elaborate rhythm. His translation run longer than the original in average, which, he believed, was permissible. He was concerned about using more words in English than in Latin. With him, English, without addition of words, was unable to reproduce the nuances of the following words: *animal* and *homo*; *genus*, *sexus* and *species*; *objection* and *subjectum*; *arbor* and *lignum*, etc. Only when used with additional words could the meaning of these words be translated. Douglas claimed that if he translated word for word the result would be unintelligible. In proof of this claim he cited Horace and St. Gregory. His general stance on translation was more for freedom than for accuracy.

Up to the middle of the 16th century, the leading figure in English translation community was **John Cheke** (1514-1557), a humanist proponent of the Reformation movement, polyglot and authority on Greek, once chaired the first guest professor at Cambridge University by the imperial edict. Largely owing to his popularity, Cambridge University then became the center of learning, translation and language study of England.

Cheke translated many Greek works, the gospel of St. Mathew and part of St. Mark. One of the striking features of his translation was that he used purely native English words, particularly words of Saxon origin, to the exclusion of imported words. His argument was that English itself had a thesaurus of native words and did not need to borrow words from other languages. Yet as he kept to the use of native English words only, he had to employ some rarely used words. The quality of his translations suffered as a consequence: they sometimes read affected and difficult. John Strype② described his translation as such:

> *And moreover, in writing any discourse, he would allow no words, but such as were pure English, or of Saxon origin; suffering no adoption of any foreign word into the English speech, which he thought was copious enough of itself, without borrowing words from other countries. Thus in his own translations into English, he would not use any but pure English phrase and expression, which indeed made his style here and there a little affected and hard: and forced him sometimes to use odd and uncouth words.* (quoted in Amos, 1920: 63)

① 《伊尼德斯》:卡克斯顿译作之一。
② 斯特里普:17 世纪英国历史学家、传记作家。

Another important translator during the 16th century England was **Nicholas Udall** (1505-1556), principal of Eton Public School. A person of wide interest, Udall was engaged, in addition to translation, in the writing and study of drama, creating the first English comedy *Ralph Roister Doister*①. He translated parts of Terence's② drama in 1533. In 1542, he translated Erasmus's *Apophthegmes*③ and later was in charge of translating Erasmus's Latin *New Testament* into English. His translation discourses gave expression to his extensive intellectual interests: dramatic, academic, and religious. The issues he touched on in his discussion included the stipend for the translator, the increase of the English vocabulary, the improvement of the English sentence structure, the style of Erasmus, the individual quality in the style of every writer—all in brief. Translation, he said, does not conform to iron rules. On the whole, Udall tended to be on the free side of the translation and believed that there was no rigid discipline to observe in translation.

The most remarkable translation during Elizabethan age was *Lives* translated by **Thomas North** (1535? -1601), a famous translator in the second half of the 16th century England. Early in his life, North studied in Cambridge University, then worked in London. In 1557, he translated Spanish writer Antonio de Guevara's *The Diall of Princes*④ via its French translation and in 1601 an oriental fable via its Italian version. North translated Plutarch's *Lives*, on which Shakespeare based his three Roman plays⑤: *Julius Caesar*, *Antony and Cleopatra* and *Coriolanus*. This is an indirect translation through a French text prepared by Amyot. He followed Aymot's translation principle that: "The office of a fit translator consisteth not merely in the faithful expressing of his author's meaning, but also in a certain resembling and shadowing forth of the form of his style and manner of his speaking." (quoted in Amos, 1920: 106) His *Lives* was a second-hand translation, but it was plain and effortless, different from Plutarch's Greek original style, which was dignified and elegant. North was also different from Aymot, his immediate source text, altering not only Aymot's words but also the substance. Like Aymot, who rewrote on the basis of Plutarch's original, North rewrote in English on the basis of the matter of Aymot's work. Shakespeare not only based his Roman and Greek tragedies on the story; sometimes he quoted outright from the translation.

Thomas Drant⑥(1540-1578) translated Horace's *Satires* into English, the first complete one of the *Satires* in English, in fourteeners⑦(rhymed iambic heptameters). He made some

① 《拉尔夫·罗伊斯特·多伊斯特》:厄代尔创作的第一部英国喜剧。

② 泰伦斯:生于希腊的古罗马剧作家。其喜剧如《福尔弥昂》和《阿德尔菲》以其巧妙的幽默和精彩的对话为特征。

③ 《箴言录》:伊拉斯谟作品之一。

④ 格瓦拉:16 世纪西班牙作家,主要作品有《王子的计时器》。

⑤ 莎士比亚以罗马历史题材为素材创作的历史剧,包括《尤利斯·凯撒》《安东尼与克莉奥帕特拉》《科利奥兰纳斯》。

⑥ 德兰特:16 世纪英国诗人。

⑦ 7 音步 14 音节的押韵的抑扬格诗体。

radical changes of content. In keeping with his Puritanism, Drant concentrated on portraying Horace as "a muche zelous controller of sinne". His version was generally close to Horace's literal meaning, but includes some drastic deletions and moralizing interventions. (quoted in France, 2000: 523) He was ready to make improvement on Horace's style: "His eloquence is sometimes too sharp, and therefore I have blunted it, and sometimes too dull, and therefore I have whetted it, helping him to ebb and helping him to rise." (Amos, 1920: 112) Drant made remarkable summary of his methods:

> *First I have now done as the people of God were commanded to do with their captive women that were handsome and beautiful: I have shaved off his hair and paired off his nails, that is, I have wiped away all his vanity and superfluity of matter. Further, I have for the most part drawn his private carpings of this or that man to a great moral. I have Englished things not according to the vein of the Latin propriety, but of his own vulgar tongue. I have interfered (to remove his obscurity and sometimes to better his matter) much of my own devising. I have pieced his reason, eked and mended his similitudes, mollified his hardness, prolonged his cortall kind of speeches, changed and altered much of his words, but not his sentence, or at least (I dare say) not his purpose.* (Amos, 1920: 113)

John Florio① (1553-1625?) is an accomplished linguist and lexicographer and a royal language tutor at the Court of James I. In 1598, he compiled and published a well-known Italian-English dictionary *A World of Words*. He is probably a close friend of and influence on William Shakespeare and is renowned for his translation of Montaigne's *Essays* (1603). As a translator, Florio was not equipped with North's fine taste, nor with Holland's knowledge, yet he was endowed with a special quality absent in them both—fantastic imagination. Florio made mistakes in his translation, and in some places his Elizabethan English was difficult as he followed the original too closely. He loved play on words, amplification of the text, and use of symmetrical construction. His translation, exquisite and elaborate, was entirely different from the original, which was frequently buoyant, plain and succinct. Despite all these defects, his translation was considered a brilliant rendition of Montaigne's liveliness, metaphors and wit. Shakespeare warmly appreciated the translation and used much of its story in his tragedy *Tempest*②. Ben Johnson③ (1572-1637) also appreciated his work. To T. S. Eliot④, Florio's translation of Montaigne's *Essays* is a classic of English literature, second only to the translation of *King James's Bible*. Montaigne was the only one to have real impact on English language and culture, thanks to the two complete renderings of Montaigne's essays, the first of which was made by Florio. His translation of Montaigne established essay as a legitimate literary genre of English literature.

---

① 弗罗里奥:英国语言学家、词典编纂家,以《意英词典》和蒙田散文的译作而著名。
② 《暴风雨》:莎士比亚的最后一部完整戏剧。
③ 琼森:英国文艺复兴时期诗人和剧作家。
④ 艾略特:美国诗人、剧作家和文学批评家,诗歌现代派运动领袖。

Philemon Holland (1552-1637) was a prolific translator of the 17th-century England. He was styled "the translator general of his age" by the ecclesiastical writer Thomas Fuller[①]. His best known translations are of Pliny the Elder's *Natural History* (1601), Plutarch's *Morals* (1603), Suetonius's[②] *Lives of the Twelve Caesars* (1606), Xenophon's *Cyropaedia*[③], and William Camden's[④] *Britannia*. He also took part in the authorized translation of the *Bible*, responsible for translation of *Matthew*, *The Acts*, and *Revelations*. Holland was criticized for using the antiquated language in his Pliny, but the work is sometimes superior to the English translations commonly available in the 20th century. His Plutarch is hardly rivaled by any later prose translator of the classics.

As a translator, Holland was inaccurate and redundant sometimes, like his fellow translators. He neglected his original, and aimed at a fresh composition which should recall the substance, if not the quality, of the Greek or Latin. Yet Holland was among the greatest of the Elizabethan translators, with a greater command of the language, a wider range of expression, and a greater sensibility to sound effect of words. His translation was characterized by energy of expression, color and variety of phrase, and invention. He enriched the language with countless borrowings from French or Latin. Holland constantly updated his translations with additions, omissions or conscious alterations. To strive for a popular style, he used contemporary terminology for certain key Roman terms. At other times, in his attempt to clarify obscure passages and references he inserted explanatory phrases or sentences. Holland's translation method was shaped by conception of his audience. His Pliny, for example, addressed itself not only to peasants and artisans but to young students, who "—by the light of the English, shall be able more readily to go away from the dark phrase and obscure constructions of the Latin" (Amos, 1920: 92).

In the 17th-century England, the deficiencies in translation theories were somewhat made up by **George Chapman**[⑤] (1559-1634), an English dramatist, translator, and poet. He is known as the first complete English translator of Homer.

Homer was among the most translated of Greek literature into the English language, but most of the earlier translations were partial. In 1616 Chapman published the complete *Iliad* and *Odyssey* in *The Whole Works of Homer*, the first complete English translation of Homer. His translation, until Pope's[⑥] Homer, was the most popular in the English language and was the way most English speakers encountered these poems. As *Iliad* and *Odyssey* are very much

---

① 福勒:英国牧师、历史学家。

② 苏埃托尼乌斯:公元1~2世纪罗马历史学家。

③ 《居鲁士的教育》:色诺芬的政治哲学著作。

④ 卡姆登:英国历史学家、古文物学家、地志学者,《不列颠》是卡姆登对英国和爱尔兰进行地志学和历史学考察的著作。

⑤ 查普曼:英国16~17世纪诗人、翻译家和剧作家,他翻译的《荷马全集》是第一部英语全译本。

⑥ 蒲柏:18世纪英国诗人、杰出的启蒙主义者,翻译过《荷马史诗》全本。

unlike each other, very few translators translated both with equal success. The biggest challenge is Homer's hexameter, with its insistent patterning, fixed epithets, speeches repeated verbatim, and lengthy catalogues. Another translation difficulty comes from the distance in time and space, namely, how to present Homer's heroes credible in the translator's time and place? Generally speaking, the most successful translators are those who allowed themselves considerable freedom. Chapman was entirely immersed in the *Iliad's* world of extravagant power and clashing princes. He identified himself unreservedly with Achilles①. He allowed him much freedom in treatment of Homeric Greek, giving up compound epithets, and coining many new words. Chapman translated *Iliad* into "fourteeners"②, a 14-syllable line that allows him to present all Homer's figures of speech and even his explanations in parentheses. A quarrel, for example, becomes a "wreathing of wraths". This kind of rhetorical excellence in his translation overwhelms the subject and becomes burdensome to the readers, distracting them away from the narrative thread.

Perhaps to show the difference between the two poems and the more domestic setting of *Odyssey*, Chapman used 10-syllable rhyming couplets when he translated *Odyssey* (1614-1615), which later developed into the heroic couplets. (quoted in France, 2000: 351) His *Odyssey*, without the extra space in the long line, becomes even more difficult to read. In the glosses, he enthusiastically praised his hero Ulysses③, sullied Ulysses' enemies, and deliberately reversed the epithets Homer used for the suitors and Polyphemus④. Chapman's *Odyssey* was translated with greater comical effect and revenge spirit in conformity with the Jacobean⑤ taste for humor and revenge. Where Homer checked Eurycleia's joy over the slaughtered suitors⑥, Chapman had her vent her joys freely, falsifying Homer's hero ethic. (quoted in France, 2000: 351) Generally speaking, Chapman's *Odyssey* was full of neologisms and more grotesque than his *Iliad*.

Chapman was concerned about laying down general principles for translation of epic poetry. Living in late 16th and early 17th centuries, Chapman served as a link between the two periods. In principle, he argued against the two extremes of too free or too literal. He pointed out that translation difficulties were inevitable but not insurmountable. He thought that

(1) Word-for-word translation was a common fault with translators;

(2) The attempt should be made to reach the "spirit" of the original;

---

① 阿喀琉斯:是荷马史诗《伊利亚特》中半人半神的英雄,在特洛伊战争中杀死特洛伊主将赫克托尔,使希腊军转败为胜。

② 7音步14音节的押韵的抑扬格民谣诗体。

③ 尤利西斯:荷马史诗《奥德赛》中的主人公的名字,译自拉丁文 Ulysses,而《奥德赛》的主人公奥德修斯则译自希腊文 Odysses,两者为同一人物的不同译法。

④ 珀涅罗珀的求婚者和独眼巨人波吕裴摩斯都是《奥德赛》剧中人物。

⑤ 詹姆斯一世时期的文学以滑稽剧和复仇剧为主。

⑥ 尤利西斯漂泊期间,其妻珀涅罗珀遭到很多求婚者骚扰,最终尤利西斯父子俩合计杀死了所有的求婚者。约克利亚是尤利西斯家里的女管家,在尤利西斯回到家后第一个认出了他,并帮助他与家人团圆。

(3) Overloose translation should be avoided by basing translation on a sound scholarly investigation of other versions and glosses. (quoted in Bassnett, 2004: 59)

Chapman's theory was largely upheld by the 17th-and 18th-century translators perhaps because he went the middle way between literalism and liberalism.

3.4.3 *Bible* Translations (Tyndale and Fulke)

Ever since the publication of Wycliffe's *Bible* in the 14th century, unauthorized translation of the *Bible* into English was prohibited and unlicensed possession of Scripture in English would lead to death sentence. Despite the strong opposition from the church, *Bible* translation had already taken a long and deep root in England prior to Tyndale's *Bible*. Under the influence of the Reformation, particularly the translation of Erasmus and Luther, *Bible* translation in England was roughly divided two camps, the Roman Catholic and the Protestant. The most distinguishing translators are William Tyndale, Gregory Martin and William Fulke.

William Tyndale① (1494? -1536) is a 16th-century Protestant reformer and humanist scholar.

In Tyndale's time, the common people of England still heard the Latin *Bible* read out and interpreted to them by the churchman, whom Tyndale found, to his shock, very ignorant about the scripture. Influenced by humanist thinking, Tyndale believed that the *Bible*, rather than the clerical, should be the only reliable source of Christian belief and practices. He was influenced by the work of Erasmus, who made the Greek *New Testament* available in Europe, and by Martin Luther, who translated the first German *Bible* for the common people. He was convinced that everyone should be able to read the *Bible* in his own language and intent upon translating the *Bible* into English.

In 1523, Tyndale finished the *New Testament* on the basis of Erasmus' *Bible*, Luther's German version and the *Vulgate*. As he translated it in Protestantism spirit, his *Bible* failed to come out in print because of the opposition from the church. In 1526, he published the first complete edition of his *New Testament* and smuggled it back to England without the permission of the church, incurring incessant attack from the clerical society. Two revised versions were later published in 1534 and 1536, both personally revised by Tyndale himself. Tyndale had only finished translating roughly half of the *Old Testament* out of a number of sources, including the *Septuagint* and Hebrew *Bible*.

Tyndale's *Bible* was important for a number of reasons: 1. It was the first *Bible* in Modern English; 2. it was a direct translation from Hebrew and Greek sources; 3. it was the first *Bible* in the Reformation spirit and played a key role in spreading Reformation ideas across the English-speaking world and eventually, on the global British Empire; 4. Tyndale's translation was the first printed *Bible* in English. His martyrdom and the growing printing industry

① 廷代尔：16 世纪英国著名的基督教学者和宗教改革先驱，英国宗教改革家和《圣经》译者。

facilitated the spread of his translation: his *Bible* witnessed unprecedented distribution in England, its reputation increasing with the passage of time. Tyndale's translation inspired the great translations that followed, including the *Great Bible*① of 1539, the *Geneva Bible*② of 1560, the *Bishops' Bible*③ of 1568, the *Douay-Rheims Bible*④ of 1582-1609, and the *King James Version* of 1611.

Tyndale's *Bible* was good for its clarity of expression and stylistic excellence. Tyndale laid particular stress on the intelligibility of the translation, using, wherever possible, the idiomatic English diction and the lively and racy narrative that came most naturally to native English speakers. His prose was clear, modern, and with unrivalled narrative force and minimized influence of Latin. For this matter his translation ran natural and effortless, devoid of all possible pedantic verbiage.

Tyndale's *Bible* was a great influence upon the English language. Many of the expressions he used were adopted in later *Bibles*. In fact, about 80% of Tyndale's phraseology was retained intact in the *Authorized Version*. (Barnstone, 1993: 208) Tyndale coined single words like *Jehovah* (from a transliterated Hebrew construction in the *Old Testament*), *Passover* (as the name for the Jewish holiday) and *scapegoat* (the goat that bears the sins and iniquities of the people), to name just a few. These coinages were adopted in the *Authorized Version*. He also introduced some phases into the English language, many of them familiar to every English reader today. Some of his famous phrases are: *lead us not into temptation but deliver us from evil*, *knock and it shall be opened unto you*, *twinkling of an eye*, *a moment in time*, *fashion not yourselves to the world*, *seek and you shall find*, *ask and it shall be given you*, *let there be light*, *the salt of the earth*, *a law unto themselves*, *filthy lucre*, *it came to pass*, *gave up the ghost*, *the signs of the times*, *the spirit is willing*, *but the flesh is weak*, and so on⑤.

His translations were condemned by Catholic Church of England. The Catholic theologians particularly hated some of the words and phrases introduced by Tyndale. *Bishop*, for example, became *overseer* in Tyndale's translations, and *priest* was translated with *elder*, *do penance* with *repent* and *charity* with *love*. These translations challenged key doctrines of the Roman Church and more or less questioned the legitimacy of the authority and hierarchy of the Catholic Church. More controversially, Tyndale used *congregation* rather than *church* for the Greek word εκκλησία (*ekklesia*). The Catholic Church had long proclaimed that the church was an

---

① 《大圣经》:科弗达尔应克伦威尔之邀修正马太圣经而成,亨利八世钦定为英国教会《圣经》。该《圣经》大部分借鉴了廷代尔《圣经》译本,但对其中敏感内容进行了改动,并根据《通俗拉丁文圣经》和德语《圣经》补译出了《旧约》。

② 《日内瓦圣经》:是一部按照新教精神翻译的英语《圣经》,是不信奉国教者推崇的《圣经》。

③ 《主教圣经》:英国国教会认可翻译的圣经,是《钦定本圣经》的主要参考译本之一。

④ 《杜埃-海姆斯版圣经》:据《通俗拉丁文圣经》翻译的一部英文天主教《圣经》。

⑤ William Tyndale. From Wikipedia, the free encyclopedia. 2009-05-23. http://en.wikipedia.org/wiki/William_Tyndale.

institution and the body of Christ on earth, apart from a group for Christian worshipers and the place for worship. The word *church* to them had come to represent the organizational structure that was the Catholic Church. Tyndale's translation was seen as a challenge to this doctrine because he favored the view that the church was made up and defined by the believers, or in other words their congregations. Some radical reformers preached that the true church was the "invisible" church, that the church is wherever true Christians meet together to preach the word of God. To these reformers the structure of the Catholic Church was unnecessary and its very existence proved that it was in fact not the "true" church. When Tyndale decided that the Greek word εκκλησία (*ekklesia*) should be more accurately translated into *congregation* rather than *church* he was undermining the entire structure of the Catholic Church. This choice posed a direct threat to the Church's ancient claim, for *congregation* emphasizes the gathering of the individual worshipers rather than the *church* as Christ's representative on earth①. Furthermore Tyndale's use of the word *congregation* attacked the Catholic Church's doctrine that the lay members and the clergy were to be separate. If the true church is defined as a congregation, as the common believers, then the Catholic Church's claim was challenged that the clergy were of a higher order than the average Christian and that they had different roles to play in the religious process.

After the publication of his *Bible*, Bishop Cuthbert Tunstall of London declared that there were upwards of 2,000 errors in Tyndale's *Bible*. Catholic theologian Thomas More harshly criticized him, too, that he had purposely mistranslated the ancient texts in order to promote anti-clericalism and heretical views. He compared searching for errors in Tyndale's *Bible* to searching for water in the sea. Tyndale was a meticulous translator who never let an error pass unattended. He urged "those that are better seen in tongues than I" to "put into their hands to amend" any faults that the critics may find in his work. (Amos, 1920: 50) Tyndale corrected his translation accordingly if the criticism was cogent but was never wavered in his basic translation principle, i. e., intelligible and edifying.

In 1528, Tyndale wrote *The Obedience of a Christian Man*, the first English book to advocate that the king of a country was the head of that country's church, rather than the pope. When a copy of the book fell into the hands of Henry VIII, who was angry over the Roman church's rejection of his divorce, the king found the rationale to break the Church in England from the Roman Catholic Church and declared himself the head of the Church of England in 1534②. This parting of ways between the Pope and the King of England not only freed the

① William Tyndale. From Wikipedia, the free encyclopedia. 2009-05-23. http://en.wikipedia.org/wiki/William_Tyndale.

② 英国国教会自公元6世纪起隶属罗马天主教会,1534年因亨利八世的再婚问题和罗马天主教会产生分歧而脱离罗马天主教会,由此揭开了英国宗教改革运动的序幕。大多数民众满足使英格兰的教会脱离罗马教皇的支配,在仪式和教义等方面并不拒绝天主教的传统。但是激进派(清教徒)希望同欧洲大陆的宗教改革一样,在教义上也作出根本的改革。

nation from the restraints of the Roman church in its modernization drive, but also opened the door to Protestantism. Tyndale's *Bible*, however, was far too sensitive for the new Church of English headed by Henry VIII, who only wanted to break away with the Roman Church for political reasons. Tyndale's public opposition to Henry VIII's planned divorce in 1530 further infuriated the king. In 1535 Tyndale was arrested, jailed in the castle of Vilvoorde outside Brussels for over a year, tried for heresy and then strangled and burnt at the stake. His last words were "God, open the king of England's eyes" (Barnstone, 1993: 208).

After the schism between King Henry VIII and the Pope in 1534, the Church in England was moving continually back and forth between Protestant or Catholic depending on whether or not the current monarch was a devout Protestant or Catholic. This Catholic/Protestant conflict in the Church of England led to the publication of many more *Bibles* that expressed contradictory religious aspirations, Protestant and Catholic.

Myles Coverdale[①] (1488-1569), or Miles Coverdale, is the translator of the *Great Bible*, also variously known as the *Cromwell Bible*, *Whitchurch's Bible*, the *Chained Bible*, or *Cranmer's Bible*[②]. This was the first complete translation of the *Bible* printed in the Modern English Language. Coverdale based his work on Tyndale's *New Testament* and Tyndale's incomplete work of *Old Testament*. Coverdale himself translated the remaining books of *the Old Testament* and the *Apocrypha*[③] primarily from Luther's *Bible*, the Swiss-German versions and Latin sources including the *Vulgate*. The revised edition of the *Bible* came out in 1539 as the *Great Bible* because of its large size. As it was wisely dedicated to King Henry VIII, it quickly won the approval of the king and became known as the first "authorized version" issued by the Church of England. As a matter of fact, Henry VIII had a *Coverdale Bible* put into every English Church, chained to a bookstand, so that every citizen would have access to a *Bible*; hence the *Chained Bible*. Coverdale's *Psalms* later became part of the common prayer, the official service book of the Church of England from 1549-1970s.

Gregory Martin (1540-1582) is the most important translator of the Douay-Rheims *Bible*, the first standard English *Bible* authorized by the Roman Catholic Church. The translation was undertaken during Elizabeth's Reign, which advocated Protestantism and banned all Catholic observances in England. Amid the religious upheaval, Martin translated his Catholic *Bible* under the cover of Protestantism until 1570, the year he openly denounced Protestantism and moved to the English College founded by William Allen[④] in Douy, France[⑤].

---

① 科弗达尔：英国圣经翻译家，用现代英语出版了完整《圣经》。

② 《大圣经》因为克伦威尔支持翻译出版，又称为《克伦威尔圣经》；因为英国印刷商 Edward Whitchurch 印刷出版，该《圣经》又称为《Whitchurch 圣经》；因为该《圣经》被铁链固定在教堂内而被称为"被固定的《圣经》"；又因为 Thomas Cranmer 为该《圣经》第二版作序，该《圣经》又被称为《Cranmer 圣经》。

③ 《次经》。

④ 艾伦：因不满伊丽莎白女王而鼓吹要维持罗马天主教的英国主教。

⑤ 杜埃：法国北部城市。

Six to seven years later he helped Allen establish the English College in Rome. Later he moved to Rheims, France①, the new site of the English College, to avoid religious persecution.

The *New Testament* was translated out of Jerome's *Vulgate* with painful literalism and met the public in 1582. It was so full of Latinism that it was difficult to understand. In the same year he published a book *A Discoverie of Manifold Corruptions of the Holy Scriptures by the Heretics of Our Days*. In the book he launched a severe attack upon all protestant versions to clear way for the reception of his *Bible*. Martin was more concerned about matters of religious belief than about abstract scholarship. He placed, without hesitation, the authority of the church fathers above the contemporary scholastics. *The Old Testament* was published 1601-1610.

Martin's translation was severely attacked by Protestant scholars, and most notably by William Fulke. For the two centuries after its publication, the Catholic *Bible* was suppressed, banned, and destroyed, but its influence could be detected in the phrasings of the *King James Bible* in the early 17th century. His version remained the official rendering for the English readers of the Roman Catholic Church until mid-twentieth century. These verbal attacks and counter attacks between Martin and Fulke revealed the bitter conflict between Protestantism and Roman Catholicism in the late 16th century England.

William Fulke②(1538-1589) was a humanist scholar. He never translated *Bible* in full, but gave insightful ideas on *Bible* translation. Following Gregory Martin's publication of his *Bible* and his *A Discoverie of Manifold Corruptions of the Holy Scriptures by the Heretics of Our Days*, Fulke published in 1583 his *Defense of the Sincere and True Translation of the Holy Scriptures into the English Tongue*. In this book he counter attacked Martin paragraph by paragraph and expounded theoretical issues concerning *Bible* translation. It was also an elaborate discussion of technical matters of *Bible* translation in Protestant spirit. Unlike Dolet, who gave a systematic elucidation of general translation principles, Fulke discussed the concrete translation problems in refutation of Martin's theory, and his theorization was therefore fragmentary.

Fulke held that translation enterprise might emancipate itself from matters of belief. Influenced by Erasmus's linguistic approach to translation, Fulke disapproved Martin's placing of clerical authority over scholarship. He maintained that a translator should, by rights, grasp a number of languages so that he would apply his right judgment to the Saint's teachings. The translator's strength lied not in his religious belief, but in his command of languages. Fulke never accepted the rigid translation formula put forward by Martin. He was unwilling to accept unsupported authority, not even that of the leaders of his own faction.

Fulke held that *Bible* translation should observe common language usage. At the center of

① 海姆斯:巴黎东北部城市,是罗马高卢地区的主要城市之一,历来为法国国王加冕之地。

② 富尔克:16 世纪英国人文主义《圣经》学者。

the controversy was the translation of ecclesiastical words. Martin accused some translators of understanding the religious words in the non-religious sense, namely, consulting secular writers like Pliny, Cicero, Vigil, etc., for the meanings of some words in a religious context. Fulke partly consented to Martin's accusation. On the other hand, Fulke doubted the ecclesiastical authority was not always a reliable guidance. As Fathers sometimes misused words, it is also advisable for the translator to consult secular writers for a more correct understanding of the difficult words. His idea was that Biblical usage would give way to general usage in confusing cases.

> *We are not lords of common speech of men, for if we were, we would teach them to use their terms more properly; but seeing we cannot change the use of speech, we follow Aristotle's counsel, which is to speak and use words as the common people useth.* (Amos, 1920: 72)

Medieval *Bible* translators invariably avoided verbose commentaries and guarded against the use of too many words in translation. As time went on, certain technical means were employed to solve the problem. Coverdale enclosed in brackets words not in the Latin text. The Geneva translators① put added words in italics. Similar technique was adopted in the Authorized Version later. Fulke was in favor of the technical device and actually accused *Rhemish New Testament* translators for neglecting the practice. On the other hand, however, he was irritated by the superstition over the number of words in translation. "To translate precisely out of Hebrew is not to observe the number of words, but the perfect sense and meaning, as the phrase of our tongue will serve to be understood." (Amos, 1920: 60)

In his own translation, Fulke resented importation of foreign idioms; he exploited English to its fullest potential, with particular emphasis on popular English expression. He admitted that English vocabulary was still deficient for translation, but the defect cannot be remedied by unwarranted coinage of words. By way of example, Fulke thought that "an image", "a worshipper of images", "worshipping of images", etc., were more proper and idiomatic than "idol", "idolater", "idolatry" respectively. His reasons were that although both "image" and "idol" were loanwords, "image", originated in Latin, took deeper root in English and became a part of common English expression. "idol", on the other hand, came from Greek, entered English vocabulary later, and was not easily accepted by Englishmen. He also pointed out that if the translator used "ancients" instead of "elders", "sages" rather than "wise men", he was speaking French, not the English language. "confide", for another example, could be translated into "have a good heart" in accordance with French usage and be "of good comfort" in conformity with English usage. But if you used "evangelized", you were not translating, but creating the neologism unfamiliar to general English readers. Fulke admitted that compared with older languages, English was noted not for its large stock of vocabulary, but this deficiency

① 《日内瓦圣经》的译者：为逃避玛丽王朝对新教徒的清洗，许多新教徒逃亡到日内瓦翻译出版《圣经》。

could be improved by the use of old words in new meanings.

Despite Fulke's caution on the use of foreign words, some foreign words he once strongly opposed have now become part of common English vocabulary. Yet his criticism of Martin was largely cogent and indeed won for him general applause among *Bible* translators.

The most remarkable English translation of the *Bible* is **the Authorized Version**.

3.4.4 The Authorized Version of the *Bible*

The battles between the Catholics and the Protestants led to the most violent persecution of the Protestants under the reign of Queen Mary, who was raised as a Catholic and saw it as her duty to purge the "evil" of Protestantism from her country. During during the reign of the Protestant Elizabeth, the Protestant doctrines and ways of life flourished and the Catholics were persecuted. The rivalry between Catholic and Reformed factions ended with the 1558 Elizabethan Settlement, which developed the understanding that the church was to be both Catholic and Reformed. The reign of King James I established a definite victory for Protestantism in England by introducing a new Protestant form of the Scriptures to church members throughout the country.

In the early 17th century, Tyndale's translation, together with many less known and uneven versions, circulated widely in England. This explosion of *Bibles* expressed contradictory religious aspirations, Protestant and Catholic, which confused the common English people. In the hope of clearing up the confusion, King James I called a conference in 1604, in which he asked a *Bible* be made that was "answerable to the truth of the original" (quoted in Baker, 1998: 338). The translators retained traditional understandings, as in the *Bishop's Bibles*①, as much as possible, censored other religious dogmas and achieved a higher degree of accuracy. The result of the work was the Authorized Version published in 1611, which was more a revision than a new translation, because many translations extant then were used to make "a principle good one out of many" (quoted in Baker, 1998: 338).

At the command and under the auspices of the King and Bishop Bancroft of London, 47 translators worked in 6 committees on the project, all members of the Church of England and all clergy except Sir Henry Savile. They worked on certain parts separately and then converged to compare and revise the drafts for harmony with each other. The translators were not paid directly; instead they were rewarded by a circular letter of recommendation sent to bishops for appointment of well-paying positions.

The King played an active role in developing the rules for translators and encouraging the completion of the work. As the committees included some scholars with Puritan sympathies, as

① 《主教圣经》:英国国教会认可翻译的圣经,是《钦定本圣经》的主要参考译本之一。

well as High Churchmen①, the King's instructions were given to limit the Puritan influence on this new translation. For example, the King instructed the translators to guarantee that the new version would use the old ecclesiastical words in conformity to the ecclesiology of the Church of England. Certain Greek and Hebrew words were to be translated in a manner that reflected the traditional usage of the church. For example, *church* was to be retained and not to be translated as *congregation* proposed by Tyndale, because *church* would reflect the Episcopal structure of the Church of England and traditional beliefs about ordained clergy. The translation was made with reference to the *Bishop's Bible*. If the *Bishops' Bible* was deemed problematic in any situation, the translators were permitted to consult other five translations from a pre-approved list: *the Tyndale Bible*②, the *Coverdale Bible*③, *Matthew Bible*④, and the *Geneva Bible*⑤. As a result, the translation was made in the spirit of religious reconciliation, rather than contestation.

The *Bible* was made with great faithfulness to the original message. In the preface to 1611 version it was declared that "niceness in words was always counted the next step to trifling" (Amos, 1920: 61). Reflected in it is a profound respect for the original truth, a conception of the translation merely as a mouthpiece of the original content and the English language nothing but a medium of divine thought. On the other hand, the version also tried to be intelligible to and popular with the common readers.

James' instructions included several requirements that kept the new translation familiar to the readers. The text of the *Bishops' Bible* would serve as basis for the translators, and the familiar and current proper names of the Biblical characters would all be retained; the original chapter division should be altered as little as possible and notes should be used only for explanations of hard Hebrew or Greek words; the 8th to the 11th rule detailed the standard procedures through which the translation should be made. It started by prescribing that each man in each committee shall separately examine the same chapter and render it as well as he could. The whole committee must then come together, compare what they have done, and agree on the final version. As a result, seven to ten distinct and carefully rendered revisions would be produced in each committee, depending on the size of the committee, all to be

---

① 高教会派：基督教新教圣公会派别之一，专指英国国教会信徒，主张在教义、礼仪和规章上大量保持天主教的传统，要求维持教会较高的权威地位，因而得名。

② 《廷代尔圣经》：廷代尔是16世纪著名的基督教学者和宗教改革先驱，按照宗教改革的精神用现代英语翻译了《圣经》，对后来的英语圣经翻译产生了深远的影响。

③ 《科弗达尔圣经》：又称为《大圣经》《克伦威尔圣经》《Whitchurch 圣经》《Cranmer 圣经》。科弗达尔是英国圣经翻译家，用现代英语出版了完整圣经。该圣经大部分借鉴了《廷代尔圣经》译本，但对其中敏感内容进行了改动，并根据《通俗拉丁文圣经》和德语《圣经》补译出了《旧约》。

④ 《马太圣经》：圣经翻译家约翰·罗杰斯1537年以"汤玛斯·马太"之名出版的英语《圣经》译本。该《圣经》大部分采用了《廷代尔圣经》，廷代尔未完成的部分由科弗达尔补译完整，约翰·罗杰斯本人只从法语翻译了《玛拿西忏悔诗》，未译完就被处死。

⑤ 《日内瓦圣经》：是一部按照新教精神翻译的英语《圣经》，是不信奉国教者推崇的《圣经》。

compared, and digested into one final copy of the particular portion of the *Bible*. Then the final version of a particular portion of the *Bible* would be sent to each of the other committees, to be critically reviewed by them all. If anything doubtful or unsatisfactory was discovered during the review, the problematic version would be sent back to the responsible committee with problems marked, for correction or check. If the responsible committee should not concur in the suggested correction, the matter was to be finally decided at a general meeting of the committee chiefs of all the companies at the end of the work. The eleventh rule requires that in case of any special difficulty or obscurity, any learned man in the land would be called in for his judgment. This rigorous methodology ensures that every part of the *Bible* would be closely scrutinized, individually or collectively, at least five times, before it took its final shape.

This version, also called *King James Bible*, was a second large-scale organized translation since the making of the *Septuagint* and one of the supreme achievements of English Renaissance. This translation has incorporated the merits of the previous *Bibles* and became a remarkable masterpiece of English literature for its profusion of literary images, plain and beautiful language and musical effects. The Authorized Version has been called "the most influential version of the most influential book in the world, in what is now its most influential language", "the most important book in English religion and culture", and "the most celebrated book in the English-speaking world"①.

As statistics show, 93% of the words are of Anglo-Saxon origin, which makes it popular among the common English readers. It has contributed 257 idioms to English, more than any other single source, including Shakespeare. Examples include *feet of clay*, *reap the whirlwind*, *clear as crystal*, *still small voice*, *arise as one man*, *broken reed*, *eye for eye*, *tooth for tooth*, etc. Indeed, the version has produced a tremendous influence upon the development of the English language and literature and, through its translation, of the small languages of British colonies as well. The main defect, if any, with this Version lies in the inconsistent style as a result of varying language habits of many different translators.

Further Readings

Amos, Flora Ross. *Early Theories of Translation*. New York: Columbia University Press, 1920.

Baker, Mona. *Routledge Encyclopedia of Translation Studies*. London & New York: Routledge, 1998.

Barnstone, Willis. *The Poetics of Translation: History, Theory, Practice*. New Haven & London: Yale University Press, 1993.

Bassnnet, Susan. *Translation Studies*. Shanghai: Shanghai Foreign Language Education

① King James Version. From Wikipedia, the free encyclopedia. 2012-06-11. http://en.wikipedia.org/wiki/Authorized_King_James_Version.

Press, 2004.

Delisle, Jean & Judith Woodsworth. *Translators through History*. Amsterdam: John Benjamins Publishing Company, 1995.

France, Peter. *The Oxford Guide to Literature in English Translation*. New York: Oxford University Press, 2000.

Robinson, Douglas. *Western Translation Theory: From Herodotus to Nietzsche*. Shanghai: Foreign Language Teaching and Research Press, 2006.

William Tyndale. From Wikipedia, the free encyclopedia. 2009-05-23. http://en.wikipedia.org/wiki/William_Tyndale.

King James Version. From Wikipedia, the free encyclopedia. 2012-06-11. http://en.wikipedia.org/wiki/Authorized_King_James_Version.

谭载喜:《西方翻译简史》,商务印书馆 2004 年版。

Topics for Discussion

1. In Renaissance England, domesticating translation or naturalization became increasingly widespread when the translators were constantly caught up in the tension between ideological renewal and traditional morality. Do you find similar strategy in the translation history in the West? Account for the translation strategy from socio-cultural perspective.

2. Compare Tyndale's *Bible* with Wycliffe *Bible*. Point out the similarities and dissimilarities. Why was Tyndale burned at the stake? Is linguistics an important consideration in the suppression or acceptance of a translation?

3. Why was Fulke considered a humanist translator and translation scholar? In what way did he respond to Renaissance spirit in his discussion of translation?

4. Compare the French *Lives* by Aymot and English *Lives* by North. And comment on what make them famous translations in world translation history.

3.5 Chapter Summary

After the fall of Eastern Roman Empire in 1453, many Greek manuscripts, including the Greek *New Testament*, were discovered and brought back to Western Europe. Availability of paper and the invention of metal movable type accelerated the dissemination of knowledge from the late 15th century. For the first time since the antiquity, ancient texts were accessible to Europeans in comparatively standardized edition and at lower price. Renaissance scholars were engaged in research and study of ancient texts with renewed human interest.

Renaissance translations of classical cultures were different from medieval translations of classical cultures. First, Renaissance translators held the classical authors in high esteem and insisted on restoring them to their true colors. Second, Renaissance translators translated with Renaissance spirit of freedom and humanism. As a result, many ancient texts were modernized and naturalized before they took root in the target culture system. Third, as the classical culture was now available to renaissance translators in the Greek or Latin original, most Renaissance translators abandoned indirect translation.

In addition to the classics, the renaissance translators also translated from Italian, Spanish, German and French sources that represented the latest renaissance achievement. *Bible* translation was an essential part of the Reformation Movement across the Europe. In the deepening crisis of the Church, Erasmus published a Greek *New Testament* in parallel with a new Latin translation to eradicate textual corruptions in the existing Vulgate versions and to restore simple Christian faith based on true Scriptures with humanist techniques. His Latin *New Testament* (2nd edition) replaced the *Vulgate* as the official *Bible* of the Church. Subsequent editions of his *Bible* produced felt influence on important *Bible* translation of the Renaissance period. Luther's Germanized *Bible* provided the Reformation Movement with an ideological program and laid the foundation for the evolution of German national language and literary tradition. The Catholic/Protestant conflict in the Church of England led to the publication of many *Bibles* that expressed contradictory religious aspirations, Protestant and Catholic. The earliest modern English Protestant *Bible* was translated by Tyndale. The Authorized Version (1611) marked a compromise between Protestant and Catholic denominations.

Practical and academic translations were largely made by lay people in the hope of disseminating useful knowledge. Literary translation was more difficult to describe largely because they happened under more diversified conditions.

Serious attempts were made to formulate a theory of translation, though. Erasmus set the keynote for renaissance *Bible* translation with the following ideas: (1) The authority of the theologians should be questioned and the original texts respected; (2) The individual translator had the right and latitude in interpreting and translating the *Bible* relying on his knowledge of the two languages; (3) *Bible* should be translated into all languages. Luther advocated the return to the original language of the *Bible* and adhered to the principle that the word should follow the meaning of the text and not the other way around. In relation to his meaning-based translation, Luther raised seven systematic principles for linguistic changes in translation. His ideas were upheld by William Tyndale of England and Reina① and Valera② of Spain in their *Bible* translation.

In the manifesto of the Pleiade, Du Bellay detailed a program of literary renewal and revolution, maintaining that French was a worthy language for literary expression. He argued against slavish translation, recommending creative imitation of Greek and Roman poetic forms into French by way of emulation of classical literary models and the creation of new terms from

---

① 雷纳:16 世纪西班牙圣经翻译家,据希伯来文本与希腊文本把圣经完整译为西班牙语,后经瓦勒拉修订出版,称为《雷纳-瓦勒拉圣经》。

② 瓦勒拉:17 世纪初负责修订出版雷纳圣经译本。

Greek and Latin. Dolet formulated five principles of a good translation. He rejected word-for-word translation, described the stages of the translation process, and emphasized the importance of the language knowledge and literary competence. His idea was reiterated by George Chapman① and others. Pasquier's lists of translation difficulties touch on all the important factors, socio-cultural and linguistic, that make translation impossible. He also introduced the effect of translation on the audience, which becomes the heated topic for discussion in 20th century translation theories. Theoretical discussion in Renaissance England was deficient in depth and scope. In spite of the large number of translators, the theories were in chaotic motley and some insightful ideas, if any at all, were fragmentary and unsystematic. The translators continued to talk about translation in metaphorical terms. The comment they make is incidental and only applicable to the particular translation problem on hand. No statement is made concerning what translation should be in general.

① 查普曼:英国16~17世纪诗人、翻译家和剧作家,他翻译的《荷马全集》是第一部英语全译本。

Chapter Four
Cultural Dissemination in the Modern Era[①]

4.1 Socio-cultural Background

Modern European history refers to the historical period following the Middle Ages, with the European Renaissance in between as an important period of transition. "Renaissance" spirit of freedom continues into the Modern era, which is characterized by the emancipation from religion, specifically the hegemony of Christianity, and the consequent secularization of intellectual life. Modern era in translation history roughly refers to the period following Renaissance encompassing the Age of Reason[②] in the 17th century, the Age of Enlightenment[③] in the 18th and 19th centuries. But as human culture is dynamic and continuous and as renaissance is far from a uniform process across Europe, this division should be understood as an expedient rather than distinct concept and the overlap between late Renaissance and early Modern Era is not uncommon.

From a global standpoint, the globalizing character of the Renaissance period (sometimes referred to as early modern period) continued into modern times, which witnessed the rise of sustained contacts between previously isolated parts of the globe and the global trade between the historically isolated powers. Some of the more notable trends and events of the early modern period included the religious conflicts the Reformation provoked, including the French Wars of

① 欧洲历史上的"现代史"大致指15世纪至19世纪初的历史,但在欧洲不同地区"现代史"的历史发展不尽一致,文艺复兴晚期和现代在不同地区有不同程度的重叠,有的学者将文艺复兴视为欧洲现代史的开端。"现代"一词在世界其他地区也有不同含义。

② 理性时代:17世纪早期的哲学思潮,它摆脱了中世纪占统治地位的基督教哲学,认为人的理性思考和感觉经验是通向所有知识的大门。

③ 启蒙时代:18世纪的欧洲文化思潮,主张理性,质疑传统教条权威,推崇个人主义,强调进步的普世观念。

Religion[①] (1562-1598) and the Thirty Years' War[②] (1618-1648), the rise of capitalism and modern nation states. Other notable trends of the period include the development of experimental science, improvements in transportation and communications, increasingly rapid technological progress, secularized civic politics in various regions of the world[③]. All these led to radical changes in the theory of literature and hence the role of translation. The subject matter of modern translation was expanding into more secular and recent works, in addition to classical antiquity and Biblical texts. The languages of translation were more diverse than ever, many translations happening between young national languages.

Translation strategy and theorization were immediately influenced by the general intellectual movement. The 17th-century philosophy is often called the Age of Reason or Age of Rationalism, a cultural movement of intellectuals emphasizing reason and individualism rather than tradition. The development of the movement in the 18th century is known as the Age of Enlightenment (sometimes synonymous with the Age of Reason), with its purpose to reform society using reason, to challenge ideas grounded in tradition and faith, and to advance knowledge through the scientific method. In the West, the period is typified in Europe by the great system-builders like Rene Descartes[④] (1596-1650) and Immanuel Kant[⑤] (1724-1804)—philosophers who present unified systems of epistemology, metaphysics, logic, and ethics. Similar attempts to formulate system were reflected in the endeavors of literary critics to formulate general rules of aesthetic production. Translation theories likewise have witnessed substantial development, the discussion growing rapidly in both depth and scope. The investigation on the nature of translation, particularly in Germany, is posited within the more general framework of language and human mind and the discussion on translation thus takes a philosophical aspect.

With their rise in politics and economy, England and France took the lead in both translation performance and theorization in early Modern Era. Translation of the classics increased considerably in France from 1625 to 1660, the great age of French classicism and of the flowering of the French theatre. French writers and theorists were in turn translated with enthusiasm into English.

---

① 法国宗教战争：又称“胡格诺战争”，是法国天主教势力同胡格诺派（即法国新教的加尔文派）在1562～1598年间进行的一场战争。它虽然带有明显的宗教色彩，但就其性质和内容而言则是法国内战。战争的结果是天主教、胡格诺教派各有所得，有助于王权的重新振兴和加强，为民族国家的统一和经济的复兴创造了条件。

② 三十年战争：由神圣罗马帝国的内战演变而成一次遍及全欧的大规模国际战争。这场战争是欧洲各国争夺利益、霸权以及宗教纠纷激化的产物，是现代史上耗时最长、极具破坏性的战争。德意志为主要战场，战争以波希米亚人民反抗奥地利帝国哈布斯堡王朝统治为肇始，最后以哈布斯堡王朝战败而告终。

③ Early modern period. From Wikipedia, the free encyclopedia. 2013-10-01. http://en.wikipedia.org/wiki/Modern_history.

④ 笛卡儿：17世纪法国伟大的哲学家、物理学家、数学家、生理学家，解析几何的创始人，欧洲哲学界和科学界最有影响的巨匠之一，被誉为“近代科学的始祖”。

⑤ 康德：德国哲学家、思想家、德国古典哲学创始人。他被认为是对现代欧洲最具影响力的思想家之一，也是启蒙运动最后一位主要哲学家。

4.2 Translations in Modern France

Translation Terms

The Belles Infideles 美而不忠的翻译

A term (meaning unfaithful beauty) invented by Gilles Menage to criticize D'Ablancout's translation that was morally and stylistically agreeable but very distant from the source text. It was later used to mock free imitations that were pleasant to the audience but unfaithful to the original. This method of translation was popular during the 17th-century France, with D'Ablancout as its representative.

Back translation 回译

Back translation is the process of translating a translated text back into the source language. In ancient and medieval times when communications were very difficult, the relationship was very complicated between the source and target texts because of frequent use of anonymous translation, indirect translation and retranslation. A translated text was sometimes retranslated back to its source language without the translator's knowledge. Back translation is still used today for research purpose, i. e., to refute the idea of equivalence.

4.2.1 Socio-cultural Background

In France, Enlightenment was based in the salons. Parisian salon culture set standards of discriminating taste from the 1630s, and with Pascal, Descartes, Bayle, Corneille, Racine and Molière①, France became the cultural center of Europe. The French language became the lingua franca of the European continent.

It is difficult to generalize over translations made in France over three centuries, for Modern France was a culturally dynamic period and Modern French translation responded warmly to the vibrant intellectual movement. For the convenience of discussion, Modern France is divided into early modern (17th century) France, 18th-century France and 19th-century France, each period with distinctive features in terms of subject matter translated, translation strategy or translation theory.

Generally speaking, early modern France was the age of *Les Belles Infideles* (unfaithful beauty), when translators cared only to produce a text that was morally and stylistically agreeable, with little respect for the original. In the 18th century, the English language and culture were catching on among polite French society. Three types of novels were particularly translated in the time: sentimental, Gothic and historical, with the method of *Les Belles*

① 法国17世纪哲学家帕斯卡、笛卡儿及贝勒和法国17世纪古典戏剧三杰高乃伊、拉辛及莫里哀。

Infideles. In the 19th century a profusion of translations were made from English, German, Italian, Spanish and Latin literatures. With the rise of romanticism in Germany, French translation returned back to literalism. Many classics were retranslated with accuracy for the purpose of restoring the ancients to their original reputation. Translation of Shakespeare started in the 18th century and flourished in the 19th century. Shakespeare was introduced to France in real earnest and triggered a craze for the study of the English playwright.

4.2.2 D'Ablancout and *the Belles Infideles*

Succeeding the Renaissance, the early part of the 17th century France was another dynamic age for translation. In addition to ancient Latin texts on architecture, contemporary works on medicine and pharmacology and texts in Flemish and Portuguese were translated. A growing number of Spanish, Italian and English works, literary and non-literary, were also translated during the 17th century. The translated works included Cervantes' *Don Quixote*①, Giambattista Marino's *Adonis*②, Machiavelli's *Discourse*③, Francis Bacon's *Moral Essays*④, John Locke's treatises, *Civil Government* and *Essay on Human Understanding*⑤. Nevertheless, Renaissance interest in the classical antiquity continued into French classicism⑥, which was represented in French theatre developed by the 17th century French playwrights from what they judged to be the rules of Greek classical theatre. Examples of classicist playwrights are Pierre Corneille, Jean Racine and Moliere⑦, who wrote under the "classical unities" of time, place and action, found in the *Poetics* of Aristotle. Under the influence of French classicism, classical texts were still among the most translated in the 17th-century France. Classical translations were increasingly expected to observe established French literary concepts and moral conceit. The flexible and innovative translations, known as *Les Belles Infideles*, took pains to provide texts that were agreeable to the French audience. This strategy to please continued well into the 18th century. The most remarkable translator of the school was Nicolas Perrot D'Ablancout (1606-1664).

Nicolas Perrot D'Ablancout⑧, a master of Latin language and a scholar of wide

① 塞万提斯:16～17世纪西班牙作家,著有《唐·吉诃德》。

② 马里诺:16～17世纪意大利诗人,著有取材于罗马神话的长诗《阿多尼斯》。该诗多用修辞,辞藻华丽,反映了17世纪意大利文学衰落时期贵族阶级的趣味,在意大利盛行一时。

③ 马基亚维利:16世纪意大利政治思想家和历史学家。1513出版《君主论》,书中提出的为君原则对政治哲学产生很大影响。

④ 弗朗西斯·培根:16～17世纪英国文艺复兴时期最重要的散文家、哲学家。

⑤ 洛克:17世纪英国哲学家、经验主义的开创人,同时也是第一个全面阐述宪政民主思想的人,在哲学以及政治领域都有重要影响,著有《政府论》(1685)、《人类理解论》(1690)等。

⑥ 古典主义:17世纪流行在西欧、特别是法国的一种文学思潮,直到19世纪初浪漫主义文艺兴起才结束。因它在文艺理论和创作实践上以古希腊、罗马文学为典范和样板而被称为"古典主义"。古典主义在创作理论上强调模仿古代,主张用民族规范语言,按照规定的创作原则(如戏剧的三一律)进行创作,追求艺术完美。

⑦ 法国17世纪古典主义戏剧三杰高乃伊、拉辛及莫里哀。

⑧ 阿伯兰库或阿布郎古尔:法国17世纪翻译家,其译作不求忠实,只求优美,被称为"美而不忠"的译本。

learning, was born to a lawyer's family. He was trained in law, but he completed his classical education at 13. In his twenties, he raised a sensation by converting from Protestantism to Catholicism and then back to Protestantism again. Valentin Conrart① encouraged him to translate some orations of Cicero, as a result of which he was elected to the Academy② in 1637. Encouraged by the success he made a major version of Tacitus③, then a spate of publications based on Greek and Spanish as well as Latin originals. In the meantime, he retired to his family estate, D'Ablancout, where he stayed until his death. He translated many Greek and Latin authors, including Cicero, Tacitus, Xenophon④, Arrian⑤ and Thucydides⑥, covering a range of subject matter: historical, rhetoric and moral. His translation of Tacitus' *Annals*, in particular, had seen one after another print.

He was renowned in his day for his free imitation which gave top priority to the elegance of the target text. And translation in his understanding bordered very much on liberal adaptation. He not only censored these works in the course of translating them but also corrected any factual errors he encountered and generally aimed to "improve" on the source text. He adapted the classical texts through omissions and improvements so that some of his translations were considered travesties. When accused of making French originals in disguise of translation of Greek and Latin models, D'Ablancout's reply was: most so-called original works in French were but disguised translations, and that "to serve one's country a man ought rather to translate valuable authors than to write new books, which seldom contain anything new" (quoted in Robinson, 2006: 157).

In the preface to his French translation of Lucian⑦ (1654), he discussed translation difficulty and justified the changes he made:

> *At every turn, the author quotes from Homeric verses, which would nowadays be pedantic, let alone from the old, excessively hackneyed myths, from the proverbs, examples, and antiquated similes, which would at present make an impression quite contrary to his intention; for we are talking here about elegance, and not about erudition. It was thus necessary to change all that in order to have a pleasing result. Otherwise it would not be Lucian; and what is pleasing in his language, would be intolerable in ours. Moreover, as with beautiful faces, there is always something that we wish were not there, so with the best authors, there are sections that must be changed or clarified, particularly when things are only done to please; for one cannot then tolerate the slightest fault, and what little is lacking in refinement becomes annoying*

① 考拉特:17 世纪法国作家,法兰西学术院的创立者。

② 法兰西学术院:法兰西学院下属的五个学术院之一,成立于 1635 年,是五个学术院中历史最悠久、名气最大的学术权威机构。

③ 塔西佗:古罗马的执政官和历史学家,著有《历史》和《编年史》,记述了上起公元 14 年,下迄公元 98 年罗马帝国的历史。

④ 色诺芬:公元前 430 ~ 354 的古希腊将军,历史学家,著有《远征记》。

⑤ 阿里安:古罗马历史学家。

⑥ 修昔底德:公元前 5 世纪古代希腊最伟大的历史学家,著有《伯罗奔尼撒战争史》。

⑦ 卢西恩:又译为琉善,古希腊讽刺作家。著有《神的对话》和《死者的对话》,讽刺了希腊哲学和神话。

instead of enjoyable. Therefore, I do not always bind myself either to the words or to the reasoning of this author; and I adjust things to our manner and style with his goal in mind. (quoted in Robinson, 2006: 158-159)

In the preface to his translation of Thucydides, he made a remark in the similar vein (1662): "*But those strict translators produce only a carcass from a living body and make a monster from a miracle. —But it is better to be unfaithful in the small in order to be faithful in the great.*" (quoted in Robinson, 2006: 160, my ellipsis)

D'Ablancout aimed at making the translation in element with the taste of the contemporary readers. To this end, he took over the general idea of the original and rewrote it in accordance with target language conventions, with little regard for the original subject matter and literary style. His translations appealed to the readers who had no idea of the original, but they were naturally full of unscrupulous omissions and additions. Unfaithful as they were, D'Ablancout's translations won general applause from many common readers and translation critics. They had a major impact on the formation of classical taste in the middle 17th century and contributed considerably to the evolution of French prose style. Under his influence, many translators went blindly for the translation that was stylistically fine, and some classics, although renowned for their simplicity and lucidity, put on fine French clothes. Claude Favre de Vaugelas① (1585-1650) spent as many as 30 years polishing his translation of Quintus Curtius Rufus②, with the sole purpose of rendering it stylistically exquisite. Elated with his translation of Virgil's *Aeneid* in 1648, Pierre Perrin③ (1620-1675) claimed in the preface of his translation that he was the first one who dolled up *Aeneid* in the guise of French knight and with magnificent plumes and foils. Some other translators were intent upon improving the translation by tailoring it to current French sensibility, too. Among them were Louis Giry④ (1596-1668), Isaac de Benserade⑤ (1613-1691), Paul Pellison⑥ (1624-1693), and Jean Segrain⑦ (1624-1701).

D'Ablancout's principles met with some opposition, though. Gilles Menage⑧ (1613-1692) invented an expression *the Belles Infideles* (unfaithful beauty) to describe his translation, saying that his translation reminded him of his mistress, who was beautiful but not faithful. Ever since then D'Ablancout's translation was invariably termed *the Belles Infideles*, a term that later literal translators used to mock free imitations that were pleasant to the audience but

---

① 沃日拉:法国语法学家和文学家。沃日拉采用宫廷与贵族阶层的用语,摒弃平民大众的口语,制订正规法语的规范。

② 鲁斐斯:1世纪的古罗马历史学家,著有《亚历山大史》。

③ 佩兰:法国17世纪诗人、歌剧作家。

④ 吉里:法国17世纪翻译家、学者。

⑤ 邦斯拉德:法国17世纪翻译家、学者。

⑥ 佩里森:法国17世纪翻译家、学者。

⑦ 塞格雷:法国17世纪翻译家、学者。

⑧ 梅纳日:法国17世纪翻译家、学者。

distant to the original. Antoine Furetiere[①](1619-1688) also attacked D'Ablancout for clothing the translation with stylish costume tailored to his own mind. Pierre-Daniel Huet[②](1630-1721) urged the translator to pay more respect to the original author.

4.2.3 The Quarrels of the Ancients and the Moderns[③]

Concerning translation of classical antiquity a heated contention broke out over the respect for the present or the antiquity. The quarrel was at first a literary and artistic debate that heated up in the early 1690s at the French Academy over the question of "Is Modern culture superior to Classical culture?" On one side of the debate were the Ancients or Revivalists, led by Nicolas Boileau[④] (1636-1711), who recognized the merits of the ancient authors, and contended that a writer could do no better than imitate them. On the other side were the Moderns or anti-revivalists, who respected the merits of the contemporary authors, arguing that the learned ancients were bound by their times and never up to the extent of modern authors. Pierre Carlet de Marivaux[⑤](1688-1763) sided with the moderns in establishing the sentimental comedy, a new genre of theatre unknown to the Ancients. Jean Racine[⑥](1639-1699) sided with the Ancients by constraining his choice of subjects to those drawn from the literature of Antiquity, and especially by confining his tragedies within the bounds of the three classical unities from Aristotle's *Poetics*: a single, consistent action must happen within 24 hours at one and the same location.

In the field of translation, Moderns gave top priority to the present and adapted classical texts to current canons and genres, exhibiting an unrestrained freedom in their translation. They held that human history was an uphill road, that men today were comparable to, or even better than, their forefathers, and that the ancient texts were not inviolable and should be open to improvements and modifications. The original, moderns argued, might be good in its time and place, but was no longer popular with contemporary readers. As the times had changed dramatically since Greek and Roman era, the original classics need to be updated, too. *The Belles Infideles* translators largely belonged among the moderns. D'Ablancout, for instance, held that classical pieces left something to be desired, and therefore were not necessarily the prototype for slavish imitation.

Ancients insisted on due respect for the ancient authors through accurate translation, but

---

① 富尔迪埃尔:法国小说家、讽刺作家和词典编纂家。

② 于埃:17~18世纪法国翻译家、学者。

③ 分别译为崇古派和厚今派。

④ 布瓦洛:法国文艺理论家、诗人,1674年发表《诗艺》,阐明了文学的古典主义原则,对当时法国和英国的文坛影响很大。

⑤ 马里沃:法国作家,以浪漫喜剧闻名,作品包括《双重背叛》与《爱情与偶然狂想曲》。

⑥ 拉辛:法国戏剧家。法国古典主义时期最伟大的悲剧作家,作品包括《不列颠》(1669年)和《菲德拉》(1677年),取材于希腊和罗马的古典主题。

with little effect. Their only argument was old and weak: any change in the transferring process made the translation worse than the original and that the translations produced by the moderns were travesties. Gaspard Bachet de Meziriac①(1581-1638) published an article (1635) in which he prescribed three laws of translation, i. e., no addition, no deletion and no change of the original idea. In the same article he also accused Amyot of adding to and detracting from the original. Lemaitre de Sacy②(1613-1684) translated a Latin version of the *Bible* into French with a more literal approach. But he used a freer method when he translated Terence③. In the preface to his Terence, he confessed that he introduced some changes into the book because it contained something that might be morally dangerous to the young people.

One outcome of the quarrel was the spreading of the term "modern". Underlying the quarrel between the Moderns and Ancients were deeper and opposing views, one in support of the very idea of progress and the other the ancient authority. The renewed interests in ancient works led to critical reassessment of the products of the classical antiquity. The Moderns' attack on ancient authority in literary criticism had a parallel movement in the rise of scientific inquiry, which subsequently extended to systems of politics and religion.

Another notable translation scholar in the 17th century France is **Gaspar de Tende**④ (1618-1697), who published a popular treatise on translation in 1660. In his book he discussed Latin-French translation from language teaching, putting forward nine specific rules for Latin-French translation. These rules cover the common topics in translation theory, ranging from how to be faithful to the original spirit, what linguistic means to use in order to render the original niceties, how to avoid additional modifiers without damaging the original ease and smoothness, how to adjust the original sentence construction and how to capture and reproduce the stylistic excellence, and so on. He went the middle road between the two extremes. He was an ardent lover, but not a slavish imitator, of classical antiquity.

Also involved in the debate was **Pierre Daniel Huet**⑤(1630-1721), a French churchman and scholar, chief editor of the *Delphin Classics*, an edition of the Latin classics. Born to parents who died in his early childhood, Huet was raised by neglectful foster parents. He began to draw attention when he was 18, with a translation of Longus' Greek romance *Daphnis ad Chloe*⑥(1648). Later he translated Origen's⑦ *Commentaries on St. Matthew* into Latin. He collected his observations on translation in the book *De Interpretatione* (*On Translation*)

---

① 梅齐利亚克:17 世纪法国数学家、语言学家、诗人和古典文化学者。

② 萨西:波尔·罗雅尔修道院神父、17 世纪法国神学家和人文主义学者。他翻译的《波尔·罗雅尔圣经》在 18 世纪的法国传布最广。

③ 泰伦斯:生于希腊的古罗马剧作家。其喜剧如《福尔弥昂》和《阿德尔菲》以巧妙的幽默和精彩的对话为主要特色。

④ 坦德:法国 17 世纪翻译家、学者。

⑤ 于埃:法国 17 世纪神学家、学者。

⑥《达夫尼斯和郝洛亚》:公元 2 世纪古希腊作家郎戈斯的田园爱情小说。

⑦ 奥瑞金:公元 3 世纪亚历山大城最知名的神学家和《圣经》学者。

(1661), in which he discussed the principles of translation in the form of dialogue.

He advocated accurate translation and criticized the Moderns like Desmaret de Saint-Sorlin[①] (1595-1676) and D'Ablancoutrt. In his Latin *On Translation*, he strongly attacked flexible translators like Cicero, Horace and Jerome, and the *Belles Infideles* of his day.

> *If anyone takes on the role of translator, his efforts should especially be focused, not on using his skill in writing, if by chance he has some such skill, and not on deceiving people with the charm of his language, but on displaying in his own words the author, whom he is trying to translate, as if the author were to be preserved in a mirror and picture. The translator should take away every deceptive ornaments as if it were a covering or, rather, as if he were scrubbing off an overlying pigment from the original color.* (quoted in Robinson, 2006: 164)

In Heut's opinion, a good translator should let the readers see the real author as he is, not the shape the translator thinks the author should assume. He should show the original author in his true colors, not to dress him up under the excuse of making him prettier or easier to understand.

> *I say that the best method of translation is when the translator adheres very closely, first, to the meaning of the author, then also to the actual words themselves, if the capacities of the two languages permit, and finally, when he sketches the innate character of the author, insofar as can be done, and concentrates on one thing only, namely, faithfully to present him diminished in no way and increased in no way, but whole and very like himself in every way.* (quoted in Robinson, 2006: 167)

Huet's theory won the approval of some celebrated classicists and remained current among many translators today.

Involved in the practice and argument about classical translation were two religious groups known as **Jesuit**[②] and **Jansenism**[③], who represented two rivaling schools of Catholic theology in France. Jansenism was a distinct movement within the Catholic Church. It had its theological centre at the Parisian convent of Port-Royal, which was a center of high education as well as a haven for writers including du Vergier[④], Antoine Arnauld[⑤], Pierre Nicole[⑥], Blaise Pascal[⑦], and Jean Racine. The Jansenist group of Port Royal strived for accuracy in their translation of religious texts. Arnauld (1612-1694), among others, translated with accuracy the *New*

---

① 索尔兰:法国作家、剧作家,法兰西学术院创立人之一。

② 耶稣会派:罗马天主教教派耶稣会的成员,组织严密,教规严明,其成员均为男性,在教育、学术研究和文化创造方面均有贡献。

③ 詹森派:天主教教派内詹森的信条及信众。詹森派强调宿命论,反对自由意志和耶稣会的道德论学说(或然说),认为得救只能靠上帝恩宠,主张虔诚地严守教会法规。被罗马天主教会视为异端。

④ 恩·杜·弗吉尔:法国天主教牧师,将詹森派学说传入法国。

⑤ 阿尔诺:17 世纪法国天主教神学家、数学家、詹森派领袖。

⑥ 尼科:17 世纪法国最知名的詹森派领袖。

⑦ 帕斯卡:法国 17 世纪哲学家。

Testament and theological works by Augustine, yet the effect was unhappy because they lacked the original enthusiasm and their language so stiff to the point of unreadable. Amid the general hostility between Catholics and Protestants across Europe, there arose the Jesuits, another group of zealous Catholics who detested Protestantism and intended to reform Catholicism from within to make it less vulnerable. To this end the Jesuits promoted elementary education to eliminate illiteracy among Catholics, which they saw as a serious impediment to Catholicism. The Jesuit schools in central and Eastern Europe contributed much to the Counter-Reformation in those lands. Heavy emphasis was placed on the mastery of Latin in the Jesuit schools, not only because it was the liturgical language of the Catholic Church, but also because it was necessary for serious study in all disciplines. Translations made under the Jesuit influence, by contrast, invariably exhibited a tendency to place the language above the substance. Jesuit translators evangelized classics at the cost of the original message and spirit, sometimes to the damage of the original author. The inaccurate translation in the 17th-century France was more or less influenced by the Jesuits.

With the passage of time, the distinction became increasingly noticeable between the free translations of the moderns and accurate translations of the ancients. Up to the end of the 17th century, free translation, represented by the prevailing translation strategy known as the *Belles Infideles* was in the vogue, with only a few translators in favor of accurate translation. The free strategy continued well into the 18th century until the elegant and beautiful translations of the classics gradually lost appeal both as a literary genre and an instructional tool. It was gradually replaced by an interest in contemporary foreign works in the field of science and literature.

In the 17th and 18th century France, many classical poems were translated with poems, yet the general quality of the translations was not desirable. The controversy revived over translation of Homer between the moderns and the ancients. At the center of the debate was the question: should Homer be translated into poetry or prose.

Antoine Houdar de La Motte① (1672-1731) was a French author, a champion of the moderns in the revived controversy of the ancients and moderns. He knew no Greek, but he made a verse translation (1714) based on Anne Dacier's 1699 prose translation of the Greek *Iliad*. In his poetical version of the *Iliad*, La Motte abridged and altered to suit his own taste. In the preface to the translation he defended the moderns and his work: "I have taken the liberty of changing whatever I thought disagreeable. I am a translator in many parts and an original author in many others." (quoted in Lefevere, 2004a: 29) La Motte insisted that the translator had the right to treat the original as he deemed proper. He announced in self-flattery that he condensed 24 volumes of *Iliad* to half as long and still thought it too long. He stated in the introduction to his translation of the *Iliad*:

---

① 拉莫特:法国作家、文艺批评家、法兰西学术院成员,散文观点独到,文笔优美。在17~18世纪围绕古典作品的翻译而再度兴起的古今之争当中,拉莫特是最坚定的厚今派。

—I have reduced the twenty-four books of the Iliad to twelve, which are even shorter than Homer's. At first sight you might think that this could only be done at the expense of many important features. But if you pause to reflect that repetitions make up more than one sixth of the Iliad, and that the anatomical details of wounds and the long speeches of the fighters make up a lot more, you will be right in thinking that it has been easy for me to shorten the poem without losing any important features of the plot. I flatter myself with the thought that I have done just that, and I even think I have brought together the essential parts of the action in such a way that they are shaped into a whole better proportioned and more sensible in my abbreviated version than in the original. (quoted in Lefevere, 2004a: 29)

Upon publication, the translation won the approval of the King, and la Motte made a large fortune out of his work. But Homer by La Motte's translation was very bad from poetic perspective, so bad that the readers doubted if the French poetry form was able to express Homer in his original splendor.

4.2.4 Madame Dacier

Anne Marie Dacier① (1654-1720), better known as **Madame Dacier**, was a famous prose translator of Homer and one of the central figures of the debate.

Dacier began to receive her classical education at 11 by her father, who, in the course of teaching her brother, discovered her special gift in classics. She soon outshone her brother and once told her father that a French translation of Quintus Curtius Rufus②, a favorite with her father, was defective in many serious respects. She received her name *Dacier* from Andre Dacier, one of her father's classical students she married.

In her twenties Dacier made a prose version of Anacreon③ and Sappho④ in 1681, and in the next few years, she published prose versions of Terence⑤ and some of the plays of Plautus⑥ and Aristophanes⑦. In 1699 she produced a prose translation of the *Iliad* and of the *Odyssey*, upon which her reputation in French literature was based. Dacier's version was the first Homer that was known to many French men of letters including Antoine Houdar de la Motte, who was her major opponent in the famous literary controversy over translation of Homer between the moderns and ancients.

Dancier's translation of Homer was made amid the heated debate between ancients and

① 达西埃夫人:法国女文学评论家、翻译家和编辑,于1711年和1716年把荷马史诗《伊利亚特》和《奥德赛》译成了极其典雅的散文。

② 鲁菲斯:公元1世纪的古罗马历史学家,著有《亚历山大史》。

③ 阿那克里翁:古希腊诗人,诗歌以歌颂爱情和美酒为主题。

④ 萨福:约公元前7~前6世纪古希腊著名的女抒情诗人,写过不少情诗、婚歌、颂神诗、铭辞。

⑤ 泰伦斯:生于希腊的古罗马剧作家。其喜剧如《福尔弥昂》和《阿德尔菲》以巧妙的幽默和精彩的对话为主要特色。

⑥ 普劳图斯:罗马喜剧作家,其作品影响了莎士比亚和莫里哀。

⑦ 阿里斯托芬:约公元5~4世纪古希腊早期喜剧代表作家,有"喜剧之父"之称,现存《阿卡奈人》《骑士》《和平》《鸟》《蛙》等11部。

moderns across France and England. She sided firmly with the ancients against such figures as Charles Perrault[①](1628-1703) and Bernard de Fontenelle[②](1657-1757). She wrote *Of the Causes of the Corruption of Taste* in 1714 in defense of her translation against la Motte.

Madame Dancier was a fervent worshipper of Homer, determined to repair the damage incurring in inaccurate translation that had falsified her idol. She translated *Iliad* and *Odyssey* into prose, taking pains to model the original style line after line. Through her own translation she demonstrated to the world that Homer was modest and urbane, not vulgar and tough as was understood by the Moderns. She restored Homer's reputation in the minds of the French readers and received high respect, which was rare for women of her day.

Dacier made insightful remarks on translation in the notable preface to her *Iliad*, which is good prose style in its own right. Her preface was superior to the one written by John Dryden[③](1631-1700), a more renowned English contemporary. She underscored the inaccessible beauties of Homer and the failures of many modern translations, discussed the merits and demerits of prose and verse translation of Homer, and insisted that she was translating not for the learned few scholars, but for the greater number of readers. Dacier insisted that Homer should better be translated into prose:

> *A translator, in prose, may say all that Homer has said; this he can never do in verse, especially in our tongue, where he must of necessity be always altering, retrenching, adding—Our poetry is not capable of expressing all the beauties of Homer, and soaring to his heights—I am not afraid to say, and could be able to prove it, that poets translated into verse cease to be poets.* (quoted in Robinson, 2006: 188, my ellipsis)

She distinguished "servile" from "noble and generous translation", which resembles the vague division of translation word-for-word and sense-for-sense. Only that a "noble" translation stays true to the "letter" or formal qualities of the original too.

> *When I speak of a translation of prose, I do not mean a servile translation, I mean a noble and generous translation which, adhering strictly to the way of thinking in the original, searches out the beauties of its language and represents the images without retaining the words. The first sort of translation becomes unfaithful through too scrupulous a faithfulness, for it loses the spirit to preserve the letter, which is the work of cold and barren genius; whereas the other, though chiefly aiming to retain the spirit, yet fails not, in its greatest liberties, to retain the letter; and by means of its bold but true strokes becomes not only a faithful copy of its original, but even a second original; which cannot be executed but by a solid, noble, and fruitful genius.* (quoted in Robinson, 2006: 189)

In his letter to Madame Dancier (1720), Voltaire revealed his modernist view about

① 佩罗:17 世纪法国诗人、学者、律师,其童话作品《鹅妈妈的故事或寓有道德教训的往日故事》称颂一时。
② 枫丹奈尔:18 世纪法国哲学家、作家。
③ 德莱顿:17 世纪英国剧作家、评论家、桂冠诗人,在欧洲文学批评史上享有盛誉。

translation of Homer: "I am convinced that we have two or three poets in France who would be able to translate Homer very well; but I am equally convinced that nobody will read them unless they soften and embellish almost everything because, Madame, you have to write for your own time, not for the past." (quoted in Lefevere, 2004a : 30)

4.2.5 Batteux

The translator who made significant contributions to translation theorization was **Charles Batteux**① (1713-1780), a French philosopher and writer on aesthetics. His works on literature and the fine arts and lengthy passages on translation were well-known across Europe. He was a prolific translator, translating the moral writings of Epicurus② and the poetics of Aristotle, Horace, etc. He contributed *Principles of Literature* (1747-1748), the fifth part (*Principles of Translation*) devoted to a detailed discussion of translation.

He meant his principles primarily for young readers and practicing translators, for he thought that the general assumptions on translation are too general to be significant to translation performance. He believed that the chief translation difficulty lie not in comprehending the original, which could be resolved with the assistance of good editions and commentaries, and above all, by examining the natural relations and connections of the ideas. The greatest difficulty consist in giving the source text as it is to the readers in its true colors, degrees, shades, without adding or diminishing or misplacing, for to do this requires as much genius and taste as to compose, or even more. He went on to observe that the translator's job is different from the author's in that "The translator has nothing in his own power; he is obliged in everything to follow his author, and to submit to all his variations with an unreserved compliance" (quoted in Robinson, 2006: 196). In chapter three of the same essay he maintained that "languages are like men, who have one common nature which unites, and peculiarities which separate them" (quoted in Robinson, 2006: 196). If, in the course of translating, the original peculiarities were transferred into the target language, there would be Latinism, Anglicism, Gallicism and Hebraism, etc. Batteux saw languages as consisting of two aspects, that is, words and their arrangements. Languages have also two peculiarities: that of the words and that of their turns, and ways of expression. A French word and a French sentence structure may be Latinized. He believed that the first principle of translation is "to leave the turns of expression such as they are in the author, when the two languages equally admit them" (quoted in Robinson, 2006: 197). From this cardinal principle many secondary rules of translation may be derived as below:

1. That the order of things, whether facts or reasonings, is not to be altered; since that

① 巴特:法国 18 世纪哲学家、文艺理论家。

② 伊壁鸠鲁:古希腊哲学家、无神论者,伊壁鸠鲁学派的创始人,主张要达到不受干扰的宁静状态,提倡享乐主义。

order is the same in all languages; seeing it depends on the nature of man, rather than on the particular genius of nations;

2. That we ought also to preserve the order of the ideas, or at least of the members;
3. That the periods should be preserved, how long soever they be; because a period is but a thought, composed of several other thoughts, connected together by intrinsic relations; and this connection is the life of those thoughts, and the principle object of the speaker.
4. It follows that all the conjunctions ought to be preserved. They are, as it were, the articulations of the members; One ought not to change their meaning, nor their position;
5. That all adverbs should be placed beside the verb, before or after, according as the harmony or energy permits. It is always on these two principles that their place is regulated in Latin;
6. That symmetrical sentences be rendered with their symmetry, or in terms equivalent;
7. That bright thoughts, in order to preserve the same degree of clearness, should be nearly of the same extent of words. If they are contracted, there is danger of obscuring; if extended, of weakening their luster;
8. That we must preserve the figures and forms of the thoughts, because the thoughts are the same in all minds: they are capable of taking everywhere the same arrangement, the same configuration, the same attitude.
9. That the proverbs, which are popular maxims, and which are never but short pithy things, should be rendered by other proverbs, or by phrases so natural that they deserve to become such.
10. That any paraphrase is faulty and imperfect; it is no longer translating; it is commenting. However, where there is no other way to communicate the meaning, necessity excuses the translator.
11. That we must entirely give up the expression in the text translated when the sense requires it for perspicuity, the sentiment for vivacity, or the harmony for delight.

(quoted in Robinson, 2006: 197-198)

Batteux believed that the ideas may be presented in different forms and still be the same, and be compounded or decompounded in the words used to express them. They may be presented by way of verb, of adjective, of substantive, or of adverb. Batteux made an ingenious metaphor of the translator's job: "he will act only like a traveler, who, for his convenience, exchanges one piece of gold for several of silver, sometimes several pieces of silver for one of gold." (quoted in Robinson, 2006: 198) He agreed that there are certain things that are incapable of translation and there are also "certain things depending on the taste, and on the manners of the people, which cannot be transferred" (quoted in Robinson, 2006: 199).

Batteux was a practitioner of his own theory, as was illustrated by his translation of Aristotle's *Poetics*. The translation kept the original word order and followed the original sentence length. But his insistence on literalism came in conflict with his emphasis on perspicuity, vivacity, and delight.

4.2.6 France's Infatuation with the Gothic Novels①

In the 17th century France, English culture was little known and studied. With the rise of British Empire in the world, there appeared a wave of interest in England and English literature in the 18th-century France. The English language and culture were rapidly catching on among polite French society. Three types of novels were particularly influential at the time: sentimental②, Gothic and historical③. Amid the general political and military hostility between England and France over overseas territorial disputes in North America, cultural exchange continued well into the late 18th century across the strait, notably in the massive and systematic import of English Gothic novels to France.

English Gothic novel dominated the book market for nearly fifty years, exerting a tremendous influence upon French literary aesthetics until it gradually died out in the 1830s. The primary period of translation, though, was from 1790 to 1800. The most translated Gothic writers included William Godwin④ (1759-1836), Ann Radcliffe⑤ (1764-1823), Matthew Gregory Lewis⑥ (1775-1818) and Mary Shelly⑦. As time went on, the French translations appeared almost simultaneously with their English originals on the other side of the channel. Two translations of Lewis' *The Monk* were made in 1797, less than a year after the publication of the original in England. Godwin's *St. Leon* came out in 1799 in France, the same year when the English original met the English audience. The same went for Radcliffe's *The Italian* (1797). Some bestselling originals were available in several French versions for literary

---

① 哥特小说:18 世纪后期在英国出现的一种通俗小说流派,以霍勒斯·沃波尔(Horace Walpole)的《奥特兰托城堡》(*The Castle of Ortanto*)为发端,18 世纪末达到高潮,以惊险神秘、阴森恐怖为特征。后来因为情节过度离奇而逐渐衰落,但哥特式手法影响了勃朗特姐妹、爱伦坡、霍桑、狄更斯等作家。

② 感伤主义小说:18 世纪后期欧洲资产阶级启蒙运动中出现的文学思潮。因英国作家斯特恩的小说《在法国和意大利的感伤旅行》而得名。又称"主情主义"。排斥新古典主义崇尚的克制和理性,认为感情高于理性,将感情的自然表达升华为艺术,也称"前浪漫主义"。

③ 历史小说:以历史事件或人物为题材进行适度虚构创作的小说流派,司各特的《威弗利》(1814)是最有代表性的历史小说,为 19 世纪现实主义小说奠定了基础。

④ 戈德温:英国作家、牧师,创作了大量的小说、儿童文学、传记、剧本和历史剧等作品。

⑤ 拉德克利夫:英国女作家。以写浪漫主义的哥特小说见长,被司各特称为"第一位写虚构浪漫主义小说的女诗人"。作品融恐怖、焦虑、悬念和浪漫主义情调于一体。代表作有《林中艳史》(1791)、《奥多芙的秘密》(*The Mysteries of Udolpho*)(1794)和《意大利人》(*The Italian*)等。

⑥ 刘易斯:英国作家和剧作家,代表作为哥特小说《修道士》(*The Monk*)。

⑦ 玛丽·雪莱:英国著名小说家,因其 1818 年创作里文学史上第一部科幻小说《弗兰肯斯坦》(又译《科学怪人》),而被誉为"科幻小说之母"。她是英国著名浪漫主义诗人雪莱的第二任妻子。

rivalry. Godwin's *Caleb Williams*[①], for example, was translated three times from 1795 and 1797. Anna Maria Mackenzie's *Fratricide*[②] was rendered in two separate translations too, one in 1798 and the other in 1799. *The Monk* and *The Italian* were both put in two separate renderings. (quoted in Delisle & Woodsworth, 1995: 211)

It needed to be pointed out that not all Gothic novels were received with similar enthusiasm in France. Horace Walpole's *The Castle of Otranto*[③] (1764), which gave the name to the genre and was reprinted several times in England, received only lukewarm response in France perhaps because it was too grotesque and disturbing. Lewis' *The Monk*, although immoral, was far more popular with the French market, witnessed 25 editions and was immediately adapted for the theatre. The translators of the Gothic novels were named in the catalogue of the booksellers. (quoted in Delisle & Woodsworth, 1995: 211)

The underlying reason for this intense translation rivalry is not purely commercial; it is also attributable to ideological and psychological causes. Gothic novels emphasized the grotesque, mysterious, and desolate. They carried subtle values that opposed papist Catholicism and fueled anticlerical sentiments among general French readers. The devotion to the supernatural, the demonic, the terror, and the gloom distracted the readers from the general political and military tension in French society[④]. In one word the genre provided a psychological asylum for the French viewers.

To appeal to the readers' taste, the translators gradually followed the tradition of "unfaithful beauty" in opposition to the rising literalism across the whole Europe at the beginning of the 19th century. They made bold to change the titles, delete passages and entire pages and even introduce entirely new elements, all for the purpose of pleasing the popular taste of their French readers. When Bernard de la Mare translated Sophia Lee's *The Recess* (1783-1785)[⑤], he abridged the work under the excuse that the events were more bizarre than interesting. The word "God" was replaced by a French word meaning "the supreme being". Similar corrections and improvements were common among Gothic translators, who only cared for the share of their translation in book market. Gothic translators served as moral censors and literary revisers of the English originals so as to make them suit the reading habits of the French readers, to achieve good French style, to bring out the potential of the French language and to conform to the current literary norms.

Under this general enthusiasm for foreign literature, there came in France a strange

---

① 《凯莱布·威廉斯》：戈德温的哥特小说。

② 麦肯兹的哥特式小说《弑兄》。

③ 《奥特兰托城堡》：霍勒斯·沃波尔的成名作，副标题为"哥特小说"，哥特小说由此得名。

④ 指 1789～1799 年的法国资产阶级革命，是法国和全欧洲政治社会剧烈变动时期。法国大革命推翻了统治法国多个世纪的君主制封建制度和宗教特权，新兴的天赋人权、君主立宪、三权分立、主权在民等的民主思想深入人心。革命期间充满暴力和血腥，影响波及整个欧洲。

⑤ 《幽屋》：索菲亚·李的哥特式作品。

phenomenon: every text, French original included, assumed the look of a translation. As English texts enjoyed a higher reputation of foreign literatures, the notation "translated from English" became a mark of prestige in book market and many original French books claimed themselves translations of English authors. Some famous French authors used the prestige of English text to promote their literary career. This was a period of pseudo-translation or literary hoaxes. Translation became free adaptation, open imitation or a trick played by authors in search of literary fame. French writers wrote with an imagined presence of the source text, and the borderline between translation and original writing was further blurred. Many translators listed themselves on the title page as authors without a qualm. Retranslation of the same source text and back-translation of thc translatcd text only further complicated the scene of translation. Consequently, the notion of translation was abused. (quoted in Delisle & Woodsworth, 1995: 213)

The abusive translation and plausible contribution of the French Gothic novel had double effects on French literature. The immediate result was that the genre was soon stereotyped, degraded into a low parody and finally rejected by the French readers as full of cliché and mediocre stuff. In the long term, however, it inspired the domestic literature in raw materials, plot development, settings, etc., providing sources of inspiration for later French writers like Victor Hugo.

4.2.7 French Translation of Shakespeare

For over a hundred years after his death, the English poet was almost unknown in France. **Francois Marie Arouet Voltaire**① (1694-1778) made the name of Shakespeare familiar to France and was regarded as an authority on the English poet. Shakespeare's plays were an antithesis to French theatrical classicism that emphasized order, rule and moderation. Voltaire's reaction to Shakespeare was mixed: he was at once attracted by his genius and force and disgusted by his disregard of the rules of unities, by his mingling of the comic and the tragic, by his description of the low people, by his scenes of violence, and by his vulgarity and coarseness of speech. Voltaire translated *Julius Caesar* with accuracy.

> *I put into prose what is prose in Shakespeare's tragedy and I used blank verse where Shakespeare uses it. What is lowly and familiar has been translated in the same way. I have tried to soar with the author where he soars and I have taken great care not to add or take away anything where he is turgid and bombastic.* (quoted in Lefevere, 2004a: 40)

He hastened to call the attention from French dramatists to his strange and wonderful discovery of Shakespeare. Voltaire's brilliant criticism aroused general interest in Shakespeare's

① 伏尔泰:法国启蒙思想家、文学家、哲学家,18 世纪法国资产阶级启蒙运动的旗手。

work. In 1730, Montesquieu① wrote that he had noted the difference between the two dramatic systems. But La Place's translation undermined Voltaire's authority as a Shakespearean critic, triggering another spirited discussion on Shakespeare.

Pierre Antoine de la Place②(1707-1793) published *Théatre Anglais* in 1745, which contained *Othello*, the third part of *Henry VI*, *Richard III*, *Hamlet* and *Macbeth*. Upon the publication of the book, there appeared seven reviews in high praise of the translation and in spirited discussion of Shakespeare. The initial volumes being so popular, he followed them up by the other two, which contained *Cymbeline*③, *Julius Caesar*, *Antony and Cleopatra*, *Timon of Athens*④ and *The Merry Wives of Windsor*. La Place selected these plays for translation because he wanted to acquaint his country fellow with Shakespeare's wide range of subject.

He adopted a controversial translation strategy, namely, he translated the dramatic paragraphs in full and the less interesting paragraphs only in summary. Of all these plays, he translated only *Richard III* in its entirety; as for the rest of the plays he summarized what seemed to him the less important scenes in a connecting narrative. He frequently omitted whole scenes, gave merely an analysis of others, and passed over important passages. In consequence, the original thought was distorted and the meaning changed. He translated Shakespeare mostly in prose, with a few rhymed lines at intervals. The result was a mixture of both prose and verse. Strictly speaking, his translation should be more properly called adaptation. But it pleased the French readers and was counted as the formal debut of Shakespeare in France.

In the preface to his translation, he gave a high opinion of Shakespeare, of his disregard of the unities and his scenes of violence, which offended sensitive French taste for drama. Although very mediocre as a translation his work marked an important epoch in the history of French dramatic taste. It diffused the knowledge of Shakespeare, offered an easy means for the study of him, introduced new and much-needed elements for dramatic reform, and imported a distinct addition to French literature.

The Dramatis **Jean-Francois Ducis**⑤(1733-1816) is another important translator, or rather, adaptor of Shakespeare after La Place. He is one of those translators who translated from the language of which he did not know a word. His ignorance of the English language left him at the mercy of the translations of Pierre Letourneur⑥(1736-1788) and of Pierre de la Place.

---

① 孟德斯鸠:法国伟大的启蒙思想家、法学家,也是近代欧洲国家较早系统研究古代东方社会与法律文化的学者之一。著有《论法的精神》《波斯人信札》《罗马盛衰原因论》等。

② 拉普拉斯:法国翻译家、学者。

③ 《辛白林》:莎士比亚根据薄伽丘的故事创作的关于不列颠国王辛白林的浪漫喜剧。

④ 《雅典的泰门》是莎士比亚悲剧时期的最后一部作品,也是莎士比亚最晦涩难懂的一部作品,作品结构怪异,并留下许多空白,常被认为是未完成的作品、多个作家的作品,或尝试性作品。

⑤ 杜西:法国剧作家,编译过莎士比亚作品。

⑥ 勒图尔纳:法国学者,完整翻译过莎士比亚作品。

His *Hamlet* (1769) and *Romeo and Juliet* (1772) were more successful. *Macbeth* in 1783 was not well received, but *Othello* in 1792, supported by the superb acting, obtained immense applause. His aim was to unite the dramatic system of Voltaire with Shakespearian subjects, and to adapt the plays of the English dramatist to the French stage. Like la Place, Ducis meant his *Hamlet* in line with the classical French theatrics without any regard for fidelity. His *Hamlet* is a curious mixture of Shakespeare and his own idea on French theatre. In his *Hamlet*, 23 characters of Shakespeare were reduced to only five: Hamlet, Claudius, Polonius, Gertrude, and Ophelia. The apparition of Hamlet's father became a dream, Aphelia's insanity was removed, and the incestuous king and his queen were put to death in the end. A confidant was introduced for Hamlet, and another for Gertrude. Ophelia was made the daughter of Claudius①, and the whole play turned upon the plots of Claudius to dethrone Hamlet. The tomb-diggers, as they were low and vulgar, were removed outright from the story, to cater to the fine taste of French viewers. Still, *Hamlet* of Ducis appealed very much to the French audience. Encouraged by the success, Ducis ventured to try his skill still further. In 1772 he produced *Romeo and Juliet* which had little in common with Shakespeare except the name and the rivalry between the houses of Capulet and Montague. The plot was different, the characters were different, the motif different, and the scenic arrangement different. Ducis also provided an alternative ending to *Othello*.

Pierre Le Tourneur (1737-1788) translated complete works of Shakespeare, the first volumes of which appeared in 1776 and the last in 1783. These first two volumes contained, besides much introductory matter, translations of *Othello*, *The Tempest* and *Julius Caesar*. The volumes were greeted with enthusiasm by the public and incurred a violent storm of criticism and protest from Voltaire and his friends, the most picturesque and one of the fiercest wars in the history of literature. The entire literary world was divided into two camps. The conservatives defended French drama and decried the English poet; the liberals on the other side cherished a tolerant and impartial judgment of the English poet and acclaimed the value and power of English play. Until the publication of the first two volumes, Shakespeare had appeared to the French audience not in the true glory, but in a kind of ridiculous travesty. Le Tourneur was the first translator who noticed Shakespeare's unique style and set more emphasis on faithfulness to the original. His translation was not only the first complete translation of the English poet, but the first that had real literary value and inspired all other French translations of Shakespeare down to the middle of the 19th century.

He maintained that slavish literality in letters could only result in unfaithfulness to the spirit. And literal translation in his reference was faithfulness to the original spirit. He disapproved modifying and improving the original in conformity with French taste and insisted

---

① 《哈姆雷特》的次要剧情是他与奥菲利亚的爱情，奥菲利亚为国王大臣波隆尼尔的女儿，克劳狄斯是弑兄娶嫂、篡夺王位的新国王。

that the original image and the spoken language should be transferred over.

Translation of Shakespeare of the 18th century was merely a prelude compared to that of the 19th century, when Shakespeare was introduced to France in real earnest and triggered a craze for the study of the English playwright. From 1800 to 1910 alone, at least 8 complete works of Shakespeare were published, the most notable of which was made by François-Victor Hugo[①] (1828-1873). With the assistance of his father, the renowned French writer Victor Hugo[②], Hugo the young translated Shakespeare's complete works from 1859-1867. The translation retained the poetic rhythm of the original drama and was glorified as the second milestone translation of Shakespeare in France. Its impact surpassed the versions of Le Tourneur at the end of the 18th century. Many of the translations were collected in *Shakespeare's Complete Works* edited by Gide[③] in 1950.

The Enlightenment in France culminated in the great *Encyclopédie*[④] (1751-1772) chiefly edited by Denis Diderot (1713-1784) with contributions by hundreds of leading intellectuals, notably Voltaire (1694-1778), Rousseau (1712-1778) and Montesquieu (1689-1755). Some 25,000 copies of the 35 volume encyclopedia were sold, half of them outside France. These new intellectual strains spread to urban centers across Europe through translation, notably England, Scotland, the German states, the Netherlands, Poland, Russia, Italy, Austria, Spain.

4.2.8 Translations in the 19th-Century France

In the 19th century there came another culmination in the translation of a profusion of English, German, Italian, Spanish and Latin literatures. With the rise of romanticism in Germany, French translation returned back to literalism in the 19th century, seeking to "transfer the creative power of great writer of other languages into their own" (quoted in Baker, 1998: 413).

Translation strategy of this period was determined by the status of the original work: whether it was a classic or contemporary work. Paul-Emile Littre[⑤] (1801-1881), for instance, translated the first part of the *Iliad* into a medieval French verse used before the 17th century. In 1820, Madame de Stael[⑥] (1766-1817) published her essay on the importance of translation

---

① 弗朗索瓦－维克多·雨果：法国19世纪文学家雨果的儿子，莎士比亚戏剧的著名翻译家。

② 雨果：法国19世纪前期积极浪漫主义文学运动的代表作家，作品包括《巴黎圣母院》(1831年)和《悲惨世界》(1862年)。

③ 纪德：法国著名作家，著有日记及小说，1947年获诺贝尔文学奖。作品探讨逆境中人的隔绝孤独以及对个性的追求。

④ 《百科全书》：由法国启蒙思想家、哲学家丹尼·狄德罗主编的百科全书。它把当时全部知识汇编为一部以字母顺序排列的多卷本图书，传播启蒙运动思想，是启蒙运动的杰出成果。

⑤ 利特雷：法国19世纪著名哲学家、词典编纂者。

⑥ 斯达尔夫人：法国女作家，积极浪漫主义的前驱，对法国浪漫主义文学起过一定作用。

to the national literature and culture. In the preface to the *Iliad* Leconte de Lisle① announced that the era of *Belles infidels* was over. The beautiful but unfaithful translation was replaced by the style that kept closer to the original. The romantic period aimed at reproducing the strangeness of the foreign text. Translation grew into an important literary genre on an equal footing with original construction. Many classics were retranslated for the purpose of restoring the ancients to their reputation. And to this end translations strived for accuracy.

A large quantity of English works was translated during the time. Among the most translated were Shakespeare, Milton, Byron, Coleridge, Shelly, Scott and Dickens. Goethe and Schiller of Germany②, Dante of Italy and some ballads from Spain were also introduced. Another interesting practice in the 19th-century France is that verse translations went in parallel with prose translation of the same poems. And as the difficulty of verse translation was recognized, many poems were translated into prose.

François-René de **Chateaubriand**③(1768 -1848) was noted for his faithful and beautiful translation of Milton's *Paradise Lost*, one of the most remarkable translations in French literature. **Gérard de Nerval**④(1808 -1855) earned his reputation with his prose translation of Goethe's *Faustus* (1828). The translation was so good that Goethe, after reading it in 1830, considered it better than his original. In the 1840s, Nerval introduced Heinrich Heine's⑤ poems to French readers.

Another notable French translator of American literature was **Charles Baudelaire**⑥(1821-1867), who, in 1846 and 1847, became acquainted with the works of Edgar Allan Poe⑦. In the tales and poems of Poe, Baudelaire discovered something he announced that had long existed in his own brain but never taken shape. As a poet, Baudelaire was surprisingly like Poe in many respects. Like Poe, Baudelaire developed the macabre and supernatural turn of mind; Like Poe, Baudelaire believed in the doctrine of original sin, denounced democracy and the idea of progress and of man's natural goodness; more interestingly, Poe held a disdainful aristocratic attitude similar to Baudelaire's dandy. Poe even had a similar life experience as Baudelaire: they both struggled with illness, poverty, and melancholy throughout much of their life. Baudelaire saw his parallel in Poe and strived to be Poe's parallel in French literature. Up to 1865, Baudelaire was largely engaged in translating Poe's works, which were generally praised as among the best translations of Poe. The most notable translations included

① 李勒:19 世纪法国“高蹈派”诗人的杰出代表,著有《古诗》(1852)、《野诗》(1862)及《悲诗》(1884)等。

② 歌德和席勒:均为德国浪漫主义作家。

③ 夏多布里昂:法国浪漫主义作家、政治家、外交家和历史学家。

④ 奈瓦尔:法国浪漫主义诗人、散文家和翻译家。

⑤ 海涅:19 世纪德国浪漫主义诗人。

⑥ 波德莱尔:法国 19 世纪最著名的现代派诗人,象征派诗歌的先驱,代表作有《恶之花》。他翻译了爱伦・坡的《奇异故事集》《奇异故事续集》和《皮姆历险记》。

⑦ 爱伦・坡: 19 世纪美国诗人、小说家和文学评论家。

Extraordinary Stories (1852), *New Extraordinary Stories* (1857), *Aventures d'Arthur Gordon Pym*, and *Grotesque and Serious Stories* (1865), etc. His translation established Allan Poe's reputation in France before he was publicly recognized in his home country.

The retranslated literary classics included Virgil's *Eclogues*, *Pastoral Poems* and *Aeneid*, and Homer's epics. Practical and academic translations were growing at the same time. Classical works were retranslated like Aristotle's *Metaphysics*①, *Politics and Logic*. More contemporary works in the fields of medicine, natural science and geography were also translated. Paul-Emile Littre② retranslated the complete works of Hippocrates (1839-1863), Pliny's *Natural History* (1848-1850), David Friedrich Strauss's *Life of Jesus*③ (1839-1840) and Johannes Peter Müller's *Elements of Physiology*④ (1851).

Further Readings

Baker, Mona. *Routledge Encyclopedia of Translation Studies*. London & New York: Routledge, 1998.

Delisle, Jean & Judith Woodsworth. *Translators through History*. Amsterdam: John Benjamins Publishing Company, 1995.

Lefevere, Andre. *Translation/History/Culture: A Sourcebook*. Shanghai: Shanghai Foreign Language Education Press, 2004a.

Robinson, Douglas. *Western Translation Theory: From Herodotus to Nietzsche*. Shanghai: Foreign Language Teaching and Research Press, 2006.

Early modern period. From Wikipedia, the free encyclopedia. 2013-10-01. http://en.wikipedia.org/wiki/Modern_history.

谭载喜:《西方翻译简史》,商务印书馆 2004 年版。

Topics for Discussion

1. Do famous translations have some common qualities? What are they? Give your idea.

2. Do you think it is possible for a translation to be beautiful and faithful at the same time? If not, which quality do you think is more important?

3. Why were Gothic novels translated with such enthusiasm in late 18th-century France? Account for the phenomenon from socio-cultural perspective.

4. Comment on Batteus' 12 points on translation? Which of his points do you think may apply to translation between Chinese and English?

5. How do you like Dacier's division of translation into servile and noble and generous? Is

---

① 《形而上学》:古希腊哲学家亚里士多德的重要哲学著作,该书考察了人类知识的形成,进而提出关于普遍知识的理论,从根本上奠定了西方哲学思想的基本概念和问题。

② 利特雷:法国 19 世纪著名哲学家、词典编纂者。

③ 施特劳斯:19 世纪德国神学家,著有《耶稣传》。

④ 缪勒:德国 19 世纪生理学家和解剖学家,现代生理学的奠基人,著有《生理学手册》。

it an improvement on Cicero?

6. List at least four important French translators of Shakespeare and their contributions.

4.3 Translations in Modern Germany

Translation Terms

Translatability 可译性

In Modern German translation theories, it is generally accepted that translation between human languages is possible because underneath the seemingly different or unique languages lie the meanings that are present and transferable (Goethe, Schleiermacher, Humboldt). But this degree of translatability is limited because there is always difference between source text and translation (Humboldt). Schlegel held that the best poetic translation is an imperfect approximation.

Translation as a Communication 作为交际的翻译

Schleiermacher redefines translation as a communication not only across languages, but also within one's language or dialect, and in some cases involving rewording of one's own idea in a different way. Schlegel asserted that all acts of speaking and writing are forms of translation because the nature of communication is to decode and interpret messages received.

4.3.1 Socio-cultural Background

After the German Renaissance and German Reformation (1500-1650), humanism spread to the various German states and principalities. The Reformation and printing press combined to mark a major breakthrough in the spread of literacy. In spite of the Thirty Years' War① from 1618-1648, German literature entered one of the most fertile times of the Baroque period② (1600-1720). At that time, many writers reflected on the horrible experiences of the Thirty Years' War in poetry and prose. French classicism, a movement beginning in the early Baroque, with its emphasis on the rational, occupied a central position in arts, sciences and politics in the 17th- and 18th- century Europe. The most translated genre in Germany was French drama which embodied the highest level of French classicism. Not only the material but also the theatrical models were introduced into German theatre. The source languages of translation were diverse and for some time in the early 18th century the most prominent

① 三十年战争：由神圣罗马帝国的内战演变而成一次遍及全欧的大规模国际战争。这场战争是欧洲各国争夺利益、霸权以及宗教纠纷激化的产物，是现代史上耗时最长、极具破坏性的战争。德意志为主要战场，战争以波希米亚人民反抗奥地利帝国哈布斯堡王朝统治为肇始，最后以哈布斯堡王朝战败而告告终。

② 巴洛克：16 世纪下半期在欧洲兴起的一种艺术风格，以繁复夸饰、富丽堂皇、气势宏大、富于动感为特征。是反宗教改革的改革运动的产物，于 17 世纪达到鼎盛，18 世纪后逐渐衰落。

intermediary language was French.

German translation of English culture through the French language began early in the 18th century and reached its climax in the 1720s. Although some classics were available in the original language, most German translators preferred to use a French translation as their intermediate source text. Through the French mediation, the German readers learned about Locke, Pope, Addison, Defoe, Swift, Richardson and Fielding, etc. The most translated of English author was Shakespeare.

English play, with Shakespeare as the representative, was an antithesis to French theatrical classicism that emphasized order, rule and moderation, yet Shakespeare was translated the most in Germany, i. e., directly from English into German, read in the French translation or even in its English original. German scholars were interested in discussions on the deviations of Shakespearean plays from French theatrical convention and the idiosyncrasies of British novels. Christoph Martin Wieland[①] (1733-1813), an important Enlightenment writer, translated altogether 22 plays of Shakespeare from 1761 to 1766 into prose. The translations actually influenced the revolutionary literary movement known as Sturm und Drang (literally Storm and Stress)[②]. Johann Joachim Eschenburg[③] (1743-1820), German art critic and literary historian, produced the first complete prose translation of Shakespeare, which is virtually a revised edition of the translations by Wieland. Friedrich Schiller[④] (1759-1805) translated Shakespeare's *Mecbeth*[⑤]. Wilhelm Schlegel[⑥] (1772-1829) finished translating 13 of Shakespeare's plays by 1810. Ludwig Tieck[⑦] (1773-1853) translated the *Tempest*[⑧] and many other Elizabethan dramas. From 1818 to 1829, Johann Heinrich Voss[⑨] (1751 ~ 1826) published a translation of William Shakespeare's plays in 9 volumes with the help of his sons, though the result has been characterized as less successful than Schlegel's work. His translations displayed not only sound scholarship but also a thorough mastery of the laws of German diction and rhythm. Of all translated Shakespeare's plays, *Hamlet* occupied a central place in German literature.

As time went on, however, some German writers grew weary of the distorted British culture filtered through the French language. The 18th century witnessed the gradual change

---

① 维兰德:德国启蒙运动时期的重要作家,翻译过莎士比亚作品。

② 狂飙突进运动:18 世纪 70 年代至 80 年代初发生于德国的一场声势浩大的浪漫主义文学运动,是德国启蒙运动的继续和发展。运动的名称源出自德国作家克林格的剧本《狂飙突进》。运动高扬个人主体性,主张情感的自由表达,以摆脱启蒙运动的理性枷锁。

③ 艾森伯格:德国文艺评论家、文艺史学家。

④ 席勒:德国浪漫主义作家,著有历史剧如《唐·卡洛斯》(1787)和《华伦斯坦》(1798 ~ 1799)及说教长诗。

⑤ 《麦克白》:莎士比亚四大悲剧之一。

⑥ 施莱格尔:德国文学理论家、作家、语言学家。德国早期浪漫主义文学运动的创始人。

⑦ 蒂克:德国浪漫主义运动早期作家和批评家、翻译家。

⑧ 《暴风雨》:莎士比亚的最后一部完整戏剧。

⑨ 沃斯:德国诗人、翻译家。

from the general acceptance to the virtual rejection of English culture translated via the French language and culture. And this emancipation from French intellectual and cultural monopoly largely coincided with the general transition in German history of thought: the rise of German Romanticism and an independent German national literature. As a reaction against the perceived constraints of rationalism imposed by the Enlightenment and associated aesthetic movements (French Classicism), German literature entered *Sturm und Drang*, a proto-Romantic movement from the late 1760s to the early 1780s that promoted free expression of individual subjectivity, especially extremes of emotion. German romanticism broke the confines of literature into the field of translation, working a parallel movement in the thinking about translation that emphasized the importance of intuition and inspiration. Modern German translation thought was distinguished also for its clear philosophical aspect as the investigation on translation is typically posited within the general framework of human mind and innate character of language. Modern German translation research was also noted for its wide-ranging academic vision as it addressed more general issues of society and culture rather than the specific translation difficulties.

Classical antiquity was still translated during this time. Johann Heinrich Voss translated Homer's *Odyssey* in 1781 and *Iliad* in 1793, for which he was praised by Goethe as an expert on classical poetry. His translation of the *Odyssey* was considered the most successful. He also translated Hesiod①(1806), Theocritus②, Bion and Moschus③(1808), the whole of Virgil (1799), Horace (1806), Tibullus④(1810), Propertius⑤(1830) and selections from Ovid (1798).

4.3.2 Herder, Goethe and Schleiermacher

John Gottfried von Herder⑥(1744-1803) is a German philosopher, theologian, poet, literary critic and a leading figure in the periods of Enlightenment, the Sturm und Drang Movement, and Weimar Classicism⑦. Herder is a scholar of wide learning, working in ten to fifteen fields simultaneously and significantly influencing the future of each. It is generally acknowledged in German translation society, with exceptions to a few revivalists, that the translator should first of all be responsible to his mother tongue and make himself "morning star

① 赫西俄德:生活在大约公元前8世纪的古希腊诗人,代表作品有《工作与时日》和《赫拉克勒斯的盾》。

② 忒奥克里托斯、比恩和摩斯库斯均为古希腊田园诗人。

③ 比埃和摩斯科斯:均为古希腊田园诗人。

④ 提布卢斯:古罗马挽歌诗人。

⑤ 普罗佩提乌斯:古罗马挽歌诗人。

⑥ 赫尔德:德国18世纪文学复兴中的重要作家、哲学家、翻译家,影响了"狂飙运动"的兴起,被认为是德国浪漫主义的先驱,其史学思想则影响了20世纪历史学家布列锡格、斯宾格勒等人的历史观点。

⑦ 魏玛古典主义:欧洲文化文学思潮。魏玛古典主义者试图调和狂飙突进运动的浪漫主义,启蒙运动的理性主义和古典主义,从而创建一种新的人文主义思潮。其代表人物包括赫尔德、歌德、席勒和维兰德,特别是1788~1905年的歌德和席勒。

of a new day in our literature", in the language of Herder. (quoted in Robinson, 2006: 207)

Herder translated the *Tempest* with the German language that is closest in effect to Shakespeare's poetry form. He was concerned about the development of German literature through translation, which is scattered through more practical considerations like German poetry forms, the use of mythology, the role of criticism and philology in the development of a national literature.

In his book *On the New German Literature*: *Fragments*, Herder held that translating is an activity that touches on the essence of the works. He expounded the translator's duties and tasks, pointing out that the translator's task consisted in making the readers who know not a word of a foreign language understand the books written in that language. In other words, the translator's task is of a hermeneutic nature. Comprehending the original is an initial step before the translator leads the readers into the understanding of special qualities of the language, and beyond that, the original nation and its history.

In the same book, Herder constantly touched on German translations, mostly from classics. He was calling for an ideal translator who is at once a philosopher, philologist and poet. Such an ideal translator shall be the morning star of a new day in German literature. Concerning translation of Homer, he stated that, the French translators should adapt all things in Homer to their natural taste, rather than try to adapt themselves to the taste of Homer's time. Homer must enter France a captive, dolled up in conformity with current French fashion, so as not to offend the French readers. Where his peasant coarseness still shows he is ridiculed as a barbarian. But Herder maintained that as the poor Germans are still in want of a fatherland and a unified nation taste, they want to see Homer the way he is. If someone were to translate Homer with all his efforts as Homer is, it would be a timeless contribution to German literature and invaluable aid to writers of genius. He suggested that the translator of Homer should use Thomas Blackwell's① investigations on Homer as a valuable guide. Then he should translate Homer as Homer is, unlike the French translators, who prettified Homer to suit their taste. Notes and glosses in the highly critical spirit should guide the readers on this foreign tour of Homer.

Herder's theory on language and translation and other fields produced far-reaching effect upon all great romantic thinkers, from Goethe, Schlegel, Humboldt brothers, to Hegel.

Johann Wolfgang von Goethe② (1749-1832) is the most brilliant writer of Modern Germany. Despite his later rejection of the movement he is one of the leading figures of German Romanticism. He is the originator of the concept of Weltliteratur (world literature). Goethe is a polymath and his works cover a wide range: literature, theology, philosophy, pantheism, and science. His *Faust* is considered one of the greatest dramatic works of modern European

① 布莱克维尔:18 世纪苏格兰古典主义学者、历史学家。

② 歌德:18 世纪中叶到 19 世纪初德国和欧洲最重要的剧作家、诗人、思想家。

literature.

In 1774 Goethe wrote his most sensational and representative novel, *Die Leiden des jungen Werthers* (*The Sorrows of Young Werther*), which contributed to the romantic literary movement Sturm und Drang (storm and stress). For his wide learning and enormous popularity Goethe was invited in 1775 by the young duke of Weimar to Weimar, where he stayed for six decades until his death in 1832. In 1786 Goethe abandoned Romanticism for Grecian Classicism. Later in his spare time between government affairs he continued to write and research. As a polyglot, Goethe was capable of translating between Latin, Greek, English, French, Spanish, Italian, Persian, medieval High German and some Southern Slavic languages. He translated Italian sculptor Celline's① *Autobiography*, Spanish playwright Calderon's② plays and some works of French philosopher and Diderot③, all standard renderings that had deep influence upon European literature. Goethe gave his views on translation in his later writings *Poetry and Truth* (1811-1814), *West-oriental Anthology* (1819), *Letters to Carlyle*, etc.

Goethe's thoughts about translation are mainly based on his fundamental reflections on nature, human, society and culture. For Goethe, translation is a gateway to Western tradition and the broader world (especially the "Orient"). Since 1813, Goethe grew increasingly interested in China, particularly Chinese drama. In Chinese literature, Goethe discovered universal patterns of human life. He concluded that the Chinese literature had much in common with German literature, but the former was much brighter and purer and more ethical. On the basis of his comparative study of literatures, Goethe introduced the concept of Weltliteratur (world literature) in 1827 to describe the growing availability of texts from other nations, including translations from Sanskrit, Islamic and Serbian epic poetry. He thought that literatures shouldn't have a border and national literatures should depend on each other for survival and development.

> *I am more and more convinced that poetry is the universal possession of mankind, revealing itself everywhere and at all times in hundreds and hundreds of men... I therefore like to look about me in foreign nations, and advise everyone to do the same. National literature is now a rather unmeaning term; the epoch of world literature is at hand, and everyone must strive to hasten its approach.* ④

Goethe thought that the right type of translation is indispensable from the intended readers of translation. He compared translator to a matchmaker in *Maxims and Reflections* (1826): "Translators should be thought of as busy matchmakers, praising a half-veiled beauty as worthy of our love; they excite an irresistible yearning for the original." (quoted in Robinson, 2006:

① 切里尼:16 世纪意大利雕塑家。

② 卡尔德隆:17 世纪西班牙剧作家。

③ 狄德罗:18 世纪法国唯物主义哲学家、文学家、百科全书派代表人物,第一部法国《百科全书》主编。

④ World literature. From Wikipedia, the free encyclopedia. 2012-10-10. http://en.wikipedia.org/wiki/World_literature.

224) In *On Carlyle's German Romance*, he remarked

> *And that is how we see the translator, as one who strives to be a mediator in this universal, intellectual trade, and makes it his business to promote exchange. For whatever one may say about the shortcomings of translation, they are and will remain most important and worthy undertakings in world communication.* (quoted in Robinson, 2006: 225)

Goethe emphasized the universality of languages and believed in translatability between human languages. He held that languages are intensely intertwined with one another in morphology, and different languages exhibit universal attributes in expressing meaning and meter, which form the basis for translatability of literary, particularly poetic texts. The reason is that underlying these seemingly differences are the meanings that are present and transferable across all human languages.

He maintained that plain and simple translation is invariably the most appropriate. The flowering rendering in emulation with the original is merely the ostentatious temper of the pedant, which will never become popular among general readers. Foreign works, poetry or prose, should be translated with easy and plain prose style, because if so, the original, Homer's epics included, would make unmistakable sense to general readers. The meter and measure are indeed important to make poetry poetry, but the most essential part of poetry is what is left behind after being rendered into prose: the writer's heart and soul that would affect the readers to the bottom of their heart. The poetic form is but a dazzling dress of the essence. Thus, he concluded, prose is a more effective vehicle of poetry translation. In *Poetry and Truth* (1811-1814) Goethe said:

> *I honor meter and rhyme, for that is what makes poetry poetry, but the part that is really, deeply and basically effective, the part that is truly formative and beneficial, is the part of the poet that remains when he is translated into prose. This residue is the pure, complete substance, which a dazzling external form can stimulate, when it is lacking, or conceal, when it is present.* (quoted in Robinson, 2006: 222)

The *Bible*, he said, was written in a great variety of genres, but Luther translated the *Bible*, poetic, historical, pedagogical and commanding, into idiomatic German prose in one whole piece without distinction. His translation worked better for spreading the words of God than the translations prepared by those people who wished to render the original poetical form, because "if you want to influence the masses, a simple translation is always the best" (quoted in Lefevere, 2004a: 75).

Goethe formulated two maxims for translation in *Oration in Memory of Wieland, Our Noble Poet, Brother and Friend* (1813).

There are two maxims for translation: the one requires that the foreign author be brought over to us so that we can look upon him as our own; the other that we cross over to the foreign and find ourselves inside its circumstances, its modes of speech, its uniqueness. (quoted in Robinson, 2006: 222)

This division points to the two directions of translation: towards the target or the source system. Goethe agreed that both strategies have strong points and most translators use them alternatively in their translation if they wish to go a middle path. But he added that a translator of feeling and taste prefers the first method in borderline cases. This division is surprisingly similar to the two opposing approaches of translation simultaneously proposed by Schleiermacher.

In *West-oriental Anthology* (1819) Goethe divided translation into three categories on the basis of the interrelationship between translation and culture: informative, adaptation and interlinear translation.

The informative translation simply aims to introduce foreign culture in a simple prose style, with Luther's *Bible* as an example. Adaptation attempts to adapt a foreign culture to the target setting in a pleasing style that is very close to original composition. Goethe used examples to show that the second type of translation is "paraphrastic, supplementary, cajoling the ear and the mind" of the target readers. (quoted in Robinson, 2006: 224) It reminds us of "imitation" current in England and France from the 16th to 17th century, in which the translator replaced the original sense with one's own in the manners comfortable to the target readers. Goethe obviously disapproved such translation by calling it "vulgar imitation". In interlinear translation the translator transcribes the original line after line in the hope that formal closeness would reproduce the original essence. In this case the translator considers not the special quality of the target language, but creates an entirely new text formally identical with the original. This formally "identical" text distances itself from the target readers with a line after line transcription that "drives us on towards the source text" (quoted in Robinson, 2006: 224). Goethe believed that the three kinds of translation form a continuous whole, because the interlinear translation would result in a close, faithful rendering comparable to the informative translation.

Friedrich Schleiermacher[①] (1768-1834) is a renowned German theologian for the creation of modern protestant theology and a founder of hermeneutics, a romantic approach to interpretation based on individual inner feeling and intuition. He was a personal friend of Wilhelm von Humboldt and helped the latter plan the University of Berlin in the humanistic spirit. Schleiermacher was a highly controversial figure of his time—he had as many fervent enemies as ardent supporters. His influence on religious circle is enormous, bringing together not only romantics and theologians but also Prussian Lutherans and Calvinists[②].

---

① 施莱尔马赫:德国哲学家和基督教新教神学家,试图调和启蒙思想和新教正教,现代阐释学的奠基人之一。

② 卡尔文教派:信仰约翰·卡尔文的宗教教义,强调上帝是万能的,以及仁慈上帝对人的救赎作用。

He was well versed in Latin and Greek and once translated Plato in 1796. As the permanent secretary of the Royal Academy of Science in Berlin, he delivered a lengthy lecture *On the Different Methods of Translating* to the Academy in 1813. The book is an important document of romantic translation theory and one of the major essays of Western translation thought. Schleiermacher viewed signifier not merely as neutrally conveying the signified, but as inextricably bound up with different languages, an idea that is inseparably connected with the problem of translatability. If every speaker is under the sway of the language he speaks and all his thinking is conditioned thereby, translation in the strict sense of the world should give way to travesty or betrayal. His ideal of translation is: bringing the reader to the author, or training the target readers to accept, even to crave, translations steeped in the foreign flavor of their original language.

In *On the Different Methods of Translating* Schleiermacher begins this historical essay by redefining translation as a communication not only across languages, but also within one's language or dialect, and in some cases involving rewording of one's own idea in a different way, which is a very broad concept of translation. Schleiermacher understood translation largely as a result of one's feelings and intuition of the moment. Hence he is associated with romantic school of translation thought.

He classified translation into two kinds: interpretation of oral texts in the world of commerce and translation of written ones in the fields of scholarship and art, each kind having its own use and purpose that can not be replaced by the other. Interpretation of practical, non-literary texts of commerce is a mechanical task and could be accomplished with more or less the same degree of success by any one with a moderate proficiency in the languages. Translation of art and scholarship, by contrast, is a totally different business partly because art and scholarship have a dual and complex relation to language. In this connection Schleiermacher touched on a complex issue between man's thinking, translation, and language, which is by essence philosophical. On the one hand, Schleiermacher said, man is bound by the language he speaks; and on the other hand, every free-thinking man makes his unique contribution to language by using it individually and originally. This is why every well-written utterance needs to be understood from two perspectives: in one direction through the spirit of the langue itself and in the other through the speaker's sense of the utterance that emerged out of his essence.

To translate a noble writer into his native language, then, the translator invariably goes to two extremes: paraphrase or imitation. Paraphrase prevails over the irrationality of language; it may succeed in reproducing the content within narrowing margins of error, but in doing so it abandons all attempts to convey the impact of the original. Imitation, by contrast, gives in to the irrationality of language and reworks the original as a kind of after-image. The imitator focuses not on bringing together the original author and the target reader, believing that it is impossible, but on making a similar impression on the target reader as the original text made on its own readers. Paraphrase is more used in scholarly translation and imitation in translation of fine arts. They are both imperfect translation methods, though.

Schleiermacher classified two approaches of translation. He is well quoted as saying that the true translator "either disturbs the writer as little as possible and moves the reader in his direction, or disturbs the reader as little as possible and moves the writer in his direction" (quoted in Robinson, 2006: 229) The two methods are different from and related to each other and a change from one to the other in the middle of a translation project often leads to unnatural result. All other translation methods, i. e., translation of letter or of sense, etc., should be grouped under these two headings. Schleiermacher conceded that each method has its own merits and demerits and the assessment of the translation is often subjective and relative.

4.3.3 Humboldt, Schlegel and Holderlin

Wilhelm von Humboldt① (1767-1835) is German philosopher, language scholar, educational reformer, and one of the most influential figures in Modern Western history. He held a romantic view on the creative use of language, an idea that has greatly informed the transformational-generative theories of the 20th century. Humboldt understood language both as an abstract system and an operational procedure, a seminal idea that was largely neglected in his time but was rediscovered by the language theory in the 20th century. He is also remembered today as the architect of Humboldt University, a forerunner of modern university. Humboldt has a younger brother Alexander Humboldt who is as influential in the fields of anthropology and biography as Wilhelm Humboldt is in arts and humanities. The elder Humboldt received a private education before he was sent to Jena University where he made friends with people like Friedrich von Schiller②. Throughout his life, Humboldt exchanged constant correspondence with Goethe.

From late 18th century up to early 19th century, Germany developed into the center for translation research in Western Europe. Humboldt played a shaping role in this formative period. German Romanticism③ broke the confines of literature into the field of translation, working a similar movement in the thinking about translation. Partly influenced by Romanticism, Humboldt published two long essays on language and its relation to people's thinking. He wrote an important introduction to Aeschylus's *Agamemnon*④. On language Humboldt believed that each language has its own uniqueness and special inner form which can not find equivalent in another language. He noted not only the differences between languages but also the universality of human minds, observing that there are mysterious connections

---

① 洪堡特:18～19 世纪著名德国语言学家、语文学家和政治家。

② 席勒:德国 18 世纪著名诗人、哲学家、历史学家和剧作家,德国启蒙文学的代表人物之一。

③ 浪漫主义:起源于 18 世纪末期欧洲的文艺思潮,以德国"狂飙突进"运动为发端。浪漫主义对大自然有强烈兴趣,注重个人情感和想象力的表达。

④ 埃斯库罗斯:与欧里庇得斯和索福克勒斯齐名,一起被称为希腊最伟大的悲剧作家,代表作有《被缚的普罗米修斯》《阿伽门农》等。

between the words and their referents.

Humboldt was the first European to study various languages from a philosophical point of view; he raised an important hypothesis we now call the *world-view* hypothesis, a strong version of the Sapir-Whorf hypothesis①. Humboldt maintained thought as being impossible without language and language as completely determining thought. Language in his sense is a platonic object that suddenly appeared one day entirely of its own accord. In this way Humboldt based his philosophy of language on subjective idealism that placed thinking above the physical world. Proceeding from this view of language, Humboldt concluded that "As the mind of the language broadens, so does the mind of the entire nation" (quoted in Robinson, 2006: 240). Words, in Humboldt's view, have a mystical connection with the referents through ideas, which, like mystical intellectual liquid, holds external physical objects in ideal solution. And this makes it possible to ground the uniqueness of words in something stable enough to permit translation. Thus language is the shell of the mind of a people. What Humboldt was hinting at is the universality of ideas, or rather, of mind that is carried in the seemingly different languages.

Closely related to the notion of the uniqueness of language and the universality of ideas is the concept of translatability. Different languages may have different ways of dividing up their life experience into verbal forms, but it is still possible to translate from one language into another, which is effected by translating a word with a phrase or a sentence as the occasion requires. On the other hand, Humboldt realized that translation in the strict sense of the word is impossible because there are normally differences between the original text and the translated text. And the more the translator clings to the word, the more divergent a translation he will produce. This is summarized as "the more faithful, the more divergent", in the words of Humboldt. (quoted in Robinson, 2006: 239) Despite its imperfections, and sometimes impossibility, that always go with a translation, Humboldt stated that translation remains an important, urgent undertaking that broadens the mind of a people and its culture.

August Wilhelm von Schlegel②(1767-1845) is the most celebrated translator in the 18th and 19th centuries. He is a German scholar, art critic, translator and poet, the son of a Lutheran minister. Along with his brother Friedrich von Schlegel, he was one of the leading figures in the spread of Romanticism. As early as 1789 he and his brother founded the famous romantic periodical *Athenaum*③. The same year he began his verse translation of Shakespeare. He translated, with Tieck's assistance, 17 Shakespearean plays from 1797 to 1810,

---

① 洪堡特的语言世界观:洪堡特认为语言反映一个民族的特征,它不仅包含着该民族的历史和文化背景,而且蕴藏着该民族对人生的看法、生活方式和思维方式。在此基础上,美国人萨丕尔及其弟子沃尔夫提出的有关语言与思维关系的萨丕尔-沃尔夫假设,认为语言决定思维,即语言决定论。

② 施莱格尔:德国浪漫主义文学评论家、语言学家、翻译家。其弟弗里德里希·冯·施莱格尔(1772~1829)也是德国文学理论家、作家、语言学家,德国早期浪漫主义文学运动的创始人。

③ 施莱格尔兄弟出版的早期浪漫派刊物《雅典娜神殿》。

Calderon's[①] Spanish plays (in romance language) from 1803 to 1809 and Dante, Tasso[②] (1544-1595), Petrarch, Ariosto[③] (1474-1533) and some other Italian writers. In 1804, he published a German version of *Bouquets of Italian, Spanish and Portuguese Literature*. As a renowned orientalist, Schlegel established Sanskrit studies in Germany.

Schlegel published his views on translation as early as in his late twenties, which went in wide circulation in his time. Heavily indebted to Herder, Schlegel produced influence, in his turn, on Novalis[④] (1772-1801), Goethe, and Schleiermacher.

Schlegel considered every literary work as an entity consisting of form and content. Herder and other Sturm und Drang poets believed that the literary entity was commensurate with nature and was unconsciously created by the artist, while Schlegel thought that the literary work is an organic form, which resulted from a conscious, intentional creative effort. Accordingly, each Shakespearean drama is a skillfully constructed organism in which every detail (each scene, character) is related to the whole, by inherent necessity, and from which, in turn, it derives its meaning. Any change, therefore, distorts and destroys the perfect organism. The language has to be light and pleasing, from which the readers have an impression that he is reading an original German text rather than a translated foreign text. It follows that the justice will be done to the original only after every detail is noted and translated by the translator. In one word, Schlegel tried to find a balance between objective and subjective translation, which combines the fidelity to the source text on the one hand, and creative transformation and naturalization in accordance with target language convention on the other. (quoted in Baker, 1998: 423) Schlegel produced fine quality translation, his Shakespearean plays being the classical literary heritage of German culture.

In *Dante: On the Divine Comedy* (1791), Schlegel expressed his idea that Dante's poetic excellence should be translated in all its entirety, with its noble rust (defects) faithfully retained. No translator has the liberty to prettify it for improvement. He noted that "The translation of poetry must be controlled by whether one directs one's efforts towards the work or its author." (quoted in Robinson, 2006: 214) In *The Works of Homer by Johann Heinrich Voss* (1796), Schlegel reiterated his view of poetic translation that best preserves the original stylistic beauty. To this he added that "Given the multiple and incommensurable divergences of languages, and the reliance of poetry not merely on overall meaning but on the subtlest nuances, all poetic translation must forever remain an imperfect approximation" (quoted in Robinson, 2006: 218). Towards the end of the document he expounded that the translator played an important role in enriching the target language. In *History of Classical Literature*

---

① 卡尔德隆:17 世纪西班牙剧作家。

② 塔索:意大利诗人,文艺复兴运动晚期的代表。写过浪漫情调的骑士长诗和牧歌剧。代表作是叙事长诗《被解放的耶路撒冷》(1575)。

③ 阿里奥斯托:意大利诗人,代表作《疯狂的罗兰》对欧洲的叙事长诗产生了一定影响。

④ 诺瓦利斯:德国浪漫主义诗人,代表作有《夜之赞歌》(1800),《圣歌》(1799)等。

(1802), Schlegel reiterated his idea on the poetic quality of verse translation. He acknowledged the difficulty of translating poetry: "It goes without saying that in the end even the finest translation is at best an approximation to an indeterminable degree" (quoted in Robinson, 2006: 220). In *History of Romantic Literature* (1803), Schlegel said that "translating poetry objectively is true writing, is creating anew" (quoted in Robinson, 2006: 220). Schlegel asserted that all acts of speaking and writing are forms of translation because the nature of communication is to decode and interpret messages received. In his understanding, translation is primarily a communication that involves decoding and interpreting of the received messages.

Friedrich Holderlin① (1770-1843) is a major German lyric poet of German Romanticism and an important thinker in the development of German Idealism.

Holderlin translated in private portions of Homer, Pindar, Sophocles, Euripides, Virgil, Horace, Ovid and Lucan②. Like his poems, his translations in general were opaque and deep as they were made with painful literalism. Indeed, Holderlin's translations were among the most difficult to read because he seemed to "compel us to experience the limits of linguistic expressions and the barriers between languages which impede human understanding" (Steiner, 2001: 341).

Despite Cowley's warning against a word-for-word translation of Pindar, Holderlin rendered six of Pindar's Olympian and ten of his Pythian odes in whole or in part with extreme literality. The devices he employed included "hyperbaton, the separation of object from predicate, the isolation of epithets either preceding or following on their substantive, the asymmetry of predicates and attributes" (Steiner, 2001: 342). The translation was not well received, but it was an important inspiration to Holderlin's own poems. For Holderlin, translation of Pindar is a hermeneutic experiment in which he penetrated to the essence of meaning in ancient Greek and spanned the linguistic and cultural distance to retrieve the universal root of poetic inspiration and language.

Holderlin translated *Oedipus*③ and *Antigone*④ sometimes word-for-word but sometimes with enhancement and corrective restructure. He accompanied the translation with very difficult notes. Critics' reaction to his Sophocles was mixed. His contemporaries mocked his Sophocles for their misinterpretations and farcical effect as well as for their apparent artificiality with the accompanying notes, while modern translation critics upheld his translation as an unrivalled reading of Sophocles as a whole.

Holderlin regarded all writings as a translation or transcription of encased, hidden

① 荷尔德林:德国诗人,古典浪漫派诗歌的先驱。

② 卢坎:罗马诗人。他写的《法撒利战记》是关于凯撒和庞培之间内战的史诗记录。

③ 《俄狄浦斯王》:古希腊悲剧作家索福克勒斯于公元前 427 年根据希腊神话中俄狄浦斯的故事所创作的一出希腊悲剧,为希腊悲剧中的代表之作。

④ 《安提戈涅》:古希腊悲剧作家索福克勒斯公元前 442 年的一部作品,安提戈涅被塑造成维护神权,不向世俗权势低头的伟大女英雄形象。

meaning. He was interested in discovering the significant meaning and ultimately the primal energies of human discourse in individual words by going back to their ancient sources. The deep signification of individual words may be intensified or made manifest by a word-for-word transfer between languages. According to Holderlin, translation is a mysterious interpretative process to retrieve the core of individual words.

In the letter to Wilmans (1803), Holderlin conceived translation as an emendation, externalization, a bodying forth of implicit meanings as well as correction. Correction and enhancement are possible, and indeed mandatory, because the translator's vision of the original is diachronic. (Steiner, 2001: 345) He believed that "the unique sense of words, particularly in tragic drama, had a material aura and consequence lacking in modern epistemology. A prophecy, an oracular dictum, a formula of anathema in Greek tragedy carried with it a literal fatality. Speech did not stand for or describe the fact: it was the fact" (Steiner, 2001: 346). To Holderlin, the conflict, adjustment and fusion of both ancient Greek and contemporary German represented the collision of being. The poet translator mediates between his own language and a foreign language. He effaces his own self in order to bring himself over to the other presence. In the process he breaks the natural division of languages and creates a new combination of the 5th-century Attic and the early 19th-century German which belongs to neither language. But this new coinage is pregnant with currents of meaning more universal, nearer to the sources of all human speech, than either Greek or German.

In the final analysis, modern Germany is a birthplace to philosophical approach to translation as the discussions on translation take on a distinctively hermeneutic turn and are based on fundamental observations of human mind, innate character of language, society and culture in general.

Further Readings

Baker, Mona. *Routledge Encyclopedia of Translation Studies*. London & New York: Routledge, 1998.

Lefevere, Andre. *Translation/History/Culture: A Sourcebook*. Shanghai: Shanghai Foreign Language Education Press, 2004a.

Robinson, Douglas. *Western Translation Theory: From Herodotus to Nietzsche*. Shanghai: Foreign Language Teaching and Research Press, 2006.

Steiner, George. *After Babel: Aspects of Language and Translation*. Shanghai: Shanghai Foreign Language Education Press, 2001.

World literature. From Wikipedia, the free encyclopedia. 2012-10-10. http://en.wikipedia.org/wiki/World_literature.

谭载喜:《西方翻译简史》,商务印书馆2004年版。

Topics for Discussion

1. Give as many metaphors of translation as possible. What do they point to about the nature of translation?

2. Comment on Schleiermacher's classification of translation into two types: interpretation of oral texts in the world of commerce and translation of written ones in the fields of scholarship and art.

3. Account for the indirect translation of English culture through the French language in early 18th Germany. What is the most translated genre of English literature?

4. List all the factors that make translation possible in German translation theories. Are you convinced by Humboldt that translation, difficult and imperfect as it is, is after all possible? If not, point out the factors that limit the possibility of translation in German translation theories.

5. Give two definitions of translation in German translation theories. How do they compare to one of the most general concepts of translation today, i. e., as a language-switching process?

4.4 Translations in Modern England

Translation Terms

Tytler's Three Laws of Translation

In 1790, Tytler raised three laws of translation in treatise *Essay on the Principles of Translation*:

1. That the translation should give a complete transcript of the ideas of the original work.
2. That the style and manner of writing should be of the same character with that of the original.
3. That the translation should have all the ease of original composition.

Newman's foreignizing translation

When translating Homer, Newman aimed to retain every peculiarity of Homer and adhere closely to Homer's manner and habit of thought on the levels of lexicon, syntax and prosody. In terms of lexicon, Newman constructed a special vocabulary, confining himself to the words of Saxon origin. One of the syntactic expedient was deliberately inverted sentence for the effect of antiquity and elevation, for emphasis or for variety to produce a quaint Homeric style. Concerning the prosody, Newman thought that ballad meter was both antiquated and popular, and therefore more suitable than hexameter for translating Homer. He oriented his translation towards the source, with the purpose of communicating the strangeness of the original.

4.4.1 Translations in Modern England: Socio-cultural Background

General conditions were unfavorable for translation enterprise in the 17th-century England, a period tormented by civil conflict[①]. Despite the rise and fall of government, the course of translation was continuous. Unlike the 16th century, in the 17th century there was an increasing confidence in the English language as a medium of translation and translation was held in high esteem. A greater body of comment was made on the methods of translation. Translation theories in the 17th century walked out of the sporadic and fragmented mode of discussion in the preceding century and became "deliberate, reasoned statements, unmistakable in their purpose and meaning" (Amos, 1920: 137). The discussions tended to narrow down to translation of a certain type of text. Denham[②] (1615-1669), for example, excluded from his consideration the texts that "deal in matters of fact or matters of faith", thus focusing on discussion of literary texts. Most translators clarified the audience they were addressing. Communication between scholars and translators was more frequent.

England (after 1707, Great Britain) in the 18th century grew into a dominant world colonial power, with France as its main rival on the imperial stage. The 18th century was a period of peace and prosperity greater than the Elizabeth Reign. Translation was regarded as a worthwhile event in the interest of the country and enlisted assistance from both the world of learning and individual patrons. Translators were more respected than before. The most favored ancient poets included Virgil, Horace, and Homer, among others. There was a notable tendency of naturalizing the Greek and Latin texts. The translations were invariably prefaced with lengthy and detailed discourse on the best rules for translation. Almost all the important questions were touched on up to the end of the century, culminating in Tytler's[③] *Essays on the Principles of Translation*.

4.4.2 Cowley and Dryden

Abraham Cowley[④] (1618-1667) was one of the leading English poets of the 17th century. He was twice expelled in his life for his fervent support of the royal court, first from Cambridge and second by Cromwell's parliament. Later he took office in different capacities at the royal court abroad until 1656. Neither rewarded by the restored Charles II nor by Cromwell, Abraham Cowley quitted politics and turned to gardening for which he wrote essays that was reminiscent of Montaigne. He was also devoted to the cause of the Royal Society and published a monograph on how to further experimental philosophy.

---

① 指 1640 ~ 1688 年的英国资产阶级革命,又称“英国内战”“清教徒革命”。以 1640 年查理一世召开新议会开始到 1688 年詹姆斯二世退位结束,最终新贵族阶级推翻封建统治,建立起英国资本主义制度。

② 德纳姆:英国诗人,因其地方山水诗《库珀山》(1642 年)而闻名。

③ 泰特勒:18 世纪至 19 世纪初英国学者、作家、翻译家。

④ 考利:17 世纪英国诗人、翻译家。

Cowley was greatly admired in his day for his translation, or rather, free imitation, of Pindar. Although his reproduction of the Pindaric Ode form in English does not accurately reflect Pindar's poetics, Cowley introduced into English a new poetry form known as English "Pindarick" Ode, or Irregular Ode, i. e., the iambic lines of irregular length, pattern, and rhyme scheme.

Under the influence of George Chapman's[①] translation theory, literal translation was viewed with general hostility in the early 17th-century England. In *Preface to Pindarique Odes* (1656) Cowley attacked literal translation of poetry: "If a man should undertake to translate Pindar word for word, it would be thought that one madman had translated another." (Amos, 1920: 149)

Cowley ignored the reasonable respect for both the original and the English language proposed by Chapman, arguing for a more radical method of supplying new beauties in place of the original beauty that got lost anyway. He openly announced in the two Odes of Pindar that he had "taken, left out, and added what I please" (Amos, 1920: 150). Cowley even proposed the term "imitation" for his free approach on the grounds that this method best preserved the spirit of the source text. (Amos, 1920: 151) Cowley's extreme liberal approach produced a reaction, primarily from such renowned poet-translator as John Dryden[②].

John Dryden (1631-1700) is a leading literary figure of the 17th-century England: dramatist, art critic, poet laureate of the restored monarchy and most brilliant translator. He dominated the literary life of Restoration England that the period came to be known in literary circles as the Age of Dryden. After the deposition of his patron King James II in 1688, Dryden turned to translation to earn a living. In his later life Dryden was a devoted translator of ancient and modern classics.

Dryden translated works by Horace, Juvenal[③], Ovid, Lucretius[④], and Theocritus[⑤], a task which he found far more satisfying than writing for the stage. In 1697 he published the complete version of *The Works of Virgil*, his most ambitious and defining work as translator. Before Dryden, *Aeneid* had been translated with different poetry forms, including hexameter, the fourteener, and the heroic couplet, the most popular meter for nearly all versions of Virgil in the 17th century. Yet Dryden was the best translator of Virgil into the heroic couplet in the English language. As a matter of fact, he borrowed phrases, rhyme-words, and sometimes whole lines from his predecessors, good and bad alike. In his notes he frankly admitted his indebtedness to Denham and the Earl of Lauderdale[⑥]. Dryden was able to polish the bad lines

① 查普曼:16～17 世纪英国诗人、翻译家和剧作家,他翻译的《荷马全集》是第一部英语全译本。
② 德莱顿:17 世纪英国剧作家、评论家、桂冠诗人,在欧洲文学批评史上享有盛誉。
③ 尤维纳利斯:古罗马讽刺作家,其作品谴责了古罗马特权阶级的腐化和奢侈。
④ 卢克莱修:古罗马哲学家和诗人。
⑤ 忒奥克里托斯:古希腊田园诗人。
⑥ 劳德戴尔伯爵:理查德·梅特兰德,是苏格兰劳德戴尔第四世侯爵,曾经翻译过维吉尔的作品。

and integrate the good lines perfectly into his own poetic style. In his translation, elevated diction and Latinism were integrated in perfect harmony. Dryden's hope was to capture the clearness, the purity, the ease and the magnificence of Virgil's style. Within the confine of the heroic couplet Dryden not only carried forward the grace and harmony of the ancient Romans but also managed to achieve a new metrical variety, suppleness and strength which left in despair the best of his predecessors. For this reason, his translation was regarded as the culmination of couplet tradition of the 17th century. His translation was praised by Walter Scott as "It is in the art of communicating the ancient poet's ideas with force and energy equal to his own that Dryden has so completely exceeded all who have gone before, and all who have succeeded him" (quoted in France, 2000: 509).

His final translations appeared in the volume *Fables, Ancient and Modern* (1700), a collection of translations of classical and medieval poetry from Homer, Ovid, and Boccaccio, as well as modernized adaptations from Geoffrey Chaucer interspersed with some of Dryden's own poems. It is his last and also one of his greatest works. All the translations are in his characteristic heroic couplet, which uses alexandrines① and triplets② to vary the movement. The Preface to *Fables* is considered to be both an interesting work of criticism and one of the finest essays in English. The *Fables* were greatly admired throughout the 18th century, and their form and versification were imitated by John Kcats③ in "Lamia".

Partly in reaction against free imitation, Dryden proposed his well-quoted division of translation into three types: metaphrase, imitation, and paraphrase. Primarily for this division, Dryden was considered by Samuel Johnson④ and many others as the first systematic translation scholar. It was argued that this reputation was undeserved on the grounds that the three terms were first used by Philo in ancient Alexandria and much repeated later and that Dryden merely revived and popularized the tradition. In *Preface to Ovid's Epistles*, Dryden stated:

> *All translations, I suppose, may be reduced to these three heads. First, that of metaphrase, or turning an author word by word, and line by line, from one language into another. —The second way is that of paraphrase, or translation with latitude, where the author is kept in view by the translator, so as never to be lost, but his words are not so strictly followed as his sense, and that too is admitted to be amplified, but not altered. —The third way is that of imitation, where the translator (if now he has not lost his name) assumes the liberty, not only to vary from the words and sense, but to forsake them both as he sees occasion; and taking only some general hints from the original, to run division on the groundwork, as he pleases.* (quoted in Robinson, 2006: 172, my ellipsis)

---

① 亚历山大体:是一种法国诗体,每行有十二个音节,在第六个音节后有顿挫。该诗体由于在《亚历山大的故事》的诗集中首次使用而得名。

② 三行诗:每段三行的押韵诗。

③ 济慈:英国19世纪初著名的浪漫派诗人,《拉弥亚》是其叙事诗。

④ 塞缪尔·约翰逊:英国作家、文学评论家和诗人,以编纂《英语大辞典》而知名。

He held that metaphrase rarely produces a work that is both faithful and good because "Tis much like dancing on ropes with fettered legs: a man may shun a fall by using caution; but the gracefulness of motion is not to be expected" (quoted in Robinson, 2006: 172). Likewise Dryden criticized imitation because "imitation of an author is the most advantageous way for a translator to show himself, but the greatest wrong which can be done to the memory and reputation of the dead" (quoted in Robinson, 2006: 173). Of the three types of translation Dryden was more in support of paraphrase provided the translator had certain qualifications. In the case of poetry translation, the translator must be a poet himself, a master of the two languages, able to understand the "spirit" of the original author and render the understanding in conformity with the translator's language.

A prevailing belief was that a good translation consisted in adding new beauties to the piece, thereby to recompense the loss which is sustained by change of language. Dryden, however, did not go with the idea. In Dryden's consideration literal translation and paraphrase are two extremes that should be avoided. The type of translation Dryden approves is one in which the translator may translate with certain latitude of expression, that is, the translator may change author's turns of expression if they sound too awkward in the translator's language, but never is he supposed to alter the sense, which is sacred and inviolable. In his *Dedication of the Aeneid* (1697), Dryden stated his stance as *Steering between Two Extremes*:

> "*On the whole matter, I thought fit to steer between the two extremes of paraphrase and literal translation, to keep as near my author as I could, without losing all his graces, the most eminent of which are in the beauty of his word. —But slaves we are, and labor on another man's plantation; we dress the vineyard, but the wine is the owner's; if the soil be sometimes barren, then we are sure of being scourged. If it be fruitful, and our care succeeds we are not thanked; for the proud reader will only say, the poor drudge had done his duty.*" (quoted in Robinson, 2006: 175, my ellipsis)

In practice, however, Dryden gave himself more freedom by updating the language of his original author and making him speak the language of his country and his day. "I have endeavored to make Virgil speak such English as he would himself have spoken, if he had been born in England, and in this present age." (quoted in Robinson, 2006: 174)

4.4.3 Pope, Johnson, Tytler and FitzGerald

Alexander Pope[①] (1688-1744) is an English poet, satirist, and translator. Pope was brought up in Roman Catholicism. His health problems (deformed spine and constant headache) made him concentrate more on his private reading and writing. He was admired for his translation of Homer and his brilliant use of heroic couplet[②], a poetry form popular in the

① 蒲柏:18 世纪英国诗人、杰出的启蒙主义者,翻译过荷马史诗全译本。

② 英雄双韵体:英语英雄史诗和叙事诗中采用的传统诗体,由乔叟引进,至德莱顿和蒲柏诗歌中臻于完善。

18th-century England.

Homer was among the most translated epic poet in the English language. John Denham[①] and John Dryden produced fragments of Homer, not to mention many other uneven sporadic translations by less known translators. Only George Chapman[②] (1559-1634), John Ogilby[③] (1600-1676) and Thomas Hobbs[④] (1588-1679) attempted to translate Homer in complete. Pope's translation was based on all the proceeding versions in the hope of bringing the art of translating Homer to perfection. So he started his translation by a critical review of earlier renderings.

He spent more than 10 years of his most productive poetical career working on the two epics. Pope cared to be loyal to the "rapture and fire" that carried the reader away, with less regard for literal equivalence. Naturally he took liberties with the *Iliad*, cutting the impediments that might damage its general force and impact and highlighting the merit of Homer wherever possible. Pope used heroic couplet that was well adapted to fluent narration, falling easily into verse paragraphs and speech. Another interesting feature was his use of footnotes, which were well phrased, witty, and learned among the best art criticisms. The *Iliad* a great success, he was incumbent to undertake the translation of *Odyssey*, in collaboration with two assistant translators. After Chapman's supervision and improvement, the two books were surprisingly homogeneous: rapid, clear and fully annotated.

He believed that the best a translator can do is to preserve this Homeric simplicity as it is and modern expressions like *platoon*, *campaign* can not be allowed. Some people consider the two peculiarities of Homer, i. e., compound epithets and repetitions, as defects and some others as beauties. Pope's idea was that the translator should translate the compound epithet into English compound where possible, that is, when the English compound is pleasant to the ear and to the received rules of composition. When there is not a ready English compound or single word to translate a Homeric compound, Pope suggested that circumlocution must be used to do justice to the original. This circumlocution includes a padded phrase for a compound, such as "the lofty mountain shakes his waving woods" in place of "leaf-shaking", which may sound absurd for a mountain in English. When a phrase, say "far-shooting", is used in two relevant meanings: the darts and bow, the ensign of Apollo, and the rays of the sun, Pope translated one meaning or the other as the context dictated. The repetition of whole speeches, sentences or half a line of verse is to be retained wherever possible unless they come so close to each other as to produce a dull effect. Homer is very expert at applying the sound to the sense. Pope flattered himself that he had the ear to Homer's versification and endeavored to reproduce

---

① 德纳姆:17 世纪英国诗人,因其地方山水诗《库珀山》(1642 年)而闻名。

② 查普曼:英国 16 ~ 17 世纪诗人、翻译家和剧作家,他翻译的《荷马全集》是第一部英语全译本。

③ 奥格比:苏格兰翻译家、制图师,翻译过荷马的作品《伊利亚特》。

④ 霍布斯:英国的政治哲学家。霍布斯晚年将《奥德赛》的四卷译为不太整齐的韵文,并于1675 年完成了《奥德赛》和《伊利亚特》的完整译本。

the beauty. To the end of the essay, however, Pope confessed that he was incapable of doing justice to Homer.

Pope's Homer was criticized for being more like Pope than Homer and erring on the side of grandeur. Richard Bentley①(1662-1742), one of the classical scholars then, thus said of Pope's translation of Homer: "It was a pretty poem, but must not be called Homer." (quoted in Robinson, 2006: 251) Still, Pope deserved the credit as the translator who put Homer into English, as Ezra Pound wrote of his translation, "out of fashion though he is, he had at least the merit of translating Homer into something." (quoted in Robinson, 2006: 192). This something in Robinson's language is "a highly stylized and personalized idiom that is grounded in his own era, as opposed to the bland, inoffensive translationese some translators prefer" (quoted in Robinson, 2006: 192). Lawrence Venuti called Pope's translation "domestication", pointing out that his Homer "continued the refinement of a transparent poetic discourse in the heroic couplet, still a literary elitism among the hegemonic classes, dependent less on court patronage than on publishers with subscription lists that were now increasingly bourgeois as well as aristocratic" (Venuti, 2004: 65-66). Susan Bassnett held that Pope followed Dryden, advocating the same middle ground, with stress on close reading of the original to note the details of style and manner whilst endeavoring to keep alive the "fire" of the poem. (quoted in Bassnett, 2004: 64)

Samuel Johnson②(1709-1784) is a renowned critic, essayist, journalist, poet, educator and lexicographer in mid-18th century British intellectual life. In 1745, he was asked by the London booksellers to write a dictionary of the English language, which came out in print in 1755, to the everlasting gratitude of the English language. The dictionary was a milestone in world lexicography for its large entries (40,000 in all), polemic and individual definitions and historical citations. His famous publications include *The Prince of Abyssinia*, 8-volume editions of Shakespeare and *Lives of English Poets*.

Imitation was a popular mode of poetic creation in Johnson's time, with Alexander Pope, Abraham Cowley, John Wilmot③(1647-1680), and John Oldham④(1653-1683) as the masters of the poetic art. Johnson himself would later define imitation in the *Life of Pope* as "a kind of middle composition between translation and original design, which pleases when the thoughts are unexpectedly applicable and the parallels lucky"⑤.

Johnson's important works *London* and *The Vanity of Human Wishes* were more or less creative imitations of the Latin poet Juvenal⑥. In both works Johnson used Juvenal's general

---

① 本特利:英国18世纪古典主义学者、评论家、神学家。

② 塞缪尔·约翰逊:英国作家、文学评论家和诗人,以编纂《英语大辞典》而知名。

③ 威尔模特:洛彻斯特第二世侯爵,是英国诗人,英王查理二世复辟王朝的朝臣。

④ 奥德汉姆:英国17世纪讽刺诗人、翻译家,模仿并翻译过罗马讽刺作家尤维纳利斯的作品。

⑤ Samuel Johnson. Poetry Foundation. 2013-11-17. http://www.poetryfoundation.org/bio/samuel-johnson.

⑥ 尤维纳利斯:古罗马讽刺作家,其作品谴责了古罗马特权阶级的腐化和奢侈。

structure, but he reworked the subject, retaining and altering sections to give expression to his own particular concerns. In *London*, for example, he left out fully half of Juvenal's section on the general helplessness of the poor and condensed the fight scene because he wanted to focus his own poem on political rather than personal conditions. Significant differences also existed between Juvenal's satire and Johnson's *The Vanity of Human Wishes*. Juvenal emphasized the physical, the sensuous, and the licentious, while Johnson was most concerned with the spiritual and the psychological. Besides, Johnson omitted Juvenal's long section on masculine beauty, preferring to focus on more general human problems and to reproduce mainly Juvenal's "stateliness" and "declamatory grandeur". As Johnson did not usually concentrate on close rendition of Juvenal, both *London* and *The Vanity of Human Wishes* became in important ways his own poems.

Johnson took most delight in Horace. On the basis of the detailed study of translations of Horace before him, Johnson paid much attention to rhyming pattern when he put Horace into English. He translated some of Horace's odes and two of his epodes[①] (II and XI), all capable and fairly accurate performances. Johnson turned to the translation of Horace's Odes of mortality in the last months of his life. Horace depicted man's finiteness and mortality in relation to the changing seasons, drawing heavily from epicurean philosophy, while Johnson shifted the motif of the poem from nature to man.

In the *Idler* (1759) Johnson reviewed world translation traditions, pointing out that translation was an early cultivated activity among the English and that Chaucer has left the English man with his version of Boethius's *Consolation of Philosophy*. He did not cherish a high opinion of the work, though. He also held that the translations published by the first English printer William Caxton were too literal to offer the audience any knowledge about the English language. This strict literality was changed in the Elizabethan age when it was found that "greater liberty was necessary to elegance, and elegance was necessary to general reception" (quoted in Robinson, 2006: 205). The literal tradition, however, was not forgotten all at once. Holland, for instance, continued to feed the nation with literal translations and in poetry translation the same degree of exactness was strictly observed. It was during the Restoration period that this servile poetry translation tradition was discarded.

In *Lives of English Poets* (1779-1781), Johnson reviewed the translating of Homer. Pope was criticized for adding what was not there in Homer and for being not Homer but Pope himself, i. e., it wanted simplicity, artless grandeur and unaffected majesty so characteristic of Homer. Johnson, however, cherished a more liberal attitude towards Pope's Homer, though, insisting that the translation should be evaluated with regard to the differences in languages and poetics and distances of time, space and customs. His idea was that as a culture grew it had a greater demand for elegance than plain sense and "Pope wrote for his own age and his own

---

① 长短句交替的古代抒情诗体。

nation: he knew that it was necessary to color the images and point the sentiments of his author; he therefore made him graceful, but lost him some of his sublimity" (Robinson, 2006: 206, my ellipsis) Johnson had a high opinion of the copious, light-hearted notes Pope added, which were attacked for bordering on frivolous and low.

George Campbell①(1719-1796) is a prominent figure of the Scottish Enlightenment②, a philosopher, minister, and professor of divinity. His major works include *A Dissertation on Miracles* (1762) and *The Philosophy of Rhetoric*. In 1789 he published a 1,500 page translation of *The Four Gospels*, which Campbell regarded as the greatest work of his life. Along with the translation, it includes critical dissertations on the problems of translating and interpreting the ancient texts, as well as his observations on the translations themselves. In the two-volume book Campbell made a detailed and systematic analysis of *Bible* translation, with far greater breadth and insight than his predecessors. He cited copious examples to show where he differed in principle and practice from earlier *Bible* translators. Campbell summarized the criteria of good translating under three principles:

(1) To give a just representation of the sense of the original.

(2) To convey into his version, as much as possible, in a consistency with the genius of the language which he writes, the author's spirit and manner.

(3) To take care that the version have, at least so far the quality of an original performance, as to appear natural and easy. (quoted in Nida, 2004: 19)

Campbell proceeded to point out the full implications of these principles not only to *Bible* translation but to translation of classical texts into contemporary English. It is obvious that he meant his principles as general laws of translation. In the following year, however, Alexander Tytler's③ *Essays on Principles of Translation* appeared, in which Tytler formulated three principles that were surprisingly identical to Campbell's. When Campbell accused him of plagiarism, Tytler insisted that his principles were a purely parallel development independent of Campbell. Today, Tytler is far better known for the three principles because he addressed more general issues with concentration on secular rather than religious translation.

Alexander Fraser Tytler (1747-1814) is a Scottish advocate, judge, writer and historian who served as Professor of Universal History, and Greek and Roman Antiquities, in the University of Edinburgh. He is known for his elegant and judicious synthesis of other peoples' work. Although he turned to law in 1770, Tytler cherished a lifelong passion for literature and history. He published several volumes of local, legal and universal history and

---

① 坎贝尔:18 世纪英国作家、神学家。

② 苏格兰启蒙运动:指 1740 年至 1800 年期间在苏格兰所发生的思想文化思潮。《1707 年联合法案》通过以后,苏格兰在世界上的地位彻底改变。随着宗教改革的完成,苏格兰进入了文化思想的繁荣期,成为欧洲文化思想最为发达活跃的地区。

③ 泰特勒:18 ~ 19 世纪初英国学者、作家、翻译家。

translated Italian poet Petrarch.①

On several occasions, Tytler read his essays on translation and poetry at the Royal Academy of Edinburg. His essays exerted deep influence on the growing generation of Edinburg, among them young Walter Scott②. These essays were later collected into an anthology *Essays on Principles of Translation*. At the beginning of the essays Tytler gave a much-quoted definition of translation:

> *I would therefore describe a good translation to be:*
> *That in which the merit of the original is so completely transfused into another language as to be distinctly apprehended, and as strongly felt, by a native of the country to which that language belongs as it is by those who speak the language of the original work.*
>
> (quoted in Robinson, 2006: 209)

Tytler defines translation in terms of the reader's response to the translated text, which is a target-centered concept of translation that distinguishes itself from prescriptive translation with focus on fidelity to the source text. Proceeding from this definition of a good translation Tytler went on to deduce three more laws of translation:

> 1. *That the translation should give a complete transcript of the ideas of the original work.*
> 2. *That the style and manner of writing should be of the same character with that of the original.*
> 3. *That the translation should have all the ease of original composition.*
>
> (quoted in Robinson, 2006: 209)

Tytler's laws of translation are prescriptive, i. e., laying down the standards for the translation to meet. His first law is a reiteration of traditional principle that the translator should faithfully render the meaning of the original author. His second law stresses the importance of the translator's ability to identify and reproduce the style of the original author in the target language, which reminds us of Dolet's fifth principle (1540). Concerning the third law of translation he realized the difficulty for a translation to remain faithful to the original sense and have the same ease of original composition. His suggestion to the translator is "adopt the very soul of his author, which must speak through his own organs" (quoted in Robinson, 2006: 211). Tytler emphasizes the importance of the order of the three laws of translation when, by necessity, a sacrifice must be made of one of them. A translation should never deviate from the original sense for the sake of imitating the original manner of speaking or copying the grace and smoothness of the original composition. It could be pardoned if, for the purpose of preserving the original sense, the translation differs from the original mode of expression or does not have the original grace. For all its overlap with earlier translation discussion, Tytler's treatise on

① 彼特拉克:意大利诗人、学者和人文主义者,曾用十四行诗创作了著名的爱情抒情诗集《抒情歌谣集》。

② 司各特:英国历史小说家,《威弗利》(1814)是其最有代表性的历史小说。

translation occupies an important position in the history of translation theory because of its hierarchical synthesis of the traditional translation thoughts.

Edward FitzGerald①(1809-1883) is an English poet and writer, best known as the poet of the first and most famous English translation of *Rubaiyat of Omar Khayyam*②, a 12th-century work consisting of four-line stanzas.

Omar Khayyam was more a mathematician and astronaut than a poet, but in his spare time he jotted down a few hundred rhymed thoughts, which, being far apart form the prevailing mystic tradition, were never popular in his own country. A few fragmented manuscripts went abroad but were not approved, either. It was Edward FitzGerald who restored the poet to life and made him a brilliant name in English literature. Although separated from the Persian poet both in time and space, FitzGerald discovered in his poem some interesting Biblical sentiments and some aptly expressed 19th-century thoughts. Perhaps as Louis Untermeyer③(1885-1977) believed, FitzGerald grew interested in this poet for two reasons: first, it afforded him an escape into fantasy; second, he was reminded that there was a connection between the Persia of Omar and the Ireland of his ancestors. (Khayyam, 2003: 78)

As he found himself identical to this Persian poet in many ways, FitzGerald set about translating him. In the first edition of *Rubaiyat of Omar Khayyam*, FitzGerald removed what he believed the vulgar parts, put together the phrases that expressed the same thoughts, rewrote the pieces that embodied the same basic theme and included some other similar Persian poems. He added some outspoken stanzas and fitted it into "a sort of Epicurean eclogue in a Persian garden" (Khayyam, 2003: 80), and published it anonymously at his own expanse. Despite his efforts, the first edition of the patch-up did not impress the readers well and remained obscure and hardly sold at reduced price.

In 1868, FitzGerald published, anonymously again, the second edition of the book. It is considerably different from the first edition. The 75 quatrains in the first edition had now grown to 110, the original lines compressed, the images sharpened and the opening stanza not as bold. The subsequent editions, again anonymous, showed more obvious changes and improvements. With the assistance of Dante Gabriel Rossetti④(1828-1882) and Algernon Charles Swinburne⑤(1837-1909), FitzGerald improved on it until its third edition made a real success. And up to its fifth edition the book had won its way into public favor. It was until after

---

① 费茨杰拉德:英国当代诗人,以自由译法翻译了波斯诗人兼数学家莪默·伽亚谟(另译欧玛尔·海亚姆)的作品《鲁拜集》而知名,成为英国文学经典。

② 《鲁拜集》:11~12世纪波斯诗人兼数学家莪默·伽亚谟的四行诗集,形式上类似中国的绝句,内容多感慨人生如寄、盛衰无常,以及时行乐、纵酒放歌为宽解。

③ 安特迈耶:美国诗人、评论家、诗歌杂志编辑。

④ 罗塞蒂:英国著名诗人、画家、翻译家。

⑤ 斯温伯恩:英国诗人、剧作家、小说家、评论家,曾参与编纂《大英百科全书》(第11版),并多次获得诺贝尔文学奖提名。

he died that Edward FitzGerald's name, which appeared on the title page of the reprint of the fifth edition, became a household translator of the Persian poet. This fifth edition of *Rubaiyat* is a miraculous unity of both FitzGerald and Omar, as Louis Untermeyer① said:

> *FitzGerald used Omar's detached thoughts and wove them into a design; imposing a continuity upon the fragments, he achieved a unity and shapeliness which the original never possessed. He adopted and adapted the Persian lines much as Shakespeare adapted the plots of his predecessors. As a result, here is a collaboration that is complete and inextricable. Separated by time, geography, and language, the two authors have become one poet: Omar-FitzGerald. They are inseparable, perfectly and permanently fused; it is impossible to think of one without the other.* (Khayyam, 2003: 90)

Thanks to his free imitation, FitzGerald introduced into English literature a new poetry form *Rubaiyat* characterized by four-line stanza, with five feet in each line and the third line unrhymed. The most quoted lines from FitzGerald's *Rubaiyat* please not only the mind but also the ear:

A Book of Verses underneath the Bough,
A Jug of Wine, a Loaf of Bread—and Thou
Beside me singing in the Wilderness—
Oh, Wilderness were Paradise enow!

(Khayyam, 2003: 97)

A comparison of his translation with a literal translation of the same lines shows the drastic changes Fitzgerald had introduced into his *Rubaiyat*. In 1889, Justin Huntly McCarthy②(1859-1936) published a prose translation of *Rubaiyat of Omar Khayyam* in which he sought for literal translation of both the word and the idea. Omar's favorite stanza was translated with painful faithfulness as below:

> *When the hand possesses a loaf of wheaten bread, two measures of wine, and a piece of flesh, when seated with tulip-cheeks in some lonely spot, behold such joy as is not given to Sultan.* (Khayyam, 2003: 95)

There is nothing striking or original about the philosophy of the poem, for it is the familiar praise of amenities of life: wine, women and song. A literal translation makes it all the more dull. After FitzGerald's perfect fusion of music and meaning and the climactic ordering, the obvious idea becomes fresh and lasting. His readjustment is so appealing that many of his famous phrases are still in use today: *a jug of wine*, *a loaf of bread*, *and Thou*, etc. FitzGerald

① 安特迈耶:美国诗人、评论家、诗歌杂志编辑。
② 麦卡锡:爱尔兰作家、民族主义政治家。

justified his free approach in a letter (1851): "It is an amusement to me to take what Liberties I like with these Persians who (as I think) are not Poets enough to frighten one from such excursions, and who really do want a little Art to shape them." (quoted in Bassnett, 2004: Introduction 14)

In another letter in 1878 FitzGerald made some cogent remarks about translation: "I suppose very few people have taken such pains in translation as I have; though certainly not to be literal. But at all cost, a thing must live; with a transfusion of one's own worse life if one can't retain the original's better. Better a live sparrow than a stuffed eagle." (quoted in Robinson, 2006: 249) And in another letter about translation of Calderon's[①] drama he reiterated his view that "I am persuaded that, to keep life in the work (as drama must) the translator (however inferior to his original) must recast that original into his own likeness, more or less; the less like his original, so much the worse; but still, the live dog better than the dead lion" (quoted in Robinson, 2006: 250). Daniel Weissbort called his translation "naturalizing reconstruction" (quoted in France, 2000: 91).

4.4.4 Debate over the Translating of Homer

Poetry translation, particularly classical poetry translation of Homer, attracted the attention of the majority of important translators from the antiquity up to the 19th century. How to render Greek poets into a different language had remained a controversial issue until very recently; the discussion continued well into the 19th century and reached its climax in the debate over translation of Homer between Matthew Arnold[②] (1822-1888) and Francis Newman[③] (1805-1897).

Newman was a classical scholar who wrote on a variety of topics, scholarly, religious and socio-political. He translated Horace's odes into English and Longfellow's *Hiawatha*[④] and Defoe's *Robinson Crusoe* into Latin. Unhappy with the former translations of Homer he made a new version of the *Iliad*, which Arnold attacked in his *On Translating Homer*, with irony and acrimony, as not retaining the nobleness of Homer. Newman replied in kind with the essay *Homeric Translation in Theory and Practice: A Reply to Matthew Arnold*. To this retort Arnold wrote another essay *Last Words on Translating Homer: A Reply to Francis W. Newman*.

Both sides shared the same romantic views of the translator's duty that he should be faithful to, and if possible, in union with, the original. The difference lied not in the basic views of translation, but in the particular approaches towards the same end. Up to the publication of Newman's *Iliad*, it was still at issue how to make a good translation. A popular idea at that time was that the translation should be such that "the reader should, if possible, forget that it is a

---

① 卡尔德隆:17 世纪西班牙剧作家。

② 阿诺德:英国诗人、教育家、评论家,英国近代教育家拉格比公学校长、托马斯·阿诺德之子。主张诗要反映时代的要求,需有追求道德和智力解放的精神。

③ 纽曼:红衣主教纽曼的弟弟,英国学者兼作家。

④ 《海华沙之歌》: 19 世纪美国浪漫主义诗人朗费罗的著名史诗,歌颂了印第安人海华沙的传奇生涯。

translation at all, and be lulled into the illusion that he is reading an original work" (quoted in Robinson, 2006: 251).

Newman aimed at precisely the opposite: he was determined to retain every peculiarity of Homer and adhere closely to Homer's manner and habit of thought. The real original is the basis on which to create a poem that will move the target readers in the same way *Iliad* is conceived to have moved the original Greek readers. This, Newman believed, is the only way to be faithful to the original. Newman opposed former translations that modernized Homer and favored a version that retained the historical remoteness. He was trying to find an analogous English form for the archaic Greek of Homer's time. Homer, in Newman's understanding, is "direct, popular, forcible, quaint, flowing, garrulous, abounding with formulas, redundant in particles and affirmatory interjections, as also in grammatical connectives of time, place, and argument" (Venuti, 2004: 127).

To retain these Homeric peculiarities, Newman took pains to develop a style on the levels of lexicon, syntax and prosody. In terms of lexicon, Newman constructed a special vocabulary, confining himself to the words of Saxon origin. He argued that Saxon-Norman was English diction of Saxon origin that could possibly produce a similar archaic effect. The result, however, was unhappy: not only did Newman overstep the confines he set himself—Latin words like *responsive*, *celestial*, etc., are found frequently in Newman's translation, thus creating a heterogeneous vocabulary; more importantly, he used the words that were highly literary and obscure, like *callant* (a young man) that appeared in Scott's *Waverley*① (1814) and *gride* (to cut gratingly) that came in Shelly's *Prometheus Unbound*② (1821). As if anticipating the possible difficulties the readers might have, Newman appended a two page glossary of the archaic words. Still his Homer was so dense and opaque as to be incomprehensible to his readers. One of the syntactic expedient was deliberately inverted sentence for the effect of antiquity and elevation, for emphasis or for variety. Newman wanted to use these artificial constructions to produce a quaint Homeric style. Concerning the prosody, Newman thought that ballad meter is both antiquated and popular, and therefore more suitable than hexameter for translating Homer, an ancient poet popular in his time. To Newman's mind, Homer is popular and primitive and should be rendered in ballad meter and Saxon-Norman language and "Wardour Street English"③ (quoted in Baker, 1998: 342) for a much larger and ordinary audience, which Newman confessed to be "the unlearned public" (quoted in Robinson, 2006: 257). The translation was thus a thesaurus of various periods of English that cut cross different literary genres. Newman's archaistic style was attacked for being too affected to be called

---

① 《威弗利》:英国著名历史小说家和诗人斯科特最有代表性的历史小说,为19世纪现实主义小说奠定了基础。

② 《解放了的普罗米修斯》:英国浪漫主义诗人雪莱的诗剧,取材于古希腊罗马神话,表达自己反抗暴政的思想。

③ 沃德街英语:沃德街是英国一条古董街,专门出售货真价实或者仿制的古董。"沃德街英语"带有贬义,指滥用古词造成的一种新旧交杂、驳杂不纯、矫揉造作的文风。

Homer, which was natural and direct.

Arnold was one of the most influential poets and art critics of Victorian England. For the most part of his adult life he traveled widely as school inspector and had a shaping influence upon the British educational system.

Arnold insisted that the best way to translate classical Homer is to adopt the classical language of the 1611 *Bible* and replicate the original hexameters for a small and learned readership. Arnold thought that Newman's general design (to retain every peculiarity of Homer, to impress his readers that he was imitating Homer in a new material, to move the target readers in the same way *Iliad* is conceived to have moved the original Greek readers) gives no real guidance. For one thing, it is impossible to tell exactly how the original Homer affected the original readers, far less to tell if the translator's readers reacted to the translation in the same way the author's readers felt about the original. For another, the unlearned reader is in no position to judge if the translator has reproduced Homer or the translator himself. The only readers that are able to judge translation of Homer are scholars of classics, who have knowledge of Greek and adequate poetical taste and feeling. They alone are the translator's tribunal.

The research on Homer attracted the attention of the majority of important translators from the antiquity up to the 19th century. Over time questions and *controversies* formed around Homer which distracted the translator's attention from the translation work. In his essay, Arnold raised his objection to the translator's detailed study of Homer research before translating him. He thought that a solution to these controversies was of no help to his translation. He maintained that Homer should be approached with simplest frame of mind possible, namely, not to be tinged with modern sentiment.

Arnold seemed to have an issue with Newman's limiting himself to the words of Saxon origin, which deprived himself a special advantage of rendering Homer. He held a rather romantic view of translation: "it may be said that union of the translator with his original, which alone can produce a good translation." (quoted in Robinson, 2006: 253) Arnold stated that the aim of the translator is to reproduce the general effect of Homer on intelligent scholars. He was rightly irritated by Newman's understanding of Homer's style, which, Arnold thought, was characterized by the four qualities: rapid in his movement, plain in his words, simple in his ideas and noble in his manner. He thought that earlier translators of Homer translated him ill because they failed to see these four qualities. Among them was Newman, who was odd in his words and ignoble in his manner.

As Arnold was an authority on classical antiquity in the 19th and 20th centuries, the method he advocated was upheld by later translators of Homer. For a time Newman's strategy was forgotten. But Newman's antiquarian version retained Anglo-Saxon poetry and alliterative verse, with the purpose of communicating the strangeness of the original (quoted in France, 2000: 92). Lawrence Venuti held that Newman's foreignizing translation method deviates "not only from Victorian standards of transparent discourse, but also from an Arnoldian concept of the national culture that favors academic elite" (Venuti, 2004: 100). Daniel Weissbort considered it one of the bold Victorian experiments that anticipated later developments. Indeed, later poet translators like Robert Southey① (1774-1843), Robert Browning② (1812-1889), William Morris③ (1834-1896) and Dante Gabriel Rossetti④ (1828-1882) adopted Newman's approach. It must be noted that Newman's foreignizing translation was strictly in terms of discourse. As far as the morality was concerned, Newman removed the sexual text of Horace and imposed on his gentle English women a Victorian sense of moral propriety, thus slanting towards domesticating translation.

Further Readings

Amos, Flora Ross. *Early Theories of Translation*. New York: Columbia University Press, 1920.

Bassnnet, Susan. *Translation Studies*. Shanghai: Shanghai Foreign Language Education Press, 2004.

Baker, Mona. *Routledge Encyclopedia of Translation Studies*. London & New York: Routledge, 1998.

France, Peter. *The Oxford Guide to Literature in English Translation*. New York: Oxford University Press, 2000.

Lefevere, Andre. *Translation/History/Culture: A Sourcebook*. Shanghai: Shanghai Foreign Language Education Press, 2004a.

Lefevere, Andre. Translation: Its Genealogy in the West. 2013-11-15. http://www.freewebs.com/keping/C_T-H-P-E-B-T-ItsGenealogyInTheWest.htm.

Nida, Eugene A. *Towards a Science of Translating* Shanghai: Shanghai Foreign Language Education Press, 2004.

Robinson, Douglas. *Western Translation Theory: From Herodotus to Nietzsche*. Shanghai: Foreign Language Teaching and Research Press, 2006.

Shuttleworth, Mark & Moira Cowie. *Dictionary of Translation Studies*. Shanghai: Shanghai Foreign Language Education Press, 2004.

King James Version From Wikipedia, the free encyclopedia.

Venuti, Larence. *The Translator's Invisibility: A History of Translation*. Shanghai: Shanghai Foreign Language Education Press, 2004.

Samuel Johnson. Poetry Foundation. 2013-11-17. http://www.poetryfoundation.org/bio/samuel-johnson.

---

① 骚塞：英国浪漫派诗人，湖畔派诗人之一。

② 勃朗宁：英国诗人、剧作家，主要作品有《戏剧抒情诗》《环与书》《巴拉塞尔士》。

③ 莫里斯：英国艺术与工艺美术运动的领导人之一。世界知名的家具、壁纸花样和布料花纹的设计者兼画家。他同时是一位小说家和诗人，也是英国社会主义运动的早期发起者之一。

④ 罗塞蒂：英国著名诗人、画家、翻译家。

谭载喜:《西方翻译简史》,商务印书馆2004年版。

莪默·伽亚谟:《鲁拜集》,爱德华·菲次杰拉德译,中国社会科学出版社2003年版。

Topics for Discussion

1. What are Tytler's three laws of translation? It is speculated that Yan Fu's famous translator's dictum of faithfulness, expressiveness and elegance came from Tytler. Compare Yan Fu with Tytler and find out the points of similarities between the two theories.

2. Is Dryden's division of translation entirely new? Point out similar points before him in Western translation history. What is Dryden's contribution to translation theories?

3. What does FitzGerald's translation of *Rubaiyat of Omar Khayyam* reveal about the nature of translation? Is translation an art, craft or science? Is *Rubaiyat* a translation, adaptation or imitation?

4. Newman translated Homer with Anglo-Saxon vocabulary, frequently inverted syntax and Ballad meter, with the purpose to preserve Homer's antiquity. What do you call his translation strategy in modern translation terms? How was his translation received? Would you translate an ancient English text into classical Chinese language of the same historical period?

5. What is the focus of the debate over translation of Homer in modern England? In what way is it different from the parallel debate in Modern France?

4.5 Chapter Summary

The subject matter of modern translation was expanding into more secular and recent works, in addition to classical antiquity and Biblical texts. The languages of translation were more diverse than ever, many translations happening between young national languages.

Translation strategy and theorization were immediately influenced by the general intellectual movement. Translation theories have witnessed substantial development, the discussion growing rapidly in both depth and scope. The investigation on the nature of translation, particularly in Germany, is posited within the more general framework of language and human mind and the discussion on translation takes a philosophical aspect.

Generally speaking, early modern France was the age of the *Les Belles Infideles* (unfaithful beauty), when translators cared only to produce a text that was morally and stylistically agreeable, with little respect for the original. The most remarkable translator of the *Les Belles Infideles was* Nicolas Perrot D'Ablancout. This free adaptation of the *Les Belles Infideles* was not generally approved, though. De Sacy, Huet and Anne Marie Dacier, among others, translated with greater faithfulness and urged the translators to show more respect for the original author. Members of Jansenism at the Abbey of Port-Royal also strived for fidelity. Translations made under the Jesuit influence, by contrast, invariably exhibited a tendency to place the language above the substance. The inaccurate translation in the 17th-century France was more or less influenced by the Jesuits.

In the 18th century, the enthusiasm with the classical texts was replaced by a growing interest in the English language and culture. Three types of English novels were particularly translated in the time: sentimental, Gothic and historical, with the method of *Les Belles Infideles*. English Gothic novels, in particular, were translated with great enthusiasm in late 18th century. Translation of Shakespeare started in the 18th century and flourished in the 19th century.

In the 19th century France there came another culmination in the translation of a profusion of English, German, Italian, Spanish and Latin literatures. With the rise of Romanticism in Germany, French translation returned back to literalism in the 19th century. The beautiful but unfaithful translation was replaced by the style that kept closer to the original. The Romantic period aimed at reproducing the strangeness of the foreign text. Many classics were retranslated for the purpose of restoring the ancients to their reputation. A large quantity of English works was translated during the time. Among the most translated were Shakespeare, Milton, Byron, Coleridge, Shelly, Scott and Dickens. Goethe and Schiller of Germany, Dante of Italy and some ballads from Spain were also introduced. Another interesting practice in the 19th-century France is that verse translations went in parallel with prose translation of the same poems. And as the difficulty of verse translation was recognized, many poems were translated into prose.

German Romanticism broke the confines of literature into the field of translation, working a parallel movement in the thinking about translation. Modern German translation thought was distinguished for its clear philosophical aspect as the investigation on nature of translation is typically posited within the general framework of human mind and language. Typical of this philosophical aspect are discussions on the uniqueness of language, the universality of human mind, translatability and untranslatability across languages, social function of translation, translation as an interpretative process or communication, the essence of translation, the division of translation as orientated either towards the source or the target, etc. Important translation theorists include Herder, Goethe, Schleiermacher, Humboldt, Schlegel and Holderlin.

The translated texts included classical antiquity and more recent, continental works. The source languages of translation were diverse, French being the most prominent intermediary language in the early 18th century. The most translated genre was French drama which embodied the highest level of French classicism. Not only the material but also the theatrical models were introduced into German theatre. Through the French mediation, the German readers also learned about English authors like Locke, Pope, Addison, Defoe, Swift, Richardson and Fielding, etc. Of all English authors Shakespeare was translated the most in Germany, i. e. , directly from English into German, read in the French translation or even in its English original. Important translators of Shakespeare include Christoph Martin Wieland, Johann Joachim Eschenburg, Friedrich Schiller, Wilhelm Schlegel, Ludwig Tieck and Johann

Heinrich Voss. Of all translated Shakespeare's plays, *Hamlet* occupied a central place in German literature. As time went on, however, some German writers grew weary of the distorted British culture filtered through the French language. The 18th century witnessed the gradual change from the general acceptance to the virtual rejection of English culture translated via the French language and culture. And this change coincided with the general transition in German history of thought: the emancipation from French intellectual and cultural monopoly and the rise of an independent German national literature.

Classical antiquity was still translated. Johann Heinrich Voss (1751-1826) translated Homer's *Odyssey* in 1781 and *Iliad* in 1793, for which he was praised by Goethe as an expert on classical poetry. His translation of the *Odyssey* was considered the most successful. He also translated Hesiod (1806), Theocritus, Bion and Moschus (1808), the whole of Virgil (1799), Horace (1806), Tibullus (1810), Propertius (1830) and selections from Ovid (1798).

Unlike the 16th-century England, in the 17th century there was an increasing confidence in the English language as a medium of translation. The sources texts for translation were classical antiquity and the most important translators include Cowley and Dryden. Translation theories in the 17th century were concerned with translation of classics, both ancient and modern. Communication between scholars and translators was more frequent. Partly in reaction against free imitation, Dryden proposed his well-quoted division of translation into three types: metaphrase, imitation, and paraphrase.

The 18th century was a period of peace and tranquility greater than the Elizabeth Reign. Translation was regarded as a worthwhile event in the interest of the country and enlisted assistance from both the world of learning and individual patrons. Translators were more respected than before. The most favored ancient poets included Virgil, Horace, and Homer, among others. The important translators were Pope, Johnson and Tytler. There was a notable tendency of naturalizing the Greek and Latin texts. The translations were invariably prefaced with lengthy and detailed discourse on the best rules for translation. Translation theories walked out the sporadic discussions in the proceeding century and became increasingly homogenous and systematic, culminating in Tytler's *Essays on the Principles of Translation*.

A notable translator in the 19th-century England is FitzGerald, who introduced *Rubaiyat*, a four-line stanza, into the English poetry, through his translation of Omar Khayyam. The discussion on poetry translation, particularly classical poetry translation of Homer, continued into the 19th century and reached its climax in the debate over translation of Homer between Matthew Arnold and Francis Newman. The debate ended without consensus since they meant their translations for different readers. As Arnold was an authority on classical antiquity in the 19th and 20th centuries, the method he advocated was upheld by later translators of Homer.

Afterword: Major Findings and Limitations

In response to the growing social-cultural approach in modern theory of translation, this book recounts translation history primarily as a socio-cultural fact in the target setting. The major findings of the book are: (1) successful translations in history are invariably initiated by the target culture with the purpose to fill a need for some idea or literary form that is absent in its own system; (2) underlying this need is the deep and unique socio-cultural background; (3) to serve this need, translations are invariably oriented towards the target, with little regard for the source; (4) the difference exists between text types and individual translators, as translation is essentially an individual undertaking as well as a socio-cultural event; (5) only translations that successfully fulfill the expectation may take long and deep root in the history of the target culture and the advance of human civilization; (6) the ideology and power relations play a decisive part while linguistics is never a really important consideration; (7) "target", "domesticating" and "ideology" are the hard facts of translation history in the West, while "source", "faithfulness", "foreignizing" and "language" are important merely as theoretical terms. As stated by Lefevere,

> *Translation can tell us a lot about the power of images and the ways in which images are made, about the ways in which authority manipulates images and employs experts to sanction that manipulation and to justify the trust of an audience-which is why the study of translation can teach us a few things not just about the world of literature, but also about the world we live in.* ①

As stated above, the underlying scenario for this book is mainly social-cultural. The insufficiency of the relevant data, however, still leaves much to be desired for this purpose. External conditions for translation, like literacy, printing industry, paper-making industry, publishing industry, linguistic background, politics, intellectual movement, communication, transportation, etc., are important factors that influence translation enterprise from ancient times. Although much of this information could be retrieved from general world history, there is problem of the imbalance of availability of that information. Translation, for example, involves

---

① Lefevere, André. Translation: Its Genealogy in the West. 2013-11-15. http://www.freewebs.com/keping/C_T-H-P-E-B-T-ItsGenealogyInTheWest.htm.

patronization and commission, a process in which a supreme religious or secular power funds or sanctions a translation event. Commission of the Toledo School of translation by King Alfonso is well documented in history, but similar information about many other translation movements is rather scanty. Likewise, information on the working procedures of the Authorized Version of the *Bible* is copious, while that about many other translations is very scarce. The book is therefore imbalanced in the availability of the socio-cultural data that influence translation. It is hoped that with my diligence this imbalance of historical data has been minimized, the insufficiency of relevant information remedied and the central idea well illustrated with ample translational facts. It is also hoped that this little textbook will be an inspiration to translation history research and an improved sourcebook for translation research in general.

2014/7/25

Acknowledgements

I would like to extend my sincerest gratitude to the following people, without whose help the completion of this book would not have been possible:

To my PhD supervisor Mr. Sun Yingchun, who wrote the Chinese preface and made valuable editorial advice for this book.

To my promoter Yu Changjin and his wife my junior PhD classmate, for their valuable suggestions.

To my husband, daughter and sisters for their support and encouragement.

I would also like to extend my gratitude to all those people from the School of Translation Studies, Shandong University (Weihai) who have contributed to the formation of this book. One is Bo Zhenjie, who reviewed the outline of this book. Cui Yinghui photocopied *Early Theories of Translation* by Amos, a book that I quoted extensively in the accounts of translations into the English language. Cui Ying and Cao Chunling worked as the English editor of part of the book. Chen Huaikai and Gu Xiuchun were in charge of the consistency in documentation format. And Wang Suhua, Sun Cuiying and Li Nan collected some valuable material for the drafting of the second chapter.

I also benefit a great deal from the sources, printed or electronic, that I quoted directly or indirectly in the book. I hereby express my respect for the authors of these valuable sources who have made the book possible.

Bibliography

Printed Sources:

Amos, Flora Ross. *Early Theories of Translation*. New York: Columbia University Press, 1920.

Bassnnet, Susan. *Translation Studies*. Shanghai: Shanghai Foreign Language Education Press, 2004.

Bobrick, Benson. *Wide as the Waters: The Story of the English Bible and the Revolution It Inspired*. New York: Simon & Schuster, 2001.

Baker, Mona. *Routledge Encyclopedia of Translation Studies*. London & New York: Routledge, 1998.

Barnstone, Willis. *The Poetics of Translation: History, Theory, Practice*. New Haven & London: Yale University Press, 1993.

Berman, Antoine. *The Experience of the Foreign: Culture and Translation in Romantic Germany*. Albany: State University of New York Press, 1992.

Copeland, Rita. *Rhetoric, Hermeneutics, and Translation in the Middle Ages: Academic Traditions and Vernacular Texts*. Cambridge: Cambridge University Press, 1991.

Delisle, Jean & Judith Woodsworth. *Translators through History*. Amsterdam: John Benjamins Publishing Company, 1995.

France, Peter. *The Oxford Guide to Literature in English Translation*. New York: Oxford University Press, 2000.

Kelly, Louis. G. *The True Interpreter: A History of Translation Theory and Practice in the West*. New York: St. Martin's Press, 1979.

Lefevere, Andre. *Translation/History/Culture: A Sourcebook*. Shanghai: Shanghai Foreign Language Education Press, 2004a.

Lefevere, Andre. *Translation, Rewriting and the Manipulation of Literary Fame*. Shanghai: Shanghai Foreign Language Education Press, 2004b.

Nida, Eugene A. *Towards a Science of Translating* Shanghai: Shanghai Foreign Language Education Press, 2004.

Pym, Anthony. Method in Translation History. Manchester: St. Jerome Publishing, 1998.

Venuti, Larence. *The Translator's Invisibility: A History of Translation*. Shanghai:

Shanghai Foreign Language Education Press, 2004.

Robinson, Douglas. *Western Translation Theory: From Herodotus to Nietzsche*. Shanghai: Foreign Language Teaching and Research Press, 2006.

Shuttleworth, Mark & Moira Cowie. *Dictionary of Translation Studies*. Shanghai: Shanghai Foreign Language Education Press, 2004.

Steiner, George. *After Babel: Aspects of Language and Translation*. Shanghai: Shanghai Foreign Language Education Press, 2001.

Wilss, Wolfram. *The Science of Translation: Problems and Methods*. Shanghai: Shanghai Foreign Language Education Press, 2001.

Ztaleva, Palma. *Translation as Social Action*. London & New York: Routledge, 1993.

Tan Zaixi:《西方翻译简史》,商务印书馆 2004 年版。

Omar Khayyam:《鲁拜集》,爱德华·菲次杰拉德译,中国社会科学出版社 2003 年版。

高华丽:《中外翻译简史》,浙江大学出版社 2009 年版。

谢天振等:《中西翻译简史》,外语教学与研究出版社 2009 年版。

孙迎春:《翻译简史》,天津教育出版社 2011 年版。

Online Sources:

Desiderius Erasmus From Wikipedia, the free encyclopedia. 2014-07-20. http://en.wikipedia.org/wiki/Desiderius_Erasmus.

Munger, Scott. *Bible*, *Babel and Babble: The Foundations of Bible Translation Section* 5-5-4. Martin Luther and *Bible* Translation. 2009-5-15. http://www.ibsstl.org/niv/munger/5-5-4.php.

Rose, Christine M. *Chaucer's Man of Law's Tale: Teaching Through the Sources* [1] College Literature. 2009-05-05. http://www.geocities.com/growonder/chaucermanoflaw.html.

Biblical literature. Encyclop dia Britannica. Encyclop dia Britannica Inc. 2012-03-04. http://www.britannica.com/EBchecked/topic/64496/biblical-literature.

Roman_Empire. 2012-05-16. http://en.wikipedia.org/wiki/Roman_Empire.

La Pléiade, From Wikipedia, the free encyclopedia. 2009-05-23. http://en.wikipedia.org/wiki/La_Pléiade.

Jacques Amyot, From Wikipedia, the free encyclopedia. 2013-10-01. http://en.wikipedia.org/wiki/Jacques_Amyot.

Hunayn Ibn Ishaq, From Wikipedia, the free encyclopedia. 2014-03-26. http://en.wikipedia.org/wiki/Hunayn_ibn_Ishaq.

Martin Luther. From Wikipedia, the free encyclopedia. 2013-10-05. http://en.wikipedia.org/wiki/Martin_Luther.

Munger, Scott. *Bible*, Babel and Babble: The Foundations of *Bible* Translation Section. 2009-5-15. http://www.ibsstl.org/niv/munger/5-5-4.php.

William Tyndale. From the free encyclopedia. 2009-5-23. http://en. wikipedia. org/wiki/William_Tyndale.

King James Version. From Wikipedia, the free encyclopedia. 2012-06-13. http://en. wikipedia. org/wiki/Authorized_King_James_Version.

Early modern period. From Wikipedia, the free encyclopedia. 2013-10-01. http://en. wikipedia. org/wiki/Modern_history.

World literature. From Wikipedia, the free encyclopedia. 2012-10-10. http://en. wikipedia. org/wiki/World_literature.

Lefevere, André. Translation: Its Genealogy in the West. 2013-11-15. http://www. freewebs. com/keping/C_T-H-P-E-B-T-ItsGenealogyInTheWest. htm.

Samuel Johnson. Poetry Foundation. 2013-11-17. http://www. poetryfoundation. org/bio/samuel-johnson.